THE SCOURGE OF THE EAGLE

THE SCOURGE OF THE EAGLE

Napoleon and the Liberal Opposition

✤

Louis de Villefosse
and
Janine Bouissounouse

✤

Translated and Edited by Michael Ross

SIDGWICK & JACKSON
LONDON

400657147

698744

940.27

Wig
20-3.72
£3.50

ZB 12/92

This translation first published in Great Britain in 1972
by Sidgwick & Jackson Limited
1 Tavistock Chambers, Bloomsbury Way
London W.C.1

Copyright © Sidgwick & Jackson Limited 1972

ISBN 0.283.48494.2

Printed in Great Britain by
Morrison & Gibb, London and Edinburgh

CONTENTS

I

The General of Vendémiaire

✦✦✦

ON the 20 Frimaire in the year VII (10 December 1797), all Paris was hastening towards the Luxembourg palace. Every window in the neighbouring streets was crowded with curious spectators. Some had even clambered on the roofs. Perhaps, with luck, they would catch a glimpse of General Bonaparte, Commander-in-Chief of the Army of Italy, for whom the Directory was preparing a state welcome. Bonaparte . . . the name had been on everyone's lips for months past. The fame of this Corsican who had suppressed the royalist rising of Vendémiaire[1] eclipsed even that of Hoche and Jourdan.[2] He had led his ragged troops from victory to victory, and now, having covered France with glory, he was returning home. He himself was unknown, but his resounding success had intoxicated the public. Bonaparte – the name spelt happiness and hope. . . .

The officials take their places in the courtyard of the Luxembourg, which is decked with Gobelin tapestries and flags from

[1] First month of the year in the Republican Calendar, 22 September–21 October.

[2] HOCHE, Lazare (1766–97). Republican general commanding the Army of the Moselle. Imprisoned under the Terror, but later reinstated, and suppressed the royalist rising in the Vendée. Commanded the tentative invasion of Ireland. One of the greatest and most dedicated men of the Revolution. JOURDAN, Jean-Baptiste, Marshal of France 1762–1833. Victor of Fleurus (1794). General of the French Army in Spain (1808–14). Later Governor of the Hôtel des Invalides under Louis Philippe. (Translator's note).

Italy. A high platform has been set up, its floor and benches covered with carpets borrowed from the former royal repositories. In the centre stands the altar dedicated to *la Patrie*, dominated by the statues of Liberty, Equality, and Peace. Seated at the foot of the altar are the five members of the Directory in capes and plumed hats. Also present are the members of the Institute, the *corps d'élite* of the State. All await with mingled respect and impatience the arrival of this diminutive hero, who advances to the rostrum followed by his aides-de-camp, all taller than their leader, but dwarfed by his presence.

Talleyrand, Minister for Foreign Relations, leads him to the altar and presents him to the Directors, who have risen to their feet. Talleyrand makes a speech: 'Ah! far from fearing what people may call his ambition, I feel that it will perhaps some day be necessary to use persuasion on him to drag him from the charms of his studious retreat. . . .'

The General makes a rapid reply and hands the Minister the treaty signed at Campo Formio. He speaks quickly in a low voice with a strong accent. Only those in the front rows can catch a few phrases here and there: 'Citizen Directors . . . you, and the Constitution of the year III have triumphed over all obstacles. . . . The era of constitutional government dates from the conclusion of the peace treaty you have just signed. . . . Once the welfare of France is established on better organic laws, all Europe will become free. . . .'

Barras, in his turn, then makes a speech. 'Your heart', he declares, 'is the shrine of republican honour.' He then embraces Napoleon while the choirs of the Conservatoire break into a hymn, with words written for the occasion by Marie-Joseph Chénier to music by Méhul, which ended thus:

> *Tu fus longtemps l'effroi, sois l'honneur de la terre,*
> *O République des Français.*
> *Que le chant des plaisirs succède, aux cris de guerre*
> *la victoire a conquis la paix.*[1]

[1] Oh Republic of the French! long were you the terror of the earth, be now its glory. Let songs of joy replace the clamour of war. Peace has come through victory.

This victory (or rather victories) was extolled in a long inscription emblazoned on a banner which the Directory, to conclude this ceremony at the Luxembourg, presented to the Army of Italy.

'The Army of Italy [it reads] has captured one hundred and fifty thousand prisoners, sixty-six regimental colours, five hundred and fifty siege guns, six hundred field guns, five bridge-trains, nine ships, twelve frigates, twelve corvettes, eighteen galleys . . . it has signed armistices with the Kings of Sardinia, Naples, and the Pope . . . concluded the Leoben Preliminaries . . . brought freedom to the peoples of Bologna, Ferrara and Modena . . . and to the inhabitants of the Aegean and Ithaca . . . sent to Paris the masterpieces of Michelangelo, Guercino, and Titian . . . victorious in eighteen fixed battles, Montenotta, Millesimo, Lodi . . . Arcola, Rivoli . . . engaged in sixty-seven actions. . . .'

Never had so many honours crowned French colours, never had a French General received such homage. The Treaty of Campo Formio was certainly the most advantageous France had ever known. It gave her Belgium and ratified her frontiers on the left bank of the Rhine. The Republic was now firmly entrenched on the continent – an entirely unforeseen outcome of a war which had lasted five years and which had nearly ended in disaster.

In France itself, both the masses and the *élite* expected to see a healthier and stronger democratic régime. Bonaparte was addressing the *élite* when he evoked the idea of the liberation of all Europe and declared that this was the beginning of an era of representative Governments, implying that reforms in the constitution could now be looked forward to.

Weighing his words with care, Napoleon's address to the Directory was loyal and deferential, but while showing respect, he nevertheless left no doubt that he was an equal speaking to equals, even perhaps with a hint of superiority. But it was in particular for the men faithful to the ideals of '89, the intellectuals and members of the Institute, that his speech had most appeal. He was intent on cultivating their confidence and friendship, and two years later, on 18 Brumaire, they did not begrudge him their support; later, however, disillusioned by the Consular dictatorship, they were to become his stubborn opponents and do their utmost to reimpose their republican principles. In some ways the Napoleonic epic has eclipsed the names and memory of these heirs to eighteenth-century ideals, who had survived the Terror. They were not men of the same stature as the new Caesar; not one of the giants of the Revolution remained, who alone could have thwarted his ambition. However, the part played by these men, all too often forgotten, was far from negligible. Who they were and what they did, we shall see later. But first let us consider this young conqueror, now hailed as the saviour of the Republic.

How was it that he gained the sympathy of such dedicated democrats? What were his opinions, reactions and behaviour at the time of the great revolutionary events, and what was his attitude to the monarchy? To what extent was he prepared to accept new ideas? In this confrontation between Napoleon Bonaparte and the ideal of Liberty, what clue can we find, from his character, origins or education, to assist our understanding?

Napoleon Bonaparte was to make his first appearance on the pages of history in 1793, when he played his decisive role at Toulon.[1]

At the end of August, the Republican troops had laid siege to this great naval base and military arsenal. The Jacobin municipality had been expelled and the Girondist sympathizers had opened the harbour, arsenal, and forts to the British Admiral Hood. The Republican forces were commanded by a former housepainter, Carteau, a sansculotte General, who did not even know the range of his own artillery. His incompetence was causing more and more alarm to the representatives of the Convention, particularly to Saliceti, who having failed to establish himself in Corsica, was at this time engaged on a mission in the Var. When Napoleon, on his way from Avignon to Nice, paid him a visit, Saliceti jumped at the opportunity to offer this '*capitaine instruit*' the command of the siege artillery. The rest of the story is well known. Bonaparte, by taking a firm stand, won

---

[1] It was after Toulon that Napoleon altered the spelling of his name from Buonaparte to Bonaparte. (Translator's note).

approval for his plans from the Committee of Public Safety, and then proceeded methodically to apply them; the enemy's key positions were systematically bombarded and then carried by assault, under the admiring eyes of Saliceti, Barras, Fréron, and Augustin Robespierre. Hood's squadron, raked by the French guns, was compelled to abandon its blazing anchorage, alight with flames of the French ships (which had defected to Hood, in the belief that they were thereby serving the cause of Louis XVII) which the English had set afire. On 19 December, the Republican troops entered the 'City of Shame' to massacre, pillage, and wreak their vengeance on the unfortunate citizens. A jubilant Fouché was there too, all agog to watch the guillotine at work. . . .

Napoleon took no part in these atrocities; indeed, according to Marmont, he even intervened to save the lives of several people. He devoted his time to the repair of the captured redoubts. On 22 December, he was promoted to General of the Brigade and shortly afterwards was sent on a tour of inspection of the coastal area between Marseilles and Nice. In February 1794, through the offices of Augustin Robespierre, the brother of Maximilien, he was appointed Artillery Commander to the Army of Italy.

The whole Bonaparte family took up residence at Antibes in the Château de Sallé. Joseph was now married to Julie Clary, the daughter of a wealthy Marseilles merchant; Napoleon was courting Julie's sister, Desirée, who was later to become the wife of Bernadotte.

It was at this time that the victor of Toulon was offered the post of Military Commander of Paris in place of Hanriot.[1] He discussed the proposal with his family. His brother Julien gives the following account of the incident in his memoirs:[2]

' "I must give my answer tonight [Napoleon said]. Well, what do you advise?"
'We hesitated a moment.
' "Hm, hm . . . it's certainly something to think about", said

[1] HANRIOT, François (1761–94). Military commander of Paris during the Terror. Executed 9 Thermidor.
[2] Th. Jung: *Lucien Bonaparte et ses Mémoires.* The last sentence is *in italics* in the text.

the General, "it's no good rushing into things. It's not so
easy to keep your head on your shoulders in Paris as it is in
Saint-Maximinin. The young Robespierre is honest enough,
but his brother is not a man to trifle with. One would have to
be his lackey. What! Be that fellow's prop . . . never! I know
just how useful I would be to him if I took the place of that
idiot Commandant of Paris, but that's the very thing I don't
want. This is not the right moment. Today the only honourable
place for me is with the Army. Be patient. *One day I shall be
master of Paris*".'

This deference to family opinion should not come as any
surprise. Nabulio was always to remain a good brother and son.
He was always to share his honours and glory with his family.
He was always indulgent to Joseph, even if he did sometimes
lose patience with his easygoing outlook and his unfortunate
habit of siding with his own opponents. As for Lucien, Napoleon
was prepared to overlook his faults, his indiscretions, and un-
governable moods; he had, after all, to admit that not all Lucien's
undertakings were bungled. As for his mother, he continued to
respect, indeed to venerate, this formidable matriarch, a true
Corsican to the marrow. She showed no more surprise at finding
herself châtelaine of the Château de Sallé, than she did later, when
she found herself installed at the Tuileries. Even there, with her
own household, and in the role of queen-mother, she would
still remain the suspicious and parsimonious Corsican that she
had always been.

At the beginning of the summer of 1794, on instructions from
Augustin Robespierre, the young General left on a mission for
Genoa, accompanied by Marmont. He returned to France on
27 July (9 Thermidor). On the following day, Augustin and his
brother, Maximilien, were guillotined.

On 5 August, as soon as he learnt the news, Bonaparte wrote
to Tilly, the French chargé d'affaires in Genoa: 'I was somewhat
dismayed at the news of the Robespierre catastrophe; I liked him,
and believed him to be uncorrupted; but I would not hesitate to
stab even my own father, if he dreamt of becoming a tyrant.'

A little later, Saliceti, now an ardent *Thermidorian*, denounced
Napoleon as a traitor, declaring that his journey to Genoa, under

the auspices of the Robespierres, had as its purpose the handing over of military secrets. As the representative of the Army of the Alps, Saliceti had watched with considerable pique the support given to his compatriot by the Robespierres, a support which seemed to favour the Army of Italy in preference to his own. A warrant was issued for Napoleon's arrest. But after ten days of close confinement in Antibes, he was declared innocent by Saliceti himself, and acquitted.

From a military point of view, Napoleon's position was still uncertain after his acquittal; since his arrest, he had had no command. The Government, remembering his friendship with Augustin Robespierre, continued to treat him as an ex-terrorist and disregarded all his requests for a posting. When, in April 1795 he was eventually ordered to the west to suppress the Chouans, he put himself in an even worse light by applying for convalescent leave. He decided to go to Paris.

A little later, on 29 Fructidor, year III (16 September 1795), the Committee of Public Safety, with Cambacérès as President, decided that 'General of Brigade Bonaparte . . . is herewith struck off from the list of serving general officers, in view of his refusal to assume the post to which he was assigned . . .', But Jean de Bry,[1] the Committee's official reporter, declared that it was essential, particularly at this moment, that 'nothing should be done to alienate an officer of such distinction from the Republic'. In the circumstances, therefore, the proposed penalty was not enforced.

*   *   *

In Paris, Bonaparte, together with Junot and Marmont, was living at the *Cadran Bleu*, a modest hotel in the rue de la Hachette. On the walls of this establishment, as elsewhere, one might have read such slogans as 'People of France! Return to your Church and King; only then will you have peace and bread'. The abolition of the *Loi du maximum* and the soaring price of bread, had plunged the country in misery. The people were hungry. On 12 Germinal (1 April) the women of Paris forced their way into the Assembly demanding bread, and the restitution of the Constitution

[1] See Chapter II. De Bry was a friend of Condorcet and one of the 'Auteuil circle'. (Translator's note).

of 1793. On 1 Prairial (20 May), the Chamber was again invaded, this time by workmen from the suburbs of Antoine and Marceau. After killing Féraud, one of the deputies, they presented his head impaled on a pike to Boissy d'Anglas, who imperturbably saluted it. For three whole days the rioters fought the National Guard and troops commanded by Pichegru, and withdrew only when the Convention threatened to bombard the faubourg Antoine. Seventeen members of the Mountain,[1] who had sided with the rioters, were arrested.

Up to the very last, the Convention had certainly had a disturbed existence. The tide had turned against mob law. The new Constitution of the year III took effect on 9 October 1795, with the formation of an Executive Directory. The Legislature was divided into two chambers, (conseils) – les Anciens and the Conseil de cinq cents, the Five Hundred. The fear, however, of reaction, whether revolutionary or royalist, taking effect at the coming (restricted) elections, inspired further modifications – in the first instance, that two-thirds of the deputies of the Council of Five Hundred must be chosen from the members of the Convention itself.

The claim that the structure of the old Assembly was still preserved in the new constitution failed to convince many Parisians, including former constituents, members of the legal profession, the bourgeois and working classes. Exploiting this discontent, the Royalists united in opposing the new decrees. The main centres of resistance were the Odéon and the Le Pelletier section.[2] At a plenary session, the Convention ordered General Menou to disarm this section and to take command of the little troop defending the Tuileries.

In the evening of 12 Vendémiaire, Bonaparte learnt that Barras was recruiting officers who had been disgraced for their 'Republicanism'. He hastened to the Assembly which was in all-night session, where he heard his own name proposed among others considered as replacements for Menou, whose conduct of the operations was considered altogether too weak. . . .

---

[1] The name given to the extremist Jacobin party who sat in the highest rows of seats in the Convention. (Translator's note).

[2] Section: a borough, or electoral constituency. (Translator's note).

In a letter to Joseph, written at two o'clock in the morning, Napoleon recounted the events of that famous 13 Vendémiaire:

'At last all is over. My first task is to give you my news. Every day the Royalists were becoming bolder. The Convention ordered the Le Pelletier section to be disarmed; the troops sent against it were repulsed. Menou was forthwith deprived of his command. The Convention next appointed Barras to command the armed forces; the Committee appointed me as second-in-command. We deployed our troops; the enemy attacked; we killed a great many. We disarmed the *sections*. Fortune is on my side. . . .'

What Napoleon did not tell his brother, was, that just before being summoned by Barras, he had said to Junot, 'Ah, if only the *sections* would put me at their head, I would guarantee to have them in the Tuileries within two hours and drive out all those miserable Conventionalists. . . .'

Three weeks later, the Convention was dissolved. On 4 Ventose, year IV (25 February 1796), Bonaparte, having suppressed the revolt which he had been prepared to abet, was given command of the Army of Italy. 'The doors of immortality were opened', as Marmont was to say.

In the meanwhile Napoleon had married. Barras, not content with giving his protégé an army, also gave him his mistress, Josephine Tascher de la Pagerie, one of the loveliest and most fashionable women in Paris, widow of the late Vicomte de Beauharnais.

'Barras promises that if I marry the General [wrote Josephine] he will give him command of the Army of Italy. Yesterday, when speaking to me of this favour (which is already making his brother officers grumble), Bonaparte said: "What! Do they imagine I need Barras's protection to succeed? Some day, they'll be only too happy if I give them my own. I have my sword at my side, and with its help I'll go far." '

Those of his brother officers who were placed under his command were not long in discovering what sort of a leader they had to deal with. On 25 March, a conference was held at his Headquarters in Nice, attended by Augereau, Masséna, and Serurier,

the Generals of Italy. They were all older than himself and somewhat scornful of 'this mathematician', who had distinguished
himself in street fighting. They looked disdainfully at the puny
little man (he was only five foot two), and probably to show how
unimpressed they were, omitted to remove their hats. Bonaparte
doffed his own. The Generals followed his example – it was,
after all, the least they could do. Napoleon, looking hard at these
gallant fellows, then replaced his own. The Generals did not dare
to move. With plumed hats in hand, they listened while he went
on to propound his plan of campaign. 'The little bugger scared
me,' said Augereau on leaving. 'I don't know what sort of power
he has over me, but at the first look he gave me I felt positively
crushed.'

He was to exercise immediately this ascendancy over the whole
Army. He galvanized his soldiers into action with inflammatory
proclamations, and won their affection with his rough familiarity.
He went through their ranks, questioning them, seemingly
interested in each man personally. He won the hearts of all by his
kindness, confidence, and simplicity. On the eve of the Battle of
Lodi, the veterans of the Army conferred on him the rank of
Corporal – or, at least, such was the legend current in Paris at the
same time as the publication of an engraving depicting the
Commander-in-Chief leading his troops across the famous bridge,
waving a standard. It was on that same evening too (if we are to
believe the passage in the *Mémorial de Sainte-Hélène*), that the
Little Corporal vowed to himself that one day he would command
all France.[1]

But he disguised his political ambitions. After entering Milan
in triumph on 15 May 1796, he planned to establish there a Transpadene Republic (i.e. north of the Po) – a very different solution
from that required by Paris – but he was careful not to disclose
his real intentions to the Directory, and for a long time was to
keep them to himself. True, the Directory had to be careful how
they handled Bonaparte, whose popularity, after Arcola (15
November), had been still further enhanced, but who, on the
other hand, was sending home to them a great deal of money.
When he set up a Transpadene republic in Romagna, the Govern-

---

[1] *Mémorial de Sainte-Hélène*, Vol. 1, quoted in *l'Ascension de Bonaparte*.

ment sent General Clarke, an officer of Irish descent, to negotiate peace with Austria in his place. But no sooner was Clarke face to face with the General, than he realized the futility of his mission. After Rivoli (14 January 1797) Napoleon's popularity was raised to such a pitch that the Government itself was infected. Even Carnot, who only a little while previously had wished to replace him by Kellerman, wrote to him that he was now the hero of all France.

What everyone now expected of Napoleon was the destruction of the Papacy. This project, partly inspired by a passionate anti-clericism ('*the torch of fanaticism, must be extinguished*') can also be explained by the alliance between Rome and Vienna and the actively belligerent attitude of the Papal States (the Papal forces had been roughly handled by the French at Castel-Bolognese) and the Pope's vain appeals to the Campagna to join in a holy war against the invader. However, the fact remained that Napoleon, although refusing to evict the Pope from the throne of Saint Peter, continued to terrify him. On 19 February 1797, he signed the compromise peace of Tolentino with the Papal plenipotentiaries, whereby the Pope renounced his claims to Avignon, Comtat,[1] Ancona, and the Legations (Bologna and Ferrara); moreover, he paid thirty millions (equivalent to one million sterling) in indemnities to France, and surrendered hundreds of works of art. But so greatly relieved was His Holiness to have preserved the essentials, that he assured the General of his 'greatest esteem', and furthermore, gave him his 'paternal and apostolic blessing'. Bonaparte immediately replied with a soothing and deferential letter in which he wrote: 'All Europe knows the pacific intentions and conciliatory virtues of Your Holiness. The French Republic will, I hope, be one of Rome's truest friends.'

Once these letters became known in Paris, the storm broke. Among sincere Republicans and in the ranks of the *parti philosophique* there was consternation and dismay. Barras gave it as his opinion that Napoleon was 'finished'; Rewbell mourned; La Révellière, the philanthropist, sobbed, swore, and thundered imprecations. Talleyrand, on the other hand, more or less openly

[1] Comtat-Venaissin. Part of the Department of Vaucluse, which had belonged to the Popes since 1274. (Translator's note).

praised the able way in which the General had handled the situation.

Talleyrand was to continue to play his own game.

On 18 April, disregarding instructions from the Directory, Bonaparte signed the Preliminary Articles of Leoben with the Austrian plenipotentiaries. Barras, La Réveillière, and Rewbell were furious, whereupon the young General submitted his written resignation. The Directory, however, fearful of the consequences if they accepted it, confirmed his right to negotiate.

In May, Bonaparte took up residence in the Castel Mombello, near Milan. He was to stay – or rather reign – there throughout the summer, surrounded by his 'court'. At Mombello he installed Josephine like a queen and Laetitia like a queen-mother. He married his sisters – Pauline to Leclerc, Elise to Bacciochi – he gave lavish receptions, and gathered Italian poets, artists, and scholars around him. From here he organized his conquests and dictated laws and, by uniting the Transpadane Republics, created the Cisalpine State. But all the time he never lost sight of what was going on in Paris.

The Babeuf conspiracy raised his fears that the Directory was not acting sufficiently firmly against 'Jacobins, royalists, and monarchists'. In the early days of 1796, a paper (*Le Tribun du Peuple*), containing a summary of the communist doctrines of the Egalitarian Society (*Société des Egaux*), was distributed all over Paris.

It was from among the disciples of Robespierre, men like the Duplays, father and son, and from 'true men of the people', that Babeuf recruited his followers. The Minister of Police (a newly created post) looked on these agitators with an indulgent eye until they seemed to be becoming dangerous. In May 1796, Babeuf's plot against the Directory was 'discovered'; the founder of the *Société des Egaux* was arrested. In September, twenty of his followers were shot in the camp at Grenelle on the orders of General Hugo, the father of Victor, the poet. After a protracted trial, Babeuf, in his turn, was executed in May 1797.

Napoleon reacted violently to the news of the conspiracy. A letter he wrote at the time to a friend, Fabre de l'Aude, a member of the Five Hundred, reveals a great deal about the political evolution of the hero of Vendémiaire, now commanding the Army of Italy.

'I am dumbfounded [he wrote] when I see Parisians indulging in such extravagant behaviour. Your Babeuf is so utterly unreasonable that I would feel sorry for him were it not that, on looking back, I realize how the tigerish ferocity of such men provoke nothing but feelings of disgust for the republican system – excellent though it may be ... I believe it only possible for a country to be strong and stable, when all authority lies in the hands of a single ruler.'[1]

Not content with confiding his personal feelings to his friend, he was determined to make clear his proposals for putting things to rights, and continued:

'The Republic is dependent on my victories and, because I am triumphant in Italy, believes itself to be invincible in France ... [but] my success will not prevent its downfall. Before I even hear of it, and before ever I could come to its assistance, it will have already fallen. You must speak seriously to Barras about all this – tell him our enemies are indefatigable and are of all sorts, but if we adopt a firm attitude, we can silence them. Tell him that I offer my support both to himself and the other members of the Directory, and if necessary, I will hasten to return. I am still the General of Vendémiaire; in time to come, that will be my first title of glory. On that day I saved the country from the Royalists; is it from Jacobins that we must preserve it today?'[2]

In the summer of 1797, it was no longer the Jacobins, but the Royalists who again threatened the Government. Frightened by the Babeuf conspiracy and the attempted rising provoked by the executions at Grenelle, the electorate returned a large number of ultra-moderates, even Royalists, to the Council of Five Hundred. The New President of the Assembly was Pichegru, the victor of Holland, who had been hailed by the Convention as the 'Saviour of the Country'. In 1795, however, he, himself an agent of Louis XVIII and England, was in contact with agents of the Coalition and made no attempt to conceal his counter-revolutionary sentiments.

[1] *Historie secrète du Directoire.*
[2] Ibid.

Bonaparte was now just as uneasy as he had been at the time of the Babeuf conspiracy – and not unnaturally, for there was little chance of survival for the General of Vendémiaire if the partisans of Louis XVIII were triumphant in Paris. After the occupation of Venice, a certain Dumolard had demanded, when addressing the Royalist Clichy Club, his dismissal and arrest. Right wing newspapers had even accused him of stealing millions from Italy. Bonaparte had reacted to these attacks with ultra-Republican energy. On 25 Messidor, he gave orders to his chief-of-staff to prohibit the circulation of all newspapers which 'tended to corrupt the Army, incite soldiers to desert, or undermine the cause of liberty'. The following day (14 July) he issued a proclamation burning with Republican zeal and loyalty to the Directory and Liberty.

He next wrote to the Directory to inform them of the indignation felt by his troops:

'I see that the Clichy Club wants to march over my dead body in order to destroy the Republic. Arrest all *émigrés*! . . . Should you need force, summon the Armies!'

But this time, the Army was not waiting to cannonade insurgents, but to make a clean sweep of deputies. Although advocating this policy, it was not Napoleon's intention to carry it out himself. Instead, he sent his lieutenant, Augereau, to Paris with further proofs of Pichegru's treason. On 17 and 18 Fructidor, Augereau, at the head of a division, carried out his mission to perfection. The *coup d'état* was over.

A fortnight later, on 19 September 1797, Bonaparte wrote to Talleyrand, outlining the course he felt the Government's policy should take. He criticized the institutions, but nonetheless, deplored the *coup d'état*, or, at least, the measures taken after the event:

'Let there be strength without fanaticism, principles without demagogy, severity without cruelty. . . . It is a great misfortune that in the eighteenth century, a nation of thirty millions should have to have recourse to bayonets to save their mother country. Such violent measures can only reflect on the legislature.'

In comparison with what he had written to Fabre de l'Aude, these are moderate and reassuring sentiments. Even if the rest of the letter makes it quite clear that he would like to see the powers of the legislature reduced in favour of the executive, it still reveals his intention of saving the Republican State from the forces of corruption which were undermining it, and of strengthening it in the face of the threat of Counter-Revolution. This is why Talleyrand considered it an opportune moment to make the contents of the letter known to such influential people as Madame de Staël, Benjamin Constant, and their friends. Nor did he omit to show it to Siéyès (as indeed, Napoleon had asked him to do) who was no admirer of the Constitution of the year III.

It was under these colours that the General wished to be known in Paris. He must remain the hope of all true Republicans; it must be known that the political convictions of the General of Vendémiaire, although now conqueror of Italy, had remained unchanged.

He had given a lot of thought to public opinion.

* * *

But there were times when his words had quite a different ring. During the course of a conversation with Miot, the French Minister to Tuscany, and Count Melzi a Milanese, in the grounds of Mombello, he revealed frankly what was in his mind. Did they imagine, he asked, that he had won his victories in Italy for the glory of the lawyers in the Directory – the Carnots and the Barras – or to found a Republic? He regarded a Republic as an impossibility for France. Glory, not liberty, was what the French demanded.

An imprudent slip of the tongue perhaps? Fortunately for Napoleon, there were many other visitors to Mombello who returned home with their heads filled with edifying thoughts. In reply to two Generals who asked him what were his intentions on his return, he said: 'I will bury myself away somewhere and work, so that one day I may be worthy of election to the Institute.'

For the time being, still in a blaze of success, he continued to treat instructions from Paris with a haughty disregard. The Directory wanted to continue the war with an advance on Vienna led by Hoche. Bonaparte, on the other hand, wanted to sign a peace with Austria, in conformity with the Preliminaries of Leoben of 18 April. On 29 September, the Directory sent him an ultimatum which he was to deliver to the Emperor. But Napoleon had already once again sent in his resignation. The Directors begged him to withdraw it, and wrote: 'The Directory places its trust in General Bonaparte and has complete confidence in his ability.'

And so it was that Napoleon negotiated and subsequently signed the Treaty of Campo Formio on 26 Vendémiaire (17 October 1797).

* * *

On his return to Paris in the evening of 3 December, Napoleon hid himself away in his little house in the rue Chantereine, shortly to be renamed rue de la Victoire.

At eleven o'clock on 6 December, Talleyrand received him at the Ministry for Foreign Relations. On leaving the Minister's office, the General looked round the crowded *salon*, and delivered one of those telling phrases, which impressed citizens no less than soldiers.

'I am grateful to you for your enthusiastic welcome. I have done my best in war, and have done my best for peace. It is up to the Directory now to make the best of both for the welfare and prosperity of the Republic.'

We already know what the subsequent ceremony in the court-yard of the Luxembourg was like. Fêtes and receptions succeeded one another. . . . When at last Bonaparte was able to get away, he kept himself to himself. His simplicity astonished everyone. He seldom went out, and then only used a carriage and pair. At the theatre, when applauded, far from acknowledging the ovations, he retreated farther into the shadow of his box and slipped away unobserved. It was the society of intellectuals and scholars that he was seeking.

On the day following his welcome by the Government at the Luxembourg, François de Neufchâteau, secretary of the Institute, invited twenty of his colleagues to honour the General. Napoleon astonished them by the scope of his knowledge, the diversity of his reading, and his extraordinary memory. He talked meta-physics with Siéyès, politics with Gallois, mathematics with Lagrange, poetry with Chénier.

Napoleon seemed particularly impressed by Daunou, one of the principal founders of the Institute, who had just completed drawing up the constitution of the Batavian Republic.[1] Napoleon told him how happy he was to see a man of his gifts devoting his talents to the welfare of the Republic. He himself, he said, wanted no more than to support the Constitution by equitable and just means.

On 25 December, he was elected to the *Classe des Sciences* (Mechanics section) and immediately sent his thanks to the President:

'I am honoured by the approbation of the distinguished members of this Institute. I well know that before ever I can become their equal, I must, for a long time, be their pupil. . . . *The only real conquests, the only ones to bring no regrets, are conquests over ignorance. The most honourable occupation, since it is the most beneficial to nations, is to contribute to the sum of human knowledge.*

'Glory bows before reason!' For these scholars of the Institute, these men who were continuing the tradition of Voltaire, Condillac, Helvétius, and Condorcet, no ideal could be more exalting. This declaration of faith gave the lie to all suspicions; it mollified the critics, especially those who had protested against the attitude of the warrior-diplomat in his dealings with the Papacy.

* * *

The Directory, indeed, declared their faith in Bonaparte by appointing him Commander-in-Chief of the 'Army of England'. But an invasion of England at this time, seemed to him impracticable. He was, in fact, thinking of quite a different expedition as he inspected the Channel ports in that February of 1798. In his carriage he had brought every book he could find on Egypt.

Why Egypt? The idea of occupying that country had already been entertained in the time of the *Ancien Régime*. Since then, Volney's famous *Voyage* had made Egypt fashionable. Bonaparte had not only read the *Voyage*, but he had also listened to Volney's accounts of the East. Now he was thinking of driving the Turks

---

[1] Batavia: the name given to the newly formed Republic of Holland. (Translator's note).

out of Constantinople and of defeating the English, not in their impregnable island, but in the East and in the Indies.

What finally decided him was a paper read by Talleyrand to the Institute on 27 July 1797, in which the Foreign Minister pointed out the advantages to be obtained by colonial expansion and stressed the fact that Choiseul, who had acquired Corsica for France, had sought to prepare the way for the acquisition of Egypt. On 16 August, Napoleon drew the Directory's attention to the advantages to be gained by conquering that country. On 14 February, Talleyrand submitted a *Rapport sur la Question d'Egypte*, which coincided exactly with the General's views.

The Directory allowed themselves to be persuaded without too much difficulty. Now that peace was concluded they were, in fact, far from displeased that this ambitious General should want to slake his thirst for conquest so far from home. But is it really fair to attribute to Napoleon only a vulgar appetite for power? His colleagues in the Institute, on the contrary, thought that one consequence of this grandiose expedition would be to enlarge *'les domains de l'esprit humain'*. Right up to the time of his departure from Paris, the General faithfully attended their meetings. Moreover, he was to do something which had never been done before – he was to be accompanied by scholars and artists – Monge, Berthelot, Geoffroy Saint-Hilaire, Denon, Larrey, and many others. Once there, they would form the nucleus of the Institute of Egypt. Bonaparte had hoped to add Destutt de Tracy, the philosopher, to their number, but he refused the invitation. Finally he asked Jean-Baptiste Say to provide a list of books to take with him. No doubt he would have liked to have had Volney with him too, but the latter had not yet returned from the United States.

On 4 May 1798, Bonaparte left Paris. At Toulon, on the eve of departure, he reviewed his strange Army of soldiers and scholars. 'I am leading you to a country [he said] where your future exploits will outshine any of those with which you have already amazed your admirers.'

He was answered by an immense shout of *'Vive la Republique immortelle!'*

* * *

While Bonaparte was conducting his campaigns in the East with alternate success and failure, the situation in France was growing increasingly serious. The Directory's political policy of annexation and extortion, which had little regard for the Treaty of Campo Formio, had resulted in the formation of the Second Coalition. The Austrians and Russians (Archduke Charles and Souvoroff) were putting tremendous pressure on the French Armies, which were spread out over an immense front, extending from the Zuyder Zee to the Gulf of Taranto. In the spring of 1799, the French suffered a series of defeats in Germany, Piedmont, and Naples.[1] Within France itself, there was growing discontent with the incompetent and corrupt régime. The elections of Germinal had produced a strong Jacobin element in the Government. In the Council of Five Hundred there was a powerful left wing opposition, led by such hot-heads as Arena, Destrem, Augereau, and Jourdan.[2] But, on the other hand, a desire to save and reconstruct the Republic was making itself felt among those moderates who had not been affected by the general rot. Men like Talleyrand and Roederer were sufficiently politically perceptive and anxious for their own interests to begin thinking of a way of putting an end to the existing chaos. The intellectuals of the *parti philosophique* of the Institute were no less anxious to save the Republic and put it on its feet once and for all. The one man acceptable both to politicians and intellectuals alike and who alone seemed capable of establishing order in the country was Siéyès. On emerging from the shadows in which he had been hiding during the Terror, Siéyès had been appointed Ambassador to Berlin. His standing had considerably increased and he was once again the man of influence he had been ten years ago, when Mirabeau had never failed to address him as 'Mon Maître' and of whom Madame de Staël had said: 'The writings and opinions of the Abbe Siéyès will establish a new era in politics, just as the works of Newton have done in physics.'

[1] The whole of Italy, in fact, with the exception of Genoa, was lost to France.

[2] JOURDAN, Matthieu Jouve (1749–94) known as Jourdan Coupetête: notorious for the atrocities committed in Provence. He is not to be confused with the Marshal, Jean-Baptiste JOURDAN, victor of Fleurus and Army Commander in the Peninsular War. (Translator's note).

On 27 Floréal, year VII (16 May 1799) Siéyès was appointed to the Directory in place of Rewbell. He forced Treilhard Merlin and La Réveillière to resign and replaced them by Gohier, Roger Ducos, and Moulin, and an obscure military officer. But there was no more agreement in the new Directory than there had been in the old. Pandemonium disrupted the meetings of the Councils. The atmosphere was incredibly tense. The former Jacobin Club, reconstituted under the name of the 'Society of the Friends of Liberty and Equality' was now installed in the famous *Manège*. Here, amid scenes of wild disorder, the most extravagant measures were voted. The nightmare of the Terror and the avenging shades of Robespierre and Marbeuf haunted Paris.

Despite these daunting circumstances, Siéyès did not disappoint his friends. He survived the attacks made on him by the *Journal des Hommes Libres* – the official organ of the *Manège* – and even dared to express the opinion that the excesses of the Terrorists were a greater danger to the Republic than any Royalist movement – a statement which made his opponents doubly angry. In the Council of Five Hundred, Cabanis and Garat both spoke in his defence. He was also certain of the support of Talleyrand, Roederer, Cambacérès, and Fouché.

'We require both a head and a sword', he said to Fouché, the newly appointed Minister of Police. Joubert, whose opinion of 'lawyers' was much the same as that of most Generals, was chosen as the 'sword'. But Joubert, who was still in Italy, was killed fighting the combined Russian and Austrian Armies at the disastrous battle of Novi. Without his 'sword', Siéyès seemed temporarily lost. If France were invaded now, the enemy from without would be helped by the enemy within. One name haunted his memory; a shadow dominated the assemblies. 'We need Bonaparte', wrote one of the newspapers. Would the young General ever be seen again? Perhaps he would never return from the East to which he had been so attached. The Directors, who had once been far from annoyed to see the hero out of the way, would now sacrifice anything, including the conquest of Egypt, to have him back.

The *Journal des Hommes Libres* (quickly copied by other Jacobin newspapers) revealed the whole seriousness of the French defeat at Novi. The Directory was determined to suppress the papers.

Editors of right wing papers, too, Fontanes, Laharpe, Flavée, and Suard, were also proscribed.

Jourdan, who despaired of the 'apathy of the Nation', sounded Bernadotte on the question of deposing Siéyès. He wanted to arrest him, dispose of Barras, and form a purely Jacobin Government, 'which alone could save the Republic'. Bernadotte cautiously avoided becoming involved. On 27 Fructidor, Jourdan delivered a speech from the Tribune of the Five Hundred, in which he declared France to be in danger (one only had to remember 1792 to see the truth of this): parliamentary rule would have to be temporarily abolished and the Constitution forgotten. Further speeches from the tribune in support of the Jacobin proposals were opposed by Marie-Joseph Chénier (in an extempore, fiery, but incoherent speech) and by a much calmer Daunou, as well as by Lucien Bonaparte, who showed remarkable presence of mind.

After that tumultuous 27 Fructidor, when deputies fought among themselves on the floor of the Assembly, Paris was paralysed with fear. Even the Palais Royal, the haunt of pleasure-seekers and lovers, was silent. So great was the alarm that for several days grenadiers were posted to guard the Luxembourg. Fear of the Jacobins was widespread. The 'Law of Hostages', which had been passed a month earlier, and which struck at ci-devant aristocrats and *émigrés*, revived the fighting spirit of partisans in the west; whole villages were abandoned: it was preferable to fight in the '*Chouannerie*'[1] than risk deportation. Conscription had the same effect; young recruits deserted to join the ranks of the '*Chauffeurs*'[2] and other bands of brigands.

Beyond the Frontiers of France, the situation was deteriorating. The Army of the Archduke Charles, advancing up the left bank of the Rhine, recaptured Mannheim; the Cisalpine Republic and Piedmont were lost. The threat of invasion was becoming a reality. Fortunately, on the anniversary of the Republic, Brune won a victory against the Anglo-Russian forces in Holland,

[1] *Chouans:* the name applied to the Royalist insurgents (mostly peasants), who organized a reactionary movement in Brittany (1792–3). The name probably derived from *chathuant* (screech owl) owing to the nocturnal habits of the guerilla bands.

[2] *Chauffeur:* the name given to brigands who practised extortion by burning the soles of the feet of their victims. (Translator's note).

Masséna recaptured Zürich and halted Souvoroff at the exit to the Saint-Gothard. Hope was in the air, and the strains of the *Carmagnole* were once more to be heard.

On 13 Vendémiaire – always an auspicious date for Napoleon – the news for which none had dared to hope burst on the country like a thunderclap: a dispatch from General Bonaparte had just been received. He was alive. He was victorious. He was on his way home.

Although Bonaparte, shortly after his arrival in Egypt in the preceding year, had reported at length to the Directory on the destruction of the French fleet by Nelson in the Bay of Aboukir (the so-called 'Battle of the Nile'), which had cut him off from Europe, the public had, at the time, only a vague idea of the magnitude of the disaster. They were therefore uninhibited in their rejoicing when, on 18 Vendémiaire, the boom of cannon signalled the news of a splendid French victory over the Turkish Army at the same spot. Bonaparte had already landed in France when the news arrived. He had embarked in the frigate *Muriot* with five Generals (Marmont, Lannes, Murat, Berthier, and Andréossy), two distinguished scholars (Berthollet and Monge), and his Mameluke bodyguard. On the evening of 17 Vendémiaire he landed at Saint-Raphaël, from where he proceeded to Paris, cheered all the way. On the evening of 21 Vendémiaire the marvellous, incredible news had already begun to spread throughout the country. On the following morning there could be no further doubt that the news was true.

Moreau, who had returned from Italy, was received by Siéyès at the Luxembourg. Negotiations? Proposals? Moreau had made up his mind. 'There is your man', he said, 'he will stage your *coup d'état* much better than I ever could!' Lucien Bonaparte was elected unanimously as President of the Five Hundred.

For Frenchmen, weary of war, Bonaparte represented peace and the true spirit of the Revolution. 'The people', said Jourdan, 'only see him as an infallible and victorious General, destined to re-establish the honour of the Armies of the Republic!' But, in the eyes of the Institute, this warrior was still the protector of principles and ideas.

On 24 Vendémiaire, year VII (16 October 1799), the soldier-philosopher entered Paris wihout fuss. He went straight to his house in the rue de la Victoire, where he rested all day. In the evening he was received by Gohier, the President of the Directory. A little later he was invited to meet the Directors at a public session. He arrived most oddly dressed, wearing an old frock coat, with a '*chapeau rond*' and carrying a scimitar. He was unable to wear uniform because all his luggage had been stolen between Fréjus and Aix by brigands. Bonaparte solemnly affirmed his loyalty to the Republic, and, laying his hand on the hilt of his oriental sword, swore that 'he would never draw it except in defence of the Republic and its Government'.

He could have been censured for abandoning his Army and for returning home without orders; indeed, he could have been arrested. Even the sincerity of his convictions might have been questioned; it was only necessary to remember with what ease this former protégé of the Robespierres had disburdened himself of their compromising friendship to obtain everything from Barras – the very man responsible for their deaths. Was Taine so far wrong when he wrote of the young Napoleon: 'None of the social or political beliefs which had such influence on other men ever had any influence on him'?

But the nation worshipped the hero. All Paris wanted to see, hear, and acclaim him. He scarcely ever left his house, which was bombarded by visitors. He found Josephine a prey to malicious gossip. He sulked. Hortense and Eugène, Josephine's children by her previous marriage, pleaded the cause of their mother. He forgave her. He informed himself of everything that had happened in his absence; he gauged public opinion; he entertained Volney, whom he congratulated on his article in the *Moniteur*, written after the Battle of the Nile, in which Volney had explained the difficulties attending the expedition. Bonaparte made a point of frequently visiting the Institute where in one of his addresses, he spoke of the famous Rosetta stone. With the help of Volney, he explained the particular interest of its three inscriptions (hiero-glyphic, Coptic, and Greek). The *Publicité*, which on 1 Brumaire had already remarked with what modesty Bonaparte had taken his seat among other members of the Institute, reported that he had attended another meeting on 5 Brumaire, when he made a speech detailing the present condition of Egypt and its ancient monuments. He had assured his listeners that a Suez canal, linking the two seas, had actually existed, and that it was possible even today, to reconstruct it on the ruins which still remained, and that he had already prepared plans and taken levels for this great work. His colleagues were exultant. All whom he met were delighted with him.

Accompanied either by Talleyrand, Siéyès, or Cabanis – or more likely, as we believe, by Volney – Bonaparte took time off to visit Madame Helvétius at Auteuil. The old lady, who had not long to live, was proud to do him the honours of her little estate. Nevertheless, she guessed that he found it a trifle small. 'You have no idea, General, what happiness can be found in three acres of land', said this friend of philosophers to the new Alexander – the man who had been forced to renounce Asia, but who was soon to appropriate for himself the 'molehill' of Europe.

2

The Society of Auteuil

✦✦✦

WHY did Bonaparte visit Mme Helvétius at Auteuil? Of course he had known for a long time that all the most illustrious French intellectuals frequented the house of this old lady who still preserved the mentality, tastes, and manners of the eighteenth century. He knew that Condorcet, the famous mathematician and one of the founders of the Republic, had at one time lived in Auteuil, and that such famous scholars as Cabanis, Siéyès, Destutt de Tracy, Daunou, Marie-Joseph Chénier, and Garat – all members of the Institute whom he admired – either lived in the village or visited it frequently. He made it his business to respect and flatter them, for the time would come when they could be useful to him.

Mme Helvétius had been brought up by her aunt, Mme de Graffigny, the friend of Voltaire. When still a girl she had been befriended by Turgot and married to Claude-Adrien Helvétius. Helvétius was of Dutch origin. At one time the *maître d'hotel* to Marie Leczynska, he later became a farmer-general and was the friend of d'Alembert and Diderot. Ambitious to make his own contribution to the Encyclopedic enterprise, he wrote *De l'ésprit*. His book, published in 1758, was condemned and burnt; in 1792 his bust was smashed by the Jacobins. Helvétius, however, without doubt owed his greatest success to his Tuesday dinner parties which were attended by everyone who knew how to talk, think, or hold a pen, including well-known foreigners such as David Hume and the Duke of Brunswick.

Now, in old age, Madame Helvétius was just as charming and

31

attractive as when young. After the death of her husband she
settled in Auteuil where she had acquired a house from the painter
Quentin Latour. Here she lived happily, apparently with no
regrets for the giddy, fashionable Paris where once she had
reigned supreme. Although relatively modest in size, Mme Helvétius's house was large enough to accommodate fifty guests in
the drawing room on the first floor. The friends whom she had
known all her life followed her out to her country retreat. Some
even made their home there. The first to do so was Morellet, the
author of a *Manuel des Inquisteurs*, whose wit so enchanted Voltaire.
Morellet worked for some time in a pavilion in Mme Helvétius's
garden, where he installed a library, but in 1789 he withdrew from
the Auteuil circle. A little later, when young Cabanis, after
finishing his medical studies, was recommended country air for
reasons of health, he was literally adopted by Madame Helvétius,
who had lost her own son. When Benjamin Franklin was in
France, he too became a firm friend of Madame Helvétius.

Everyone Franklin met at her house followed passionately
the course of the American War of Independence and all longed
for a rebel victory, none perhaps so much as Condorcet, the
friend of Thomas Paine, principal author of the Constitution of
Pennsylvania. Franklin, who had founded the American Philosophical Society in Philadelphia, made Condorcet and Daubenton
members (1775), and later added two more 'regulars' of the
Auteuil circle to their number – Volney and Cabanis. It was to
Cabanis that this great American bequeathed his Governor-
General's sword on leaving France.

Despite ill health, Cabanis insisted on visiting his patients in all
weathers on horseback. They adored him. The doctor had not
renounced his philosophical studies. Persuaded that the universe
was governed by a being of infinite intelligence and convinced
that the best means of approaching 'Him' was by consecrating
one's life to human suffering, he wrote his *Serment d'un Medecin*
in 1783. He swore before God to devote his life to the care of the
sick, the poor in particular. These were no vain words – as a member of the hospitals commission of Paris during the years 1791–
1793, he proposed reforms which, with the help of his friend
Pinel, were finally implemented. The reforms included the demand for an increase in the number of hospital beds (two patients

to a bed was not uncommon), and for assurances that the sick were really dead before burial and were not just disposed of as unwanted bodies to make room for others. He was also concerned with the lot of prisoners, who, for him, were still human beings, and also with the inhuman treatment accorded to lunatics and foundlings. Like Condorcet, who became his brother-in-law when he married Charlotte de Grouchy (the sister of Sophie, the wife of the philosopher), he believed it the duty of society to care for all who were unable to look after themselves.

It was Cabanis who introduced Volney to Auteuil. The real name of Volney (a contraction, perhaps, of Voltaire and Ferney?) was François Chassebeuf. After completing his schooling with the Oratorians at Angers and then studying law and medicine in Paris, this excellent Latin scholar went on to study Hebrew 'to show up the errors with which translations of the Bible abound'. His passion for knowledge, however, was not merely confined to book learning. In 1782 he made a voyage to the Levant where he remained for two years, travelling in Egypt, Syria, and Palestine.

In Auteuil, he received a truly intelligent and motherly welcome from Madame Helvétius, whose guest he was to be during the whole time required to complete the account of his journeys. His clearly written, unbiased book, which is primarily a socio-logical study, had a very considerable success; it was warmly received by the *philosophes* and was translated into many languages. Lamartine set great store by it, and Berthier, in his *Account of the Campaign in Egypt* (*Relation de la Campagne d'Egypte*) describes it as having been 'the guide for the French in Egypt . . . the only one never to mislead'.

In the spring of 1792, after war had been declared, a young German, by the name of 'Anacharsis' Cloots, who, like Tom Paine had become a naturalized Frenchman,[1] wrote a long letter to his mother in which he sang the praises of Auteuil. . . . 'We are all Jacobins here [he wrote] but not in the sense of Robespierre or the Robespierrots.' For Cloots, as for all the Auteuil *philosophes*,

[1] JEAN-BAPTISTE DU VAL DE GRACE, Baron Cloots (b. 1755) was a *conventionnel* and one of the founders of the *Culte de la Raison*. He was guillotined in 1794 together with other *Enragés* (the communard followers of Hébert) by Robespierre. Anacharsis was a philosopher and friend of Plato. *c.* 589 B.C. (Translator's note).

In the course of this summer of 1792, a former officer of La Fayette's army arrived in Auteuil with his family. His name was Antoine Louis Claude (formerly Count) Destutt de Tracy. He was descended from a noble Scottish family settled in France in the fifteenth century. On his grandmother's side, he was a great-nephew of the famous Arnould.[1] He had had a brilliant military career. His marriage into the Penthièvre family, at the age of twenty-four (1778), had brought him the colonelcy of the regiment of that name. Always strongly attracted to philosophy, as a young man he had avidly read the works of the *Encyclopédistes*, and, contrary to the wishes of his family had made a pilgrimage to Voltaire at Ferney.

Despite his political opinions, Destutt de Tracy was elected deputy of the Bourbonnais nobility to the Estates General (1789) where he voted for the reunion of the nobility and clergy with the *tiers état*, renouncing his own title and privileges. In 1791 he denounced his own regiment to the Assembly for its loyalty to Bouillé (who, it will be remembered, was responsible for preparing the flight of Louis XVI to Varennes). In the following year he was raised to the rank of *Marechal de Camp* (Major-General) by Narbonne,[2] the Minister of War, and placed in command of the cavalry of La Fayette's army. Destutt remained friends with La Fayette until the events of 10 August put an end to his relationship with the 'Hero of Two Worlds'.[3]

It was shortly after this event that Destutt resigned his own commission and came to live in Auteuil where he assiduously cultivated the company of Madame Helvétius, Cabanis, and Condorcet, who were later joined by Daunou.

Daunou was an Oratorian priest, a professor of philosophy and

---

[1] SOPHIE ARNOULD (1746–1802). Famous French singer, well known for her beauty and wit, who specialized in the works of Rameau and Gluck. (Translator's note).

[2] LOUIS, Comte de Narbonne-Lara (1755–1813), illegitimate son of Louis XV. (Translator's note).

[3] When La Fayette was proscribed by the Assembly for his so-called monarchist sympathies, he attempted to escape to temporary asylum in America, but was captured by the Austrians and imprisoned for five years and was only released after the signing of the peace of Campo Formio.

theology. He had adopted the principles of 1789 and welcomed the victory of 14 July; indeed, he had gone further, for when the Superior of the Oratorians – a relatively liberal order – had blessed the Revolutionary flag, Daunou had pronounced the funeral oration for those who had died fighting for liberty and had identified the cause of patriotism with religion. Moreover, he approved the Civil Constitution of the Clergy and accepted the appointment of diocesan Vicar of Arras and later that of metropolitan vicar to the Bishop of Paris. He resigned from the Church when he was elected to the Convention, where he took his seat beside the Girondists.

Despite what has been said and written of Condorcet, he himself was never a member of the Girondists. In fact, he formally stated, when he joined the Convention, 'I never have and never will belong to any party'. Indeed, far from supporting the Girondists, he was often in complete disagreement with them. But he was firmly on their side after their defeat by the *coup de force* of 2 June 1793, when twenty representatives of the Nation were expelled from the Assembly at gun point.

Now, living in retirement in his house at Auteuil, all he wanted to do was to work on the newspaper which he had recently founded in collaboration with Siéyès. This *Journal de l'Instruction Sociale* was designed to familiarize its readers with 'political language' and to explain 'the principles of natural and political rights, public Economy, and the Social Arts'. He believed that the political education of the masses was 'one of the first duties of all writers dedicated to the cause of truth and the welfare of their country'.

Siéyès – the Abbé Siéyès – shared his views completely; indeed, he went even further. According to him, it was necessary to reform the language before one could reform Society. It was the difference between ideas and words which make for errors in scientific knowledge and rendered metaphysics incomprehensible. Like Descartes, he wanted 'to efface from his mind everything that he had hitherto been taught, the better to receive the impressions of truth, whencesoever they should come'.[1]

Although they differed so profoundly in character – Siéyès was as undemonstrative, prudent, and secretive as Condorcet was

[1] *Discours de la Methode* (1637). (Translator's note).

generous, enthusiastic, and emotional – the cleric and the heir to the *Encyclopédistes* understood each other perfectly. They had known each other for years; both had demanded a Declaration of Rights at the same time. After the Constituent ssembly was replaced by the Legislative, Siéyès, who had no seat in the latter, seldom left Auteuil, except to spend a few hours in Paris with Madame Roland and Sophie de Condorcet. He was offered an archbishopric, but refused on the pretext that he had never preached and had never been to confession. As a member of the Convention he had collaborated with Condorcet in drawing up the new Constitution and had then resigned from the Committee, composed in all of nine members, just as though this Committee had not been at one time his main preoccupation.

What sort of a man was this Siéyès – a man so difficult to understand and so often slandered? His very discretion surrounded him with a kind of mystery. In the Assembly he sat motionless on his bench, taking notes and never applauding. His slightest gesture was remarked; his few words were eagerly seized upon; his silence was respected. Robespierre said of him: 'The Abbé Siéyès never shows his hand, but he never ceases to work underground. He is the mole of the Revolution.' After the Terror, everyone quoted Siéyès's famous remark: *j'ai vécu* ('I survived').

Was he a knave? Was he a coward? Probably neither, but just a calculating man, little disposed to action, but one who found refuge in political and philosophical speculation, who spent nearly all his life elaborating the ideal social constitution by which he was obsessed.

In his youth, however, this former Jesuit pupil had aspired to a military career, but ill-health had forced him to relinquish the idea. Influenced by the devout piety of his parents, he had chosen instead the Church as his profession, but once having made his decision, he was immediately to regret it. Hardly had the doors of the seminary closed on him than he began to feel assailed by scruples and entertain doubts about his faith. In 1773, at the age of twenty-five, he was ordained but, nevertheless, continued to read Locke and Condillac.[1] In the months preceding the convocation

[1] CONDILLAC (Etienne Bonnot de) (1715–80) b. Grenoble. Leader of the *école sensualiste*, author of *Traité des Sensations* and *La Logique*. (Translator's note).

of the States General, thousands of pamphlets were published, but probably none had such success as that written by Siéyès, which contained the famous sentence: 'What is the Third Estate? – Everything. What part has it played so far in the body politic? – None. What does it demand? – To become something.'

This pamphlet struck a hard blow at the established régime. Siéyès was a clear thinking theoretician and no mere dreamer. In his eyes, revolution could mean only one thing – civil war. He predicted that the privileged classes would consent to make minor concessions to the Third Estate, but he was courageous enough to declare that there was no common ground for agreement between oppressed and oppressors. The Third Estate could only depend on themselves and on no account should allow themselves to be fooled into the belief that their first duty was to obey an autocratic monarch endowed with Divine Right.

As soon as Siéyès was elected to the States General, this *philosophe*, whom a modern historian[1] has described as the 'first revolutionary thinker', was immediately recognized as a born leader. It was on 10 June 1789, that Siéyès, on entering the Chamber, exclaimed, 'The time has come for us to cut the painter'. 'On that day,' says Michelet,[2] 'Siéyès, who had calculated the course of events with such accuracy, revealed himself as a true statesman. He said what had to be done, and carried out his plans immediately.' The Third Estate became the National Assembly.

Siéyès was a revolutionary after Condorcet's heart, a man capable of opposing the 'political charlatans who wish to curry favour with the people, the better to tyrannize them'.

Although Condorcet spent most of his time on the *Journal de l'Instruction Sociale*, he still occupied himself with *La Feuille Villageoise*. This little review was a sort of popular Encyclopedia, composed of very simple articles 'written by village schoolmasters and journalists'. Its purpose was 'to reach every village in France to instruct in Laws, Events, and Discoveries which were of interest to every citizen'. *La Feuille Villageoise* first appeared in 1790 and numbered among its founders Rabaud, Saint-Etienne, and Pierre-Louis Ginguené.

[1] J. L. Talman: *Les Origines de la democratie totalitaire.*

[2] MICHELET, Jules (1798–1874). French liberal historian; author of a *History of France* and a *History of the French Revolution*, etc.

Ginguené was a curious personality, of whom a lot was to be heard in the years to come. He was a Breton from Rennes who in his youth had dreamed of occupying an important place in the world of letters, and first tried his hand at poetry and drama. But in 1780, this gifted young man entered the civil service (*controle generale*), where no doubt he might have made a sucessful career for himself, but the convocation of the States General, the capture of the Bastille, and subsequent events inspired him to take up his pen again and two years later saw the publication of his *De l'autorité de Rabelais dans la Revolution presente et dans la Constitution civile du clergé*, followed by his *Lettres sur les Confessions de Jean-Jacques Rousseau*. A devoted admirer of Condorcet, Ginguené then offered to work for *La Feuille Villageoise*.

Condorcet, who although he scarcely ever left Auteuil, still followed with the closest attention everything that was taking place in Paris, where his Girondist sympathies had made him a suspected person. On 10 June 1793, his former friend, Herault de Séchelles, read the text of the new Constitution to the Assembly. This was called the *Montagnarde*, a flagrant plagiarism on the title of Condorcet's own draft Constitution, which was entitled the *Girondine*. Indignation prompted Condorcet to write his *Letter to the Citizens of France on the New Constitution*, in which he maintained that the *Montagnarde* was a 'botched-up job put together by five incompetent officials, at a moment when the freedom of the Press was being destroyed by inquisitorial methods, by the plundering of printing presses, and when respect for private correspondence was being flagrantly violated to an extent undreamed of even in the days of despotism'.

Although the 'Letter', which was printed secretly and circulated in all *départements*, was unsigned, Condorcet was well aware that he could only expect the worst, and in order 'to remain, in all circumstances, master of himself', provided himself with poison, prepared by Cabanis, which he shared with Jean de Bry.

The identity of the author of the letter was soon known. On 8 July, a warrant for Condorcet's arrest was issued. But Auteuil, united in its resistance to the Assembly, knew how to safeguard the flight of their hero. The two police officers sent from Paris to arrest him went from house to house in vain: no one had seen the philosopher. While the police searched the village, Condorcet was able to make good his escape. Where did he go? To hide at Madame Helvétius's, only a couple of steps from his own house, would have been too risky; as for accepting the hospitality of Garat, the Minister of the Interior, who had offered him asylum, he would not dream of it. Garat, who for many years had been the friend of the philosopher, wrote in his *Memoires of the Revolution*, published in 1795:

> As soon as Condorcet was forced into hiding, I offered him a refuge in the Ministry of Interior itself; never could the residence of a member of the Republic have served a worthier purpose. . . . This was the most saintly act I ever performed.

The fugitive, instead, put himself in the hands of two reliable men recommended to him by Cabanis – Pinel, the doctor who did his best to improve conditions in Bicêtre (the old people's home and lunatic asylum), and Boyer, the second surgeon at the hospital of la Charité (who, after 1804, became Napoleon's surgeon). The two doctors took him to a hiding place which had long been prepared for him. In a house in the rue des Fossoyeurs – today the rue Servandoni – between the Luxembourg and the church of Saint-Sulpice (then known as the Temple of Victory) lived a Madame Vernet, widow of Vernet, the sculptor, who let out rooms. Pinel and Boyer had lived there when they were students. Brave to the point of rashness, the widow kept the fugitive hidden during the eight months he still had to live. It was here that he wrote his most important work, *l'Esquisse d'un tableau historique des progrès de l'Esprit Humain*.[1]

Paris was living through a nightmare. The Law of Suspects rendered every citizen guilty. After Louis XVI and Marie Antoinette had been guillotined, true Republicans were also executed; Girondists mounted the scaffold singing the Marseillaise. Condorcet knew that he could not escape death, but nevertheless, indifferent to his own fate, his work shows a serene assurance that the Revolution, which seemed to have been betrayed,

---

[1] In this work he insists on the justice and necessity of civil and political rights between the individuals of both sexes and proclaims the indefinite perfectibility of the human race. (Translator's note).

would survive, and that humanity, despite all, was advancing to a better future.

Once his work was completed, and no longer wishing to compromise Madame Vernet, he managed to escape her vigilant eye and disappeared one morning in March 1794. It was believed that he had escaped to Switzerland, but in fact he poisoned himself while in prison at Bourg-Egalité (Bourg-la-Reine). His old friends, the Suards, who had an estate at Fontenay-aux-Roses, had refused him hospitality. He was captured at an inn at Clamart (on the outskirts of Paris).

He was by no means the only member of the Auteuil circle to suffer from the Terror. Volney, Ginguené, Daunou, and Destutt de Tracy were all arrested. Volney, for his royalist tendencies; Ginguené for his journalistic activities; Daunou, like Condorcet, for having refused to vote for the King's death; 'One can no longer speak of the Revolution', Daunou had protested, 'when it depends on a rule of vultures; let us rely on an atmosphere of humanity and justice.' After denouncing the proscription of the Girondists, he was imprisoned in La Force, and thereafter in four other prisons. But neither privation nor insults could quell his courage. While Ginguené translated Plato, Daunou sustained himself by reading Cicero and Tacitus and other classical authors.

Destutt de Tracy was arrested in Auteuil on 2 November 1793, and taken to the Abbaye, where, with three hundred other prisoners he remained for six weeks. He was then transferred to the Carmelites, where he began to read and work. Here, just when he thought he had found the answer to the ideological problems by which he was obsessed,[1] he heard steps in the corridor,

---

[1] Of Destutt de Tracy's philosophy, which he called *ideology*, he published a first outline in 1801. It was an offspring of Condillac's sensationalism, but under the influence of Cabanis, Destutt refined the analysis of sensations and emphasized their physiological character. 'Ideology is a part of zoology'; but it was far more inclusive and corresponded to the anthropology of the German philosophers. The four activities of conscious life, perception, memory, judgement, and will, are all varieties and commutations of sensations. Thought is nothing but an elaboration of sensations and an activity of the nervous system. (Translator's note.)

followed by a shouting of names. It was the roll-call of those destined for the guillotine on the following day, a roll-call which never ceased. From one moment to another it might be his own name which was called, but Destutt de Tracy never allowed his thoughts to wander from his writing. It was during this terrible time that he formulated the essentials of what was to serve as the basis of all his writings.

The date of his execution was fixed for 11 Thermidor. He was saved by the death of Robespierre.

Condorcet's fate was only revealed on 30 December 1794 in an article in the *Décade philosophique*. This paper, the organ of the *parti philosophique*, was founded on 10 Floreal, Year II (20 April 1794), at the very time that Robespierre was busy eliminating the *enragés* and *modérés*. The aim of the *Décade* was to defend freedom of thought and preserve the principles of the Years of Enlightenment and republican values. From its inception Ginguené had been its leading spirit.[1] Collaborating with him were Jean-Baptiste Say, Roederer, Fauriel, Marie-Joseph Chénier, and Cabanis. Cabanis was later to write an analysis of the work of the great missing philosopher, whom Ginguené had always recognized as the inspiration behind this journal: 'A Revolution created by philosophy,' he wrote, 'should be preserved by philosophers.'

It was Condorcet's attitude which dictated the conduct of most men who remained faithful to the ideals of political liberty and human rights. If we examine the opposition to Napoleon from this point of view, we discover that everything stems from Condorcet's teachings.

Once again elected to the Convention, Daunou began work on a projected Constitution to replace the *Montagnarde*, which had never been implemented. He consulted Siéyès, the great authority

Destutt developed the consequences and applications of his theories and treatises published between 1801–15 under the general title of *Elements d'Idéologie* and dealing with grammar, logic, and political economy. He left unfinished his *Traite de la Volonté*, to which Stendhal was much indebted. (Translator's note).

---

[1] In March 1798, his collaboration with the paper was interrupted when he was sent to Turin as ambassador to the King of Sardinia.

on constitutional law, but the latter was not prepared to colla-
borate. Daunou continued his work, inspired by the *Girondine*.
Henceforth the Republic would respect the principles of 1789, as
formulated by the *Philosophes*; liberties would be restored and the
victims of tyranny rehabilitated. It was in this spirit that Boissy
d'Anglas demanded freedom of the Press, for which Brissot,
Condorcet, and Rabaud had fought so valiantly.

In this same Assembly, Marie-Joseph Chénier urged that the
deputies expelled from the Convention should be reinstated.
'They have run away, you say, to hide themselves. They have
buried themselves in the depth of caverns. Why has no cavern
been found deep enough to preserve the thoughts of Condorcet
and the eloquence of Vergniaud?...'

Long before the Revolution Marie-Joseph Chénier had already
begun to write verse; verse because he was a poet, and plays
because the theatre afforded him a platform for his beliefs. In 1788
he had finished his tragedy, *Charles IX*, and a little later,
Henry VIII. M. Suard, the theatrical censor, had, however,
obstinately withheld permission for their performance. Fearful
of compromising himself, Suard had even banned Beaumarchais's
Marriage of Figaro.

On 19 August 1789, one of the audience of the Théatre Français demanded in stentorian tones why *Charles IX* was not
performed on the boards of one of France's principal theatres.
An actor replied that authorization to present this play had been
unobtainable. The audience protested that authorization was
unnecessary. The anonymous spectator was none other than
Danton himself. Bailly brought up the question in the National
Assembly and, despite the fears of Monsieur Suard, *Charles IX*
was performed for the first time on 4 November 1789 with Talma
in the title role. Such was the eloquence of his performance that at
the fall of the curtain the audience stamped in approval for ten
minutes on end, calling for the author, whom the great actor
brought on again and again in triumph on to the stage.

We are told by Grimm that *Charles IX* attracted an even larger
audience than *Figaro* and that on leaving the performance Danton
exclaimed: 'If *Figaro* has destroyed the nobility, *Charles IX* will
destroy the monarchy'.

In February 1792, Chénier presented *Caius Gracchus*, which had a prodigious success. When this great tragedy was performed again during the Terror, and the audience heard the lines:

> *Des lois et non du sang. Ne souilles point vos mains.*
> *Romains, vous oseriez égorger des Romains . . .* [1]

the audience remained still for some moments, not daring to applaud. A few days later, Billaud Varennes denounced the play from the Tribune, as the work of 'a bad citizen'. Two years later, the dress rehearsal of another play, *Timoléon*, was interrupted by a partisan of Robespierre, who shouted, 'Chénier, you were never anything but a phoney revolutionary'.

In March 1794, André was arrested and imprisoned in Saint-Lazare. The enemies of Marie-Joseph claimed that he did nothing to try to save his brother. But in fact he made numerous efforts to obtain his freedom, but in vain.[2] If the sincerity of Marie-Joseph's revolutionary sentiments are sometimes called into doubt, it must be recognized that he was fundamentally a timid character, terrified by Robespierre. Madame de Staël, who was one of his friends, wrote of him:

> 'Chénier was a man who was both violent and timid. Although an enthusiastic admirer of the *philosophes*, he was full of prejudice; he was quite impervious to reason when his passions were roused.'

*   *   *

At the end of May 1795, the *parti philosophique* was reinforced by the arrival in Paris of two foreigners, who were to play an important role in the years to come – Benjamin Constant and Madame de Staël.

Germaine de Staël was Swiss by parentage, Swedish by marriage, and French at heart. It was three years since she had left Paris, to which she was now returning filled with republican ideals. Her beloved father, Monsieur Necker, whom she had left behind in Coppet, lavished good advice on his daughter:

[1] 'Laws, not blood. Do not soil your hands. Romans, would you dare to cut the throats of fellow Romans?'

[2] André was executed six months later (25 July), just three days before the end of the Terror. (Translator's note).

'I very much hope that you are not indulging in any secret schemes which will get you talked about. You can't have plans of this sort without incurring endless trouble. Remember all the worries you brought on yourself on former occasions.'

Germaine de Staël seemed destined always to be in the public eye. Her abundant vitality, her curiosity, and enthusiasm naturally led her to engage in an active life. No matter where she was, she always had to see everything, hear everything, and become involved in everything that was going on.

Her father, though a mediocrity as a man, was a popular and successful financier who exerted a profound influence on her life. She worshipped him, and even went so far as to say she would like him as a husband. After the intrigues which had resulted in the dismissal of the great reformer Turgot, Louis XVI had appointed Necker, while still a comparatively young man, Director-General of Finance – as a foreigner he could not be made a Minister.

The lovely, irreproachable, but colourless Madame Necker, born Suzanne Curchot, the daughter of a Lutheran pastor, had been brought up with a sound scholastic background. Despite her strict moral principles, she nevertheless managed to adapt herself to a 'futile and corrupt Parisian society'. In her *salon*, which was one of the most frequented of the capital, her little daughter, Germaine, had her own *tabouret*.[1] Here she listened to the words of the Abbé Galiani, Buffon, and Diderot, with the same enthusiasm as she was later to read the works of Rousseau and Raynal, Montesquieu and the *Encyclopédistes*.

Madame Necker wanted to marry Germaine to William Pitt. Germaine, however, resolutely opposed the match, particularly because she did not want to be separated from her father, and at the age of nineteen, in 1785, she decided to marry the insignificant but accommodating Baron Eric-Magnus Staël von Holstein, secretary to the Swedish Embassy, whom M. Necker arranged to have promoted ambassador. By this marriage, Baron Staël acquired a fabulous dowry. Germaine's father could not have arranged a more suitable life for his brilliant daughter, who attracted all Paris to her *salon* in the rue de Bac. She was less

[1] *Tabouret*. The stool of honour accorded by Louis XIV's protocol only to his most distinguished courtiers. (Translator's note).

concerned with creating a personal impression than in examining and attempting to resolve problems with her guests. At that time, politics, rather than philosophy and literature, was the principal topic of conversation. Germaine knew how to keep silent and listen, but when she felt inspired and wished to carry her point, she appeared almost beautiful, and her flowing impromptu eloquence subdued all her hearers into silent admiration. But was she really as ugly as everyone said, Napoleon in particular?

She quickly put on weight; she had no taste in dress, and the turban which she liked to wear had the effect of making her round face even plainer. But her portrait, painted in 1789 when she was twenty-three, and now hanging in the Estampes, shows a witty and attractive face. Her sharp eyes and mocking half-smile make one forget the heavy chin and her curly hair reminiscent of a poodle's.

She had seen her father, a citizen of Geneva, promoted a quasi-Minister of the King of France. All the greatest celebrities flocked to his house every Friday. His famous *Account Rendered* [*Compte rendu*], published in many editions in 1781, proved that his administration was the best in the world and revealed Monsieur Necker as the most provident of men – but unfortunately, his budget, in excess of ten millions, omitted to include the expenses incurred by the American war. However, as he disapproved of the enormous pensions paid to courtiers, these, led by Maurepas[1] and Vergennes,[2] considered it was high time to get rid of this embarrassing foreigner, a plebeian by birth, despite his recently acquired baronial title.

Accepting their disgrace with dignity, the Necker family retired to their country residence at Saint-Ouen.

After bestowing the Ministry of Finance on Calonne[3] and

[1] MAUREPAS (Jean-Frederic Phelypeaux de), 1701–81, Minister under Louis XV and XVI. He advised Louis XVI to appoint Turgot, but as a frivolous friend of Marie-Antoinette, later advocated his dismissal.

[2] VERGENNES (Charles Gravier, Comte de), 1716–87, Minister of Foreign Affairs and one-time Ambassador to Constantinople and Stockholm. (Translator's note).

[3] CALONNE (Charles-Alexandre de), 1734–1802. Appointed Controller General of Finance in 1783. Disgraced because of his improvidence by the Assemblée des Notables, he took refuge in England.

then on Lomenie de Brienne,[1] and thereby antagonizing Parliament, Louis XVI recalled Necker, who was trusted by both financiers and businessmen alike, and who, moreover, had the reputation of being a liberal.

By the end of June, Necker had again fallen out of favour with both Louis XVI and Marie-Antoinette, though to his friends, he was always to remain a great man. The people of Paris, too, rose in arms when they learnt that he had been dismissed, and demanded his reinstatement.

Monsieur Necker left for Brussels with his family. It was from there that he guaranteed Messrs Hope, the Amsterdam bankers, the sum of two million francs for a shipment of wheat on its way to Paris – a sum which he never recovered, and which Germaine ceaselessly tried to reclaim.

But the people of France wanted Necker. He was recalled again by Louis XVI. Persuaded by his wife and exhorted by his daughter, Necker, who was then in Bâle, once more took the road for Paris. Acclaimed throughout his whole journey, he was greeted at the Hôtel de Ville by a crowd delirious with joy.

Germaine on this occasion felt that she 'had reached the extreme limits of happiness'; that her father, with whom she shared all her thoughts, should have caused this wave of enthusiasm, and who, for the moment, appeared to be master of France, profoundly influenced her future conduct. The Revolution was under way and Madame de Staël thought she was at the tiller. Never had Necker's popularity been as apparent as at the *Fête de la Fédération;* but only six weeks later, after the patent ineptitude of his financial policy had been exposed, he was booed in the Assembly, and was obliged to slip out of Paris and retire to Saint-Ouen. From there he sent in his resignation. On 8 September 1790 he was back in Coppet.

Necker's departure in no way changed Germaine's situation in Paris. While the Ambassador indulged more and more in mysticism, she welcomed to her *salon* anybody and everybody of

[1] LOMENIE DE BRIENNE (Etienne de) Cardinal, 1727–94. Also disgraced because of his improvidence by both the *Assemblée des Notables* and Parliament. In 1788 he took the oath of allegiance to the Civil Constitution, i.e., he became *a prêtre assermenté* (Translator's note).

the slightest importance. Talleyrand was one of the habitués, as well as one of her lovers, but he renounced his claims to her favours to Narbonne, who gave her two sons and whom she was instrumental in making Minister of War. Sophie de Condorcet, to whom she was much attached, helped her to obtain this appointment. Siéyès attended these reunions assiduously, as did Brissot, Malouet, and Barnave, and the brothers Lameth. In this year 1791, Germaine had succeeded in her ambitions: she had gathered around her all the most intelligent men in Paris—men who were also moderate enough in their principles to allow reasonable discussion. Such was her hatred of fanaticism that, two years later, she was even prepared to help in the escape of Marie Antoinette.

Not content with holding a *salon*, she claimed to play a preponderant role in the affairs of France. When Narbonne was obliged to renounce his portfolio, it was at Madame de Staël's home that the Girondists and the followers of La Fayette held their meetings, at which Sophie de Condorcet was also present. Narbonne was not reinstated, but the fall of the Ministry was decided, and his place was taken by a Girondist (April 1792). Although unsuccessful in her plans, Germaine was still under the impression that it was she who was controlling events. Such conduct on the part of the wife of the Swedish Ambassador was naturally a source of annoyance to the King of Sweden, Gustavus III, who ordered the Baron de Staël to close down his embassy. The Ambassadress, however, in no way modified her activities and continued to entertain her friends either in her father's house or in that of Madame de Condorcet.

However, she was much disturbed by the violence of the critical days of the Revolution and, although entirely devoted to the masses who had acclaimed her father, she was frightened by their ruthlessness. Their march on the Tuileries on 20 June terrified her.

She was deeply concerned by the fate of her unfortunate compatriots, the Swiss Guard, who had defended the Tuileries on 10 August. She helped to hide her friends, sheltered Narbonne and Mathieu de Montmorency. When on 2 September the 'populace' began on a course of wholesale massacre, the Baronne de Staël drove off in her berline travelling coach, drawn by six horses, and departed for Coppet.

*   *   *

In the summer of 1793, the worthy Constant family saw the return of their Benjamin from Germany, or rather from Brunswick. His father, Colonel Juste Constant de Rebecque, who like many other Swiss, was serving with the Dutch army, had obtained for his son the post of *Kammerjunker*, or 'Chamberlain' to the Duke of Brunswick.

Thus the young man had spent five years – practically the whole period of the Revolution – at this little court, which he had entertained with his wit, and where he had married one of the Duchess's ladies-in-waiting, ten years his senior. Although he carried out his duties with discreet loyalty, he had nonetheless attentively followed events in France. But it is surprising that Benjamin, who was completely converted to the new liberal ideas, should have shown no indignation at the terms of the famous Manifesto,[1] particularly as Paris, threatened with destruction, was not yet a prey to the Terror.

Benjamin's youth had been extremely turbulent. Despite the very curious selection of tutors chosen by his father – a rascally lot who took him to gaming houses and brothels – his precocity was prodigious. At seven he was fluent in Greek and an accomplished pianist; at twelve he had written a tragedy in verse and five cantos of a heroic romance. At the age of thirteen he was enrolled at Edinburgh University, where he remained for two years.[2] In this home of intellectual and political liberalism, he listened to such great intellects as Adam Smith and Adam Ferguson. In 1785, his father sent him to Paris to complete his education with the critic, Monsieur Suard, at whose *salon* Benjamin breathed the air of the declining years of the eighteenth century.

He expressed his thoughts with a clarity and independence of mind which were quite remarkable. Paul Bastid,[3] who has made a truly masterly study of Constant, does not hesitate to put him on the same plane as Siéyès. Constant was the heir to the eighteenth century. From his youth he had been an admirer of its

[1] Issued by the Duke of Brunswick, C.-in-C. of the Coalition armies, threatening reprisals on Paris if the King or Queen suffered harm. (Translator's note).

[2] He also went to Oxford for two months, though because of his extreme youth, he was only conditionally admitted. (Translator's note).

[3] *Benjamin Constant et sa doctrine.*

literature, which – unlike that of the seventeenth century – was less concerned with perfection of style than with the propagation and defence of democratic ideals.

It is hardly surprising that in this libertarian century, it should be Voltaire who, in Constant's opinion, held pride of place. Voltaire's respect for the individual, his hatred of fanaticism, the sharpness of his thought, the probity of his style, made them akin. What is remarkable is that Benjamin so quickly appreciated the dangers of Rousseau's doctrines, which were gospel for most men of his time: Bonaparte was imbued with them.

Naturally, Constant was aware of Rousseau's powerful influence; but he also recognized that the methods he propounded to preserve freedom, would only create a new form of despotism. Bastid remarks that Constant, on 20 March 1820, speaking from the tribune of the *Chambre*, affirmed that every time laws against liberty were proposed, it was always in the name of Rousseau.

We learn from the *Cahier Rouge* that in the year 1785, when Benjamin embarked on the mighty task of writing the *Histoire du Polythéisme*, he was reading many of the works of Helvétius and was enchanted by the idea that pagan religion is superior to Christianity.

It was not only his very extensive reading which enriched the mind of this European, but also his conversations with men of the most diverse opinions from other countries. He himself was a brilliant talker. Conversation stimulated him, it helped to formulate his thoughts, and sharpened his wit: conversation was essential to him.

He was twenty-seven when he returned to Switzerland in 1793. He was in debt, and was involved in a law suit of his father's. He worked extremely hard on his *Histoire du Polythéisme*, but he was unhappy for, as yet, he had had no success.

Germaine de Staël then arrived on the scene. She had rented the château of Mézery near Lausanne. One day in September 1794, having left Coppet for Lausanne, she noticed a horseman endeavouring to catch up with her carriage. She invited him to enter her coach, and though she found him ugly she marvelled at his intelligence – and it was his intelligence she admired more than anything else.

She and Benjamin dined *en route* with some of Germaine's friends and discussed, without pausing to draw breath, the freedom of the Press. She invited him to be her guest at Mézery. It was this man on whom she relied to prepare her return to France.

'Thermidor has delivered the country from a tyrant', wrote Germaine, who had no illusions, 'and has substituted a pack of rascals who are only motivated by self-interest for one rascal, whose sole interest is a love of crime.' In other words, the period of *Virtue* had passed; now was the time for business. Many of those who had trembled in fear of their lives now seemed only to have regained their freedom in order to enrich themselves.

The Convention, dominated by the centre, feared the excesses of the Jacobins just as much as a royalist revival. However corrupt it might be, the Republic had to be saved. Helped by Benjamin, who shared her views, and whose style was better adapted to composing pamphlets than her own, Germaine wrote *Réflexions sur la paix adressées à M. Pitt et aux Français*, which was an appeal to the British Prime Minister to renounce the insensate idea of restoring the *Ancien Régime* by war, and to all Frenchmen, who were constitutional monarchists, to rally to the Republic.

Eric-Magnus was once again ambassador, and had the honour, as representative of Sweden, of arranging the signing of the peace treaty between France and Prussia. He despised the political activities of his wife, who sent him letter after letter announcing her return. 'Springtime and I will return together', she wrote on 1 March 1795. In fact, despite Monsieur Necker's misgivings, she set out for Paris on 15 May 'with Benjamin in the baggage'.

They found Paris in a state of confusion after the recent disturbances.

'The repression of the "Terrorists" was in full swing', Constant recounted much later. 'The only talk was of severe sentences of execution or deportation. . . . The members of the Convention were denouncing one another, reciprocally expelling each other and arresting their fellow members. None of these things conformed with my idea of a Republic. However . . . I said nothing and waited with some mortification and with a great deal of impatience in my heart of hearts to become myself involved in affairs of state. Madame de Staël, in whose society I often found myself, was entirely on the side of the Republic, first of all, because its ideals coincided with her own, and, secondly, because she was always frightened of being exiled as a royalist, which gave her republicanism even more fervour. But, at the same time, she was a reactionary because, like everyone else, she was revolted by the crimes of the Terror, and because the Terrorists had either killed or banished all her friends.'[1]

Constant did not have long to wait to become 'involved in affairs'. In order to stem the Counter-Revolutionary movement, the Convention, by preparing the decree of the *Deux Tiers*, turned against the right wing. It was this anti-republican motion in defence of the Republic which provoked Constant's protest. Both as a matter of principle and to please Madame de Staël, who hoped to see the doors of the new Assembly open to her moderate friends, he published three letters (unsigned) in Suard's newspaper, the *Nouvelles Politiques* (6–7–8 Messidor, i.e. 24, 25, 26 June 1795) attacking the '*décret de Deux Tiers*'. The articles made 'the devil of a noise', excited the indignation of republicans, and rejoiced the hearts of royalists, who to Benjamin's embarrassment, invited him to co-operate with them in the re-establishement of a monarchy.

'I came back home', he recounted, 'cursing all *salons*, women, and journalists and all who did not believe wholeheartedly in a permanent republic.' Pressed to exculpate and explain himself, he agreed to write a speech for a certain Louvet, a member of the Convention, 'proving that without the *conventionnels* a Republic would be impossible'. Perhaps it amused Benjamin to hear his own words delivered from the Tribune, flatly contradicting his letters in the *Nouvelles Politiques*. Perhaps, too, this new arrival in the capital, who was so impatient to play a part in public affairs, felt that he was now really part of the political scene, and was overjoyed at his initial success. This success was perhaps even more important to him than the purchase of the Abbey of

[1] Notes dictated by Constant in 1828 and quoted by Olivier Pozzo di Borgo: Benjamin Constant, *Ecrits et Discours politiques*.

Hérivaux, expropriated by the Nation, for which he has been so blamed. This purchase was certainly an excellent stroke of business, but it was also a necessity: every 'citizen', under the terms of the new constitution, had to pay taxes, but only property owners could vote.[1] Hence Constant's wish to acquire property in France, an ambition he was able to fulfil with the help of Monsieur Necker.

On 26 October, three weeks after the disturbances of 13 Vendémiaire, the Convention was dissolved. The next day, the new constitution came into force and the Directory was formed. This Constitution of the year III had been drawn up by Daunou, whose moral probity was respected by all.

In a very understandable reaction to the *Montagnard* dictatorship, the new régime initiated a return to the principles of 1789, and was distinguished by a very marked division of powers. On the one hand, there was the Directory consisting of five members, one of whom was to retire annually, the new director being elected by the two *conseils* (chambers); on the other, the two chambers – 'the Five Hundred', who initiated and prepared the laws, and the '*Anciens*' who passed or rejected them. As a result of this system, a fatal antagonism was to be born between the executive and the legislature. Moreover, in comparison with the Constitution of 1791, it represented a backward step in democratic government, because by increasing the *cens* (i.e. the tax payable before a 'citizen' had the privilege of voting) the number of electors was reduced. Not all the faults of this Constitution, however, can be blamed on Daunou, who was unable to implement all his ideas. Instead of five directors, he would have preferred a president, like that of the United States, or else two consuls, taking office alternately.

Daunou was elected President of the Council of the Five Hundred. But disinterested as he was impartial, he did not join the Directory, having refused to make any modification in the age limit required (forty – he was only thirty-four). Siéyès was recommended for the post, but also refused; the Directory was eventually formed of La Reveillière-Lepeaux, Rewbell, Letourneur,

---

[1] That is to say, only citizens who paid taxes could choose electors, and the electors chose deputies. (Translator's note).

Carnot, and Barras, who took up residence in the Luxembourg.

On the fringe of the disturbances in the capital, but still interested in public affairs, the intellectuals of Auteuil continued to meet. They had even found a new centre in Paris. Two days before disbanding, the Convention had founded the Institute (24 October 1795). The original idea for its establishment had come from Condorcet, who after the closure of the *Academies* conceived the idea of a National Society of Sciences and Arts. Taking up the project again, Daunou had concerned himself with its formation as well as the organization of public education, and in particular, of the '*Ecoles centrales*'. The Institute comprised three classes: physical and mathematical sciences; moral and political science; literature and the fine arts – 'a compendium of the intellectual world, the representative corpus of the Republic of Letters', to quote Daunou's definition. On 7 December, the Minister of the Interior summoned to the Louvre the third of the members nominated to the Institute by the Governor to elect the other two thirds. The oldest member of this illustrious assembly, the celebrated Daubenton, assumed the presidency. In the second class, were Volney, Garat, Ginguené, Cabanis, Bernardin de Saint-Pierre, the Abbé Grégoire ('the libertarian and Christian fanatic'), Roederer, Dupont de Nemours, and, of course, Daunou and Siéyès and, finally, Talleyrand.

It was Madame de Staël who was responsible for the return from exile of the former Bishop of Autun. At her request, Chénier had pleaded his cause with his usual fire: *Je réclame Talleyrand-Perigord au nom de la Patrie, de la philosophie et des lumières.* The Convention was impressed by these fine words, and Constant who reported them, added: 'M. de Talleyrand returned at the end of the following year; and at the end of six months he had quarrelled with Chénier and had allowed Madame de Staël to be exiled.' Why this exile? The subtleties that lay beneath Germaine's political conduct escaped the more insensitive minds of several of the Conventionals. Her *salon* was the meeting place of four or five different factions and her friendship with ex-noblemen, whose sympathies for a constitutional monarchy were well known, increased their suspicion.

She was therefore asked by the Directory to leave France.

The Ambassador could do nothing for her. Benjamin Constant followed her to Coppet where she proposed to finish her essay *On the influence of Passions*.

With the patronage of her friends Suard, Roederer, and Chénier, *On the influence of Passions* was favourably received by the Directory and Germaine was allowed to live in France again, provided she remained eight leagues (approximately twenty-four miles) from Paris. She stayed with Benjamin at the Abbey of Hérivaux. Since October she had been with child, perhaps by Eric-Magnus, or perhaps by Benjamin, as he himself believed. The child, Albertine, was born in Paris in June 1797. The Directors now allowed themselves to be swayed by sentiment and the Ambassadress was allowed to take up residence again at the embassy. Hardly had she recovered from her confinement than she was once more politically active. She persuaded Barras to give Talleyrand the portfolio of Minister for External Relations (i.e. Foreign Affairs), and at the same time in opposition to the Royalist Vichy Club, she founded the *Cercle Constitutionel* in the rue de Lille, also known as the Salm Club, where former Conventionalists, republicans, intellectuals, and members of the Institute met. Here, together with Talleyrand and Siéyès, one might meet Constant, Chénier, Cabanis, and Daunou.

It was at this time that the *coup d'état* of Fructidor was carried out. There had been an increase in royalist activity following on the royalist successes in the elections of May 1797. Pichegru had been elected President of the Five Hundred; numerous *émigrés* had returned to France; there had been a proliferation of newspapers hostile to the Republic; the treasonable activities of Pichegru had been proved by the documents which Bonaparte had sent to Barras through Augereau, in command of a division of troops. Barras had persuaded both Rewbell and La Revellière of the necessity for action, but of the other two members of the Directory, Barthélemy, who had only held office for a short while, was a notorious monarchist, while Carnot was not entirely convinced of the threatened danger, and, in any case, did not wish to have recourse to unconstitutional methods.

On 17 Fructidor (2 September) there was a rumour of a plot to place Louis XVIII on the throne. On the following day, the Tuileries, the seat of the two Assemblies, was surrounded by

Augereau's troops. Barthélemy and Pichegru and a dozen deputies were arrested. Carnot, who was a suspect, managed to escape. On the demand of the three remaining Directors, the republican minority of the Five Hundred and the *Anciens* annulled elections in forty-nine *départements*, suspended the freedom of the Press for a year, 'eliminated', without replacing them, seventy deputies, and had sixty-five deported to Guiana (of whom Pichegru should have been one, but he managed to escape to England). By the 19 Fructidor the operation was over, and had set a worse precedent than that of Prairial; the Army had been called in against the national representative Government and legally elected parliamentary members. Pitiless measures, reminiscent of a period which it was hoped had been put aside for ever, were to strike at the returned *émigrés* and priests, who were given a fortnight to leave France on pain of death.

Daunou, who was no longer one of the Five Hundred, watched this *coup de force* with regret, and wrote in the *Conservateur* protesting against the deportations. When he returned as a member of the Five Hundred in the following year, he bitterly criticized the conduct of the Directory.

Although Daunou condemned the behaviour of the Directory, there were republicans among his friends, including Cabanis, Chénier, as well as Benjamin Constant and Madame de Staël, who approved and encouraged the policy. *One* illegal action, in their eyes, was necessary to preserve *legality* – certainly a very subtle Machiavellian reasoning, in the name of which so many crimes against the individual have been committed. But it must be recognized that the 'Fructidorians' had some sound arguments on their side – the 'White Terror' in certain provinces, provoked by the Chouans and *émigrés*, and the certainty that the new Assemblies were preparing to overthrow both the Directory and the Republic.

Twelve days after the *coup d'état*, Benjamin Constant tried his best to justify military interference in an embarrassing and circumlocutionary speech to the *cercle constitutionel*.

Madame de Staël, for her part, devoted her energy to saving her royalist friends who had been 'fructidorized' (to use the current term), thereby making herself again suspect in two camps. She insisted that she had not played a preponderant role in the affair and had done no more than propose the appointment of Talleyrand.

The Bishop of Autun's witticism is well known: 'Madame de Staël made 18 Fructidor, but not the nineteenth.'

But to return to Constant: if he appeared somewhat embarrassed by the sequel to the *coup d'état*, at least he had the merit, in that same year, of propounding a healthy doctrine and of urging the true principles of the Revolution, and, better still, of advocating a more liberal attitude for the future. His book, *Des réactions politiques*, published in March 1797, is a thoroughly sound and perspicacious work – a condemnation of totalitarian régimes and refutation of exclusively authoritarian Governments which is certainly a century and a half ahead of its time.

Like Germaine de Staël, Constant was a Swiss protestant, imbued with the principles of eighteenth-century England, America, and France. He was a convinced believer that the only legitimate form of rule stemmed from a contract between governors and governed (in Locke's interpretation,[1] and not that of Rousseau). He also held to the theory of 'the perfectibility of human intelligence'. Thus one of the links between the philosophers of the Auteuil circle and Constant is made clear. A further example of their similarity of thought appeared in a new edition of his book published in May 1797 under the title of *Des effets de la Terreur*. It is a lucid, vigorous, and pungent indictment of Robespierre and his followers, proving that the Terror did appalling harm to the cause of Liberty. Although Constant might have believed in the necessity for a *coup d'état* to save the Republic, he would never have been the servant of a military dictatorship.

Constant became a familiar of members of the Auteuil circle, whom he used to meet at the Salm Club and also at the *Diners du tridi*[2] attended by Cabanis, Destutt de Tracy, Garat, Chénier, Daunou, Ginguené, Andrieux, and several others, and where, in a friendly atmosphere, they discussed literature, philosophy, and politics.

---

[1] 'I found that a general freedom is but a general bondage, and that the popular asserters of liberty are the greatest engrossers of it too, and not unjustly called its keepers.' John Locke. (Translator's note).

[2] *Tridi:* the third day of the *décadi*, or ten day Republican week.

On 10 Vendémiaire, Year VI (1 October 1797) an impressive ceremony was held in the Champ-de-Mars in honour of Hoche who had just died. The orator chosen to pronounce his panegyric was Daunou, to whom Madame de Staël was to write a fortnight later:

'Although I have not the advantage of knowing you personally, Monsieur, I hope I may be allowed to send you a token of my respect. . . . Your speech seemed to me more than just a written text. In it I seemed to distinguish an act of courage. I, too, feel that I must participate in the sentiments by which it was inspired. Necker Staël de Holstein.

Henceforth, Daunou was to be a constant visitor to Germaine's salon, who placed great store on his friendship.

If the memory of the deceased General Hoche evoked great emotion in Germaine, the fame of General Bonaparte, who was very much alive, stirred her with equal enthusiasm. Even before he had returned to France, she had asked Talleyrand, Siéyès, and others to arrange for her to meet the hero as soon as he arrived in Paris.

But Bonaparte was chary, and even from a distance had shown an antipathy, which was soon to turn to hatred, for this celebrated woman. From Italy he wrote to his friend Fabre de l'Aude: 'Everything I learn of that woman shows her up as a gadabout in search of notoriety, rushing from one *salon* to another, always trying to hang on to someone's coat tails, and who, because her petticoats prevent her from ruling directly, tries to obtain authority by ruse. They say she has wit, but in France who hasn't?'

When Fabre asked him to receive her, he answered, half seriously and half in a joke, 'Why wasn't Madame de Staël included among the deportees of Fructidor?' Nevertheless, he could not disregard her. Her book, *On the influence of Passions* had made a great stir; Barras and La Reveillière were her friends; Talleyrand was 'on his knees' to her.

Madame de Staël deployed her big guns. For weeks and months she was preparing for the attack. When Bonaparte's aide-de-camp, the young Marmont, was in Paris in October 1797, this scheming woman realized that in him she had an excellent go-between; she invited him to her soirées and spoke to him of the

General with enthusiasm. When she met Augereau on 18 Fructidor, she also spoke to him of Napoleon and asked him if he was
really thinking of making himself King (of Lombardy). 'Certainly
not', he assured her. 'He is much too well-brought-up a young
man to think of such a thing.'

Fabre de l'Aude refers in a very amusing way to the feverish
comings and goings of Madame de Staël on the eve of Fructidor,
which was 'her day'. On entering one of her *salons*, he found
himself in the company of some thirty persons – Directors,
members of the *Conseils*, functionaries, and military men. She
'summoned' them one after another. When it came to Fabre's
turn, she said to him, 'We are on the eve of catastrophe. But the
Directory will triumph; I have prepared the way for it. It should
recognize what I have done to restore order, but it will be un-
grateful. Never mind. I will have done my duty and my conscience
will be at rest.'

He wanted to know what she meant by 'her duty', but before he
could get a word in, she continued:

> 'Bonaparte must take advantage of this. I want him to be
> made a Director as soon as possible. I want him to be there
> with Barras, whom I am keeping on, with Siéyès, Talleyrand,
> and Constant. ... Only then will the Republic be perfectly
> administered'.

All in all, this was a combination which had its merits, however
absurd Fabre may have thought it. Fabre could not think of a
word in reply and bowed to the baroness, who, as though she
were a Head of State, continued, 'Inform your friend what I am
doing for him, so that he is aware of my interest in him. There are
nights when my sleep is strangely troubled by his triumphs. I am
sure that there will be a bond of sympathy between us.'

Knowing how much she wanted to make his acquaintance,
Talleyrand told Germaine that he was receiving Bonaparte on
the morning of 6 December. She arrived at the Ministry an hour
early for the appointment in a state of great excitement. She was
astonished to see an exhausted-looking, puny man, with olive-
coloured complexion, his cheeks framed in long locks of hair.
Talleyrand introduced her to the General, who made an effort to
assure her most politely that he very much regretted that he had

been unable to meet Monsieur Necker on his way across Switzerland. Germaine was astonished to find herself for once in her life tongue-tied and embarrassed.

To flatter a wife to gain a husband is a commonplace. But Germaine and Josephine could not abide each other. Josephine found Germaine ugly; Germaine found Josephine stupid. 'A person who thinks and behaves like Josephine', she said, 'should not be the wife of a hero, but his housekeeper. What a wonderful conversation these two must have. While he speaks of battles, she talks of dressmaking.'

While dining with Bonaparte and Siéyès, she was able to examine the General at her leisure. It is not difficult to imagine the looks that this amply-endowed thirty-year-old woman, whose superb shoulders and arms made one forget her lack of taste, cast on this still young, but exhausted hero.

How should she behave to this little Corsican General, who though covered in glory, had neither manners nor wit? Had he not cut short their conversation by replying to her question, 'Who, in your opinion, is the greatest woman alive or dead?' with the curt words: 'The one who has borne the most children'.[1] True, he had smiled as he said this, but she was quick to remark that 'his eyes held no expression . . .' and that he was always ready to smile 'to mislead anyone who wished to read his thoughts'.[2]

The General's departure for Egypt did not extinguish this flame. While in the Orient, he became a god-like figure for Germaine de Staël. Arcola, Rivoli, and Mantua – these were fine victories, but Alexandria and the Pyramids! He was truly 'the intrepid warrior, the most extraordinary and profound thinker'. What she admired most, was that he signed his proclamations *Bonaparte, general en chef et membre de l'Institut*. Furthermore, he had read her book *On the influence of Passions*. 'So there you are', the good, kind Monsieur Necker had written to his beloved daughter, 'glorified on the banks of the Nile. . . .'

Her infatuation was not only due to vanity, a wish to appropriate for herself the man of the moment. Bonaparte was most

[1] Or, 'the most fecund'. The words have been reported differently by witnesses and later by historians.
[2] *Considerations sur la Révolutions francaise*, Vol. II.

certainly inseparable from her political preoccupations. At this period she wanted an end to revolution, as did also Benjamin Constant and all French liberals.

In the days following Bonaparte's return from Egypt, all Paris looked to him to clear up a situation which was becoming more and more desperate. What the people demanded was stability. The ill feeling shown towards the young General by some Jacobins scarcely found an echo among the general public. Vandal quotes the following from a police report: 'Paris is calm. Workers, especially in the faubourg Antoine, complain of continued unemployment, but the rumours of peace which are widespread, seem to be having a very favourable impression on public morale.' Nevertheless, a little later, another report states that all commercial activity was at a standstill: 'No one dares undertake any business; it is said that a new *coup* is being prepared.'[1] Rumours of a conspiracy in fact began to spread. As time passed, the troop movements, the comings and goings of important persons, and the news that leaked out from their conferences, began nonetheless to disturb the populace. In the rue de la Victoire, visitor succeeded visitor at all hours of the day; military officers rubbed shoulders with *savants* from the Institute. Bonaparte seldom left the house.

On 15 Brumaire, (6 November) the *Anciens* gave a great banquet in honour of Napoleon and Moreau[2] (who was passing through the capital), in the Temple of Victory, the former church of Saint-Sulpice. The two men had only known each other a short while. It was a gloomy meal. Moreau remained silent. Bonaparte, having proposed the toast of unity between all Frenchmen, asked his aide-de-camp, Duroc, to bring him a roll of bread and two half bottles of wine, (according to another story, hard

---

[1] *L'Avènement de Bonaparte.*

[2] MOREAU Jean-Victor (1763–1813) was appointed Commander of the Army *du Rhin et Moselle* in 1796 and served in Italy. He was C.-in-C. of the Army of the Rhine and victor of Hohenlinden (1800) and became rival to Bonaparte. He was exiled for collaborating with the royalist faction and sought refuge in the United States. He returned to Europe to fight on the side of the Russians and was killed at the Battle of Dresden. (Translator's note).

boiled eggs), either because he feared poison or to show that he was on his guard.

On the following day it was learnt that all officers with whom he had had dealings, together with the adjutants of the National Guard, were summoned to attend at the rue de la Victoire at six o'clock in the morning of 18 Brumaire. It was still dark when a large body of troops clattered noisily into the Place de la Concorde. Were they there to defend the Tuileries? If so, against whom? Or was it only an early morning review? Early risen inhabitants of the Chaussée d'Antin district were astonished to see so many soldiers making their way to the rue de la Victoire. They watched the officers in admiration, as their gold braid glittered in the grey dawn. At about nine o'clock Bonaparte appeared on the steps at the entrance to his house, dressed in his General's uniform. Although he spoke from a script, it was difficult to distinguish his words. It was thought that he was appealing to the people to help him save the Republic. In fact he was reading the decrees of the *Conseil des Anciens* which had just been brought to him. The transfer of the two Chambers to Saint-Cloud had been voted, and Bonaparte, as newly appointed Commander-in-Chief of all military forces, was ordered to the Tuileries to take the oath. He leapt on his horse and headed the procession amid the clamour of marching feet, clattering swords, and the cheers of the multitude. A crowd had gathered round the Tuileries, a crowd rejoicing and laughing because *He* was there. Bonaparte entered the chamber of the *Anciens*, of whom only a few were present at this early hour and exclaimed in a loud voice:

'Citizen representatives! The Republic is on the verge of destruction. Your decree will save it. Woe betide any who want strife or trouble. Aided by General Lefèbvre and General Berthier and all my companions in arms I will arrest them. Do not seek for examples from the past which will delay your advance! There is nothing in history to resemble the end of the eighteenth century, and nothing in the eighteenth century to resemble the present moment. We desire a Republic founded on true liberty. . . .'

Garat endeavoured to point out that although the General had been sworn in, he had not in fact taken the oath of loyalty to the

Constitution. The President, Lemercier, objected. The transfer having been decided, no further discussions could take place except at Saint-Cloud. This was exactly what Lucien Bonaparte told the Five Hundred, thus postponing the sitting until the following day. (Because, as everyone knows, the 18 Brumaire actually took place on the nineteenth.)

Napoleon then returned to the Tuileries Gardens, where the grenadiers and soldiers he was henceforth to command were drawn up. He was about to address them when he noticed Barras's secretary, Bottot, waiting to speak to him. Barras himself had remained in the Luxembourg. Thrusting aside the dumbfounded Bottot, he apostrophized the crowd and the soldiers in words that have gone down in history.

'What have you done with the France which I left in such glory? I left peace, and return to find war! I left you victorious and find defeat! I left millions from Italy and find everywhere despoiling laws and misery! Where are the hundred-thousand Frenchmen whom I knew – my companions in arms? They are dead! This state of affairs cannot last. Within three years it would lead us to despotism; we must have a Republic firmly established on the bases of equality, morality, civil rights, and political tolerance. . . .'

Even if Bonaparte did borrow some of these fine phrases from a letter sent to him by the Jacobin Club of Grenoble a few days previously, one must admit it is a moving speech. This oration was not to be forgotten; Chateaubriand was to use it one day against the Emperor.

Warned by Constant, Germaine de Staël, who was staying at Coppet at the time, returned to Paris. She arrived in the capital on 18 Brumaire. At Charenton, where she changed horses, it was said that Barras had just passed through on his way to his estate at Grosbois, accompanied by gendarmes. The atmosphere was very tense. It was also said that Bonaparte was in charge of the Government of Paris and that the two Chambers had been transferred to Saint Cloud. Bonaparte . . . Bonaparte . . . no one spoke of anything but Bonaparte.

'This was the first time since the Revolution [she wrote] that one heard a proper name on everyone's lips. Hitherto it

had always been the "Constituent Assembly" had done something, or else it was the "People", or the "Convention".
Everything was now invested in this one man.'

As soon as she arrived in Paris, all agog for the great day to
follow, her friends told her that Bonaparte had come to an agreement with Siéyès; the Jacobins would be overthrown – the
Jacobins by whom she was so detested, and who, should they
win, would oblige her to take the road back to Coppet. According
to a resolution passed by the Directory, but never made public,
she had only been 'tolerated' in Paris. But Germaine felt protected
by her friends who were all in the plot and who kept her *au
courant* with what was happening at Saint-Cloud.

Cabanis, Chénier, and Daunou, members of the Five Hundred,
were already there. At Auteuil, Madame Helvétius, in her great
blue and white armchair awaited the news, surrounded by the
mayor, La Roche, Destutt de Tracy, Ginguené, and Volney.
Standing on the garden wall was a ten-year-old boy, Ambroise-
Firmin Didot,[1] on the look-out for the messenger bringing the
hoped-for tidings. Strollers in the village streets lingered on,
exchanging views, some, too impatient to wait, went as far as
St Cloud.

Night fell. In the *salon* of Madame Helvétius, anxiety grew.
Everyone there, however, was hoping for the success of the
coup d'état. Delivered from the excesses of the Jacobins and
protected against a return of the Royalists, France would perhaps
at last reap the benefits promised her in 1789; henceforth men
with brains would be at the head of the Government.

It was now quite dark. Still the vigil continued. There were all
sorts of contradictory rumours, but at last the messenger arrived.
The Directory was overthrown; Bonaparte had saved France!

---

[1] DIDOT, Ambroise-Firmin (1790–1876). A famous Hellenist, one of
a famous family of publishers and printers. (Translator's note).

3

The Discontented Brumairains

❋❋

THE 18 Brumaire . . . a fateful day for the Republic! And yet the most enlightened and dedicated of the republicans, not least the philosophers of Auteuil, must bear the guilt of having blindly abetted the betrayal. How far were they actively involved in the *coup*?

The outward circumstances of the *coup* are familiar from François Bouchot's well-known painting in the Musée de Versailles. Bonaparte stands bareheaded in the Chamber of the Five Hundred, hemmed in by threatening deputies with raised hands and clenched fists. The bayonets of the grenadiers are seen coming to the rescue. From the presidential rostrum, the figure of Lucien Bonaparte dominates the scene.

The sequel is hardly less familiar: Bonaparte's 'humiliating exit'; the continuing uproar; his reappearance (having recovered his presence of mind); his harangue to the troops; and finally the assault on the Orangerie, led by Leclerc and Murat, with Murat yelling at the top of his voice: '*F . . . -moi tout ce monde-là dehors!*'

All this was on the afternoon of 19 Brumaire. Up to now, the Auteuil group (dismissed by Vandal as the 'dogmatic, literary, and philosophizing element of the Revolution') had stayed in the background, alarmed by the unconstitutional turn of events, and had allowed the 'hotheads and the nonentities to hold the stage. The scholars and intellectuals – men like Daunou, Cabanis, Chénier, and Andrieux – remained at home and held their peace. The Institute seemed in danger of opting out of its own *coup d'état*.' Only Siéyès proved himself a man of decision. When news was brought to Bonaparte that he had been declared an outlaw, Siéyès turned to the shaken General and remarked: 'In outlawing you, they have outlawed themselves.' Whereupon Bonaparte drew his sword and shouted from the window: '*Aux armes!*'

During the night that followed, the outcome was decided. The *Conseil des Anciens* and a minority of the Five Hundred voted the abolition of the Directory and the nomination of three provisional consuls, Bonaparte, Siéyès, and Roger Ducos. Bonaparte immediately left Saint-Cloud, and hurried to rejoin Josephine in the rue de la Victoire. The next morning he began a series of meetings at the Luxembourg, to the second or third of which he invited Roederer and Talleyrand. Roederer's account is of some interest:

> 'We made our way to the Luxembourg, where M. de Talleyrand and I were astonished to find M. de Volney, who, so far as we knew, had had nothing to do with the operation of 18 Brumaire. No doubt his contribution had taken the form of good advice; for he had no influence whatsoever in Paris, and was by nature little inclined to meddle in political affairs. . . . The First Consul thanked all three of us collectively in the name of *la Patrie* for the zeal we had shown in making such a success of the new revolution.'[1]

If Bonaparte took the trouble to thank Volney at the same time as the two others, he probably had good reasons for doing so, reasons of which Roederer knew nothing. Was it true, in any case, that Volney had 'no influence whatsoever' in Paris? As a former *Constituant*, he would have known nearly all the members of the *Conseils*. 'He was presumably in a position to guide Bonaparte through the parliamentary jungle, and thus, on the night of the 17–18, contributed more than anybody else to the drawing up of the list of those *Anciens* whose vote would approve the transfer of the two Chambers to Saint-Cloud.'[2]

Be that as it may, it is clear that Volney's prestige in the intellectual world counted for more than his political contacts; it was this, and in particular his high standing at the Institute, which

[1] Roederer: *Mémoires sur la Révolution, le Consulat et l'Empire.*
[2] Roederer: *op. cit.*

rendered him so useful to the young General. Volney had always had a soft spot for Bonaparte, ever since their meeting in Corsica seven years previously; he had been a constant visitor to the rue de la Victoire, keeping a watchful eye, it is said, on his idol's coffee to ensure that it was neither too hot nor too cold. More to the point, he had worked on the feelings of those in the Auteuil group who were members of the Five Hundred, trying to goad their Bonapartist leanings into active support – ineffectively, perhaps, in the case of the retiring Daunou, but to more purpose with Garat, Chénier, and Cabanis. And the intervention of Cabanis was later to turn the scale on more than one occasion.

To return to Joseph and Lucien: Lucien (who had been elected President of the Five Hundred soon after his brother's 'triumphal' return from Aboukir) worked actively with Joseph in Napoleon's interest, but found it impossible to win the support of Siéyès. This key member of the Directory, deeply hurt by Bonaparte's contempt (he had completely ignored Siéyès at a dinner-party), expressed the opinion that the conceited young General, who had abandoned his army in Egypt without authorization, deserved to be shot. The animosity was not all on one side. Siéyès was the *bête noire* of Bonaparte, who put it about that he was in the pay of Prussia, and attempted to have him removed from office so that he himself could take his place. Bonaparte had also been trying to win Barras to his cause by suggesting that Barras should hold the highest executive position, while he, Bonaparte, should be the military Commander-in-Chief. When this deal fell through, there was nothing for it but to seek a reconciliation with Siéyès.

Talleyrand and Roederer were more than willing to lend their good offices in bringing about this tricky *rapprochement* (for which, indeed, Roederer was later to claim the credit). But first it was necessary to talk Siéyès into climbing down and agreeing to negotiations. It was Cabanis who undertook this delicate task; not only was he very close to Siéyès, but he had also taken pains (like his friend Volney) to remain on visiting terms with the General. The ensuing manoeuvres are described in Joseph's memoirs:

'. . . I saw M. Cabanis, who was still a member of the Five Hundred and on intimate terms, as I knew, with Director

Siéyès, with whom we were to dine the following day. Cabanis prepared him for my visit; and after our dinner Siéyès took me aside and said: "I want to go along with General Bonaparte, since there's no one in the whole army who's more of a civilian at heart. All the same, I know what to expect. As soon as he's succeeded, he'll leave his two colleagues behind him, like *this!*" With these words, he suddenly pushed his way behind Cabanis and came between us, flinging out both his arms, and thrusting us backwards against the chimney-piece, so that he was left standing alone in the middle of the room – much to the astonishment of those guests who were unused to his outbursts of Provençal temperament. When I described the scene to Napoleon, he laughed heartily and exclaimed: "*Vivent les gens d'esprit!* This is an excellent omen." '

Bonaparte had every reason to feel satified. There was nothing to prevent him from making a *démarche*, now that Siéyès, apparently, knew exactly what Bonaparte had in store for him, and was nevertheless resigned to his fate. Perhaps, however, Siéyès was less ready to accept his own deposition than his theatrical gesture implied.

Whatever the case, his prophecy did nothing to diminish Cabanis's confidence. Either he refused to believe that Bonaparte would assume dictatorial powers, or he thought he would use them only in order to safeguard liberty. Lucien now let him into the secret of the plot (at the same time as Boulay, Chazal, and Gaudin), and invited him to a meeting at the house of Mme Récamier, the current object of Lucien's affections. There the conspirators were briefed as to their respective roles in the forthcoming operation, and arrangements were made for the famous Saint-Sulpice banquet, which was to allay any suspicion of an intended *coup*. So it came about that on the crucial day, 19 Brumaire, Cabanis, the friend of Mirabeau and Condorcet, gambled his reputation as a scholar and republican by lending his support to the *coup* and by guaranteeing the good intentions of Bonaparte. Convinced republican though he was, he nevertheless believed it necessary, with things as they were, to strengthen the executive, and even, if the worst came to the worst, to impose provisionally a system of 'personal rule'. In so thinking, he could claim to be following Mirabeau, who believed that 'liberty, once achieved through insurrection, must be maintained by respect for the law; that legislation could be put into effect only by an "active force"; and that in a great empire, whose subjects were as yet unenlightened, this "active force" must necessarily rest in the hands of one man, and one man only'.[1]

It was Cabanis, then, who, on 19 Brumaire, drew up the proclamation addressed to the French people in the name of the two Chambers. He had earlier delivered a long speech to the Chamber of the Five Hundred – or, to be more precise, to those few dozen deputies who had been assembled by Lucien in the Orangerie of Saint-Cloud at about nine o'clock that evening. After opening the candle-lit session, Lucien gave the floor to Chazal, a former Girondist and friend of Siéyès, who proposed a resolution 'legalizing' the change of régime – viz., the abolition of the Directory, the disqualification of certain members because of their 'violent and criminal excesses', and the setting up of a provisional executive authority to be vested in the two former Directors, Siéyès and Roger Ducos, together with Bonaparte (all three of whom were to 'assume the title of Consuls of the Republic'). He further proposed the nomination of two Commissions, drawn from the two existing Chambers, which would be responsible for assisting the Consuls in their work of reorganization. Chazal was followed by Boulay de la Meurthe, who emphasized the need for order and stability in the face of Jacobin bigotry. When Boulay sat down, it was Cabanis's turn to speak:

> 'Can it be said that at this moment the French people possess a genuine Republic? Do they enjoy any real liberty? . . . With one voice you will answer *No!* . . . Is it possible to enjoy true liberty and security in a country where, for at least six months out of ten, annual elections raise the people's temper to fever pitch; where there is no stable legislation; . . . where the most costly and complicated form of administration ever devised bleeds the nation dry; . . . in short, where arbitrary rule and insurrection constantly threaten the people with tyranny and ruin?'

[1] Cabanis: *Journal de la maladie et de la mort d'Honoré-Gabriel-Victor Riquetti Mirabeau.*

He went on to paint a picture of the country's ruinous state, brought on by public disorders and by over-hasty legislation. While conceding some virtues to the Constitution of Year III, out of respect for his friend Daunou, he ended by saying:

'Changes must be made in this Constitution. Only a provisional Government can carry out such changes and put the necessary reorganization in hand; and the kind of government proposed by your Commission seems to me not only the best, but indeed the only possible one in our present circumstances.'

His address to the French people, which was adopted after a vote had been taken, was no less republican in its sentiments. 'Frenchmen!', he began, 'the Republic has once again escaped from the raging storms of party strife. Your devoted representatives have shattered the dagger clutched within those murderous hands.' After recalling the aftermath of the Terror – first, the feelings of relief, then the hopes raised by the Constitution of Year III, then the attacks by 'seditious elements' upon the 'weak links' of the Constitution, and finally, the present anarchy – he concluded, 'The Royalists will never raise their heads again. The hideous scars of the revolutionary Government will be effaced. ... Republicanism and Liberty will cease to be mere empty words. A new era is beginning. ... *Vive la République*!'

It is easy to smile at such innocence. Yet how was Cabanis to see (as we can, in retrospect) what the future was to bring? At the very least, his diatribes against the country's present ills must be seen as sincere and well-founded; such feelings were wellnigh universal in that autumn of 1799, when the wind of popular derision was blowing Tallien and Barras away like rotting leaves. And as for his exaggerated confidence in Bonaparte, this was shared by most of his friends at Auteuil and at the Institute – Volney, Garat, Destutt de Tracy, Jean-Baptiste Say – to say nothing of Benjamin Constant and Mme de Staël.

Much the same can be said of the officers who acted as Bonaparte's spokesmen: none of them doubted the purity of his intentions. Marshal Lannes declared: 'The Republic was on the brink of ruin. ... Make no mistake, citizens, the 18 Brumaire is not a party triumph; it is a victory of the Republic, won by republicans.' Lefebvre wrote in the same vein to Mortier, describing the wave of enthusiasm that was sweeping Paris. He had just been administering the oath to the National Guard: 'Never', he declared, 'was there such a whole-hearted response from the men . . . I thought I was back in 1789, in the dawn of the Revolution. As for the *coup*, *ça ira*, you can take my word for it!'

Were the people of Paris really so enthusiastic? Historians seem unable to agree on the point. But as far as the provinces are concerned, we can be certain that there was no serious opposition to the *coup*, except in the West. The only protest of any significance came from one Barnabé, a *président de tribunal* in the Yonne, who refused to enter the law of 19 Brumaire in his register.

After ten years of violent upheavals, the nation could scarcely fail to respond to the promise of a general reconciliation. The actions, no less than the words, of Bonaparte answered the deepest longings of most Frenchmen; they saw in him, as he intended they should, the impartial judge who would bind up their wounds, settle their differences, and make peace at home and abroad.

As early as 22 Brumaire, the four-months-old 'law of hostages', directed against the families of *émigrés*, was repealed. Five days later, the *Gazette de France* reported that Bonaparte had visited the interned hostages, and had personally questioned them as to their food and treatment. At the Temple he had ordered the immediate release of the internees, telling them: 'An unjust law has deprived you of your freedom. My first task is to give it back to you.' He promised the other inmates, before leaving the prison, that he would speedily look into the reasons for their detention.[1]

Shortly afterwards, almost all the victims of the Fructidor proscriptions (though not Pichegru) were permitted to return; and Bonaparte further intervened to secure the release of a group of *émigrés* – all technically liable to the death penalty – who had been shipwrecked at Calais while making for the Vendée. Thanks to these acts of clemency, the tension in the Vendée was eased; negotiations were opened which led to a cessation of hostilities on 3 Frimaire. There was, however, some uneasiness in republican circles. Cabanis felt it necessary to reassure his colleagues (in the

[1] Aulard: *Paris sous le Consulat.*

Ami des Lois of 30 Brumaire). There would be no going back, he wrote; the men of 18 and 19 Brumaire were still the same men who had crushed the 'royalist brigands' by the measures of 18 Fructidor.

Despite such assurances, the relaxations in favour of the right wing seemed to call for some similar concessions towards the extreme left. Yet Siéyès was opposed to any move in that direction; since the *coup* had been justified by the allegation of a 'terrorist plot', he expected it to produce a rigorously anti-Jacobin policy. He had obtained from Fouché a list of fifty-nine Jacobins, to be deported to Ré, Oléron, and Guiana; the order was confirmed by Bonaparte on 20 Brumaire. In addition to some genuine 'killers' of 1793, the list included the names of men whose only offence was their ardent republicanism, among them deputies who had made an obstinate stand for legality at Saint-Cloud; there was also General Jourdan, who had refused to take part in the *coup*. The deportation of such an illustrious soldier would obviously have created a scandal, and Bonaparte lost no time in striking his name off the list; in a letter to Jourdan he made it clear that he personally deprecated the proscriptions, for which he blamed Siéyès; he begged the General 'not to doubt his friendship', and expressed his desire that he might 'always see the victor of Fleurus taking the path which leads to a happy and well-ordered society'.

Soon afterwards, the whole decree was dropped, and the deportions commuted to 'house arrest'. Thus the Brumaire revolution was accomplished without executions or imprisonments, and with no vindictive reprisals. Several weeks after the *coup*, the intellectuals were still firmly behind the new règime, as can be clearly seen in the *Décade Philosophique*. Before Bonaparte's arrival in Paris, the *Décade* had already been demanding reforms in the law regarding hostages and *émigrés*; on 30 Brumaire it gave cautious approval to the 'Revolution of 19 Brumaire' ('. . . there are, then, more grounds for hope than for apprehension . . .'), while at the same time calling for the speedy establishment of a new Constitution. Similarly, on 10 Frimaire it was expressing satisfaction at the stability of the new régime ('. . . from all parts of France congratulatory addresses are streaming in . . .'), and expatiating, in glowing terms, on the decision to revoke the deportations; while on 20 Frimaire it returned, with a hint of impatience, to the question of the new Constitution, now announced as being almost ready: 'Let us hope that it will be followed by a second, and no less great, blessing – peace!'

A new Constitution was indeed a pressing requirement, if the régime was to achieve any stability or permanence. We have already seen that two Commissions – one drawn from the Five Hundred, the other from the *Conseil des Anciens* – had been set up by the law of 19 Brumaire. Each Commission, which consisted of twenty-five members and wielding the same powers as the Chamber it had replaced, was to designate a sub-committee known as a *section de Constitution*. That of the Five Hundred comprised seven members, including Lucien Bonaparte, Daunou, Boulay de la Meurthe, Chénier, Chazal, and Cabanis; while that of the *Anciens* amounted to five members, among them Garat and Régnier. The big question was: who should preside over their deliberations?

An obvious choice would have been Daunou, regarded only five years before as the supreme law-maker of France. His friends Cabanis and Chénier had strongly pressed him to accept membership, first of the Commission, and subsequently of the *section*, of the Five Hundred. Everyone stood in awe of his extensive learning and his absolute integrity. On the debit side, however, he had lent no support to the *coup* (though he had not actually opposed it); and in the days before the return from Egypt, when Siéyès was already on the look-out for a strong man capable of overturning the Constitution, Daunou had refused to have anything to do with his schemes. As the author of the Constitution of Year III, he was in no hurry to volunteer his services for rewriting it. Besides, during the latter years of the Directory, he had virtually retired from public life, apart from solemn national occasions, at which his oratory was still much in demand. He had secured the post of administrator to the Panthéon Library, and was doing his best to bury himself in scholarly work.

With Daunou out of the reckoning, the only conceivable alternative was Siéyès – Siéyès, whose rather tarnished halo had, in the preceding months, begun to gleam with something of its former brilliance. He was a man of few words, whose cold, disdainful manner did not make for popularity; but he had

laboured patiently to build up a reputation, not only as a statesman, but also as a political theorist, as the constitutional expert
par excellence. Now at last he would be able to show his true
mettle – now, when brains, rather than swords, were at a pre-
mium. He had some old scores to settle with the Year III Constitution, and it was no secret that his plans had been laid well in
advance. This, then, was the 'oracle' to whom the constitutional
sections now turned; and in answer to their prayers, the oracle
condescended to let fall, one by one, the details of his master-
plan. As for Bonaparte, he seemed preoccupied with other matters; he gave Siéyès a completely free hand, and attended hardly
any of the meetings.

Siéyès's system turned out to be a strange and intricate piece of
machinery. The principle of national representation was ostensibly safeguarded by a 'three-tier' suffrage: five million electors
were to elect a preliminary list of 500,000 (the *liste communale*);
these 500,000 were then to pick, from their own number, a
'departmental list' of 50,000, who in turn were to select a 'national
list' of 5,000. Municipal officials would be appointed from the
half million, departmental officials from the 50,000; while the
5,000 would supply the major offices of state, the judiciary, and
the legislative assemblies.

The appearance of democracy was misleading, since the pro-
cess of selection for the various lists was in fact subject to other
kinds of pressure. For example, the selection of the 'national list'
was put in the hands of a *jury constitutionnaire* (destined to become
the *Collège des Conservateurs* and ultimately the Senate). Since this
body was directly nominated by the Consuls, the people were in
no real sense able to elect their own representatives.

A further stipulation was that all former members of the revolutionary assemblies, whether national or provincial, together with
all those who had held public office since 1789, should be auto-
matically included in the appropriate lists, without election. These
men would continue to enjoy the sacrosanct position that had
already been theirs during the Directory – a position which they
claimed as their right, not because of the people's suffrage, but by
virtue of their revolutionary past. In defence of this provision,
Siéyès could point to the reactionary tendencies of the rising
generation; was it not imperative to ensure that elements

hostile to the Revolution should not take over the Republic?

Siéyès's most original stroke was the division of the legislature into three assemblies: a Council of State to initiate legislation; a Tribunate to discuss and amend; and finally, a Legislative Body to accept or reject. Over and above these, the *Collège des Conservateurs* (later to be renamed the Senate) was to act as a kind of Supreme Court, empowered to overrule any unconstitutional acts should the necessity arise. Its main function, however, would be to nominate, not only the members of the three assemblies, but also the Head of State. The holder of this post – to be known as the *Grand Electeur* – would have no executive powers, his chief function being the designation of two Consuls (a 'Peace' consul and a 'War' consul), who between them would rule the country with the help of ministers of their own choosing. All the major functionaries of state, including the Grand Elector and the Consuls, could be removed from office by decree of the Senate, into which they would in such case be 'absorbed'.

The essence of Siéyès's blueprint was a division of power such that, by a delicate balance of checks and counter-checks, any move in the direction of autocracy would be doomed to failure. In his eyes, theoretical perfection was everything: 'True statesmanship', he declared, 'is not the science of *what is*, but of *what ought to be*.'[1] He had no use for the pragmatic approach, which he regarded as 'being a slave to the force of circumstances'.

It remained to be seen how Bonaparte would react to this extraordinary Constitution, 'almost Byzantine in its complexity', as someone described it. In the initial stages he had steered clear of the *sections*' deliberations; but Roederer and Talleyrand had kept him informed of their rather slow progress. As Siéyès continued to enjoy playing the oracle, vouchsafing his secrets crumb by crumb, Bonaparte turned to Fouché, who gave his old friend Réal the task of 'pumping' Chénier, Siéyès's closest confidant. After a dinner at which there was 'no shortage of wines and spirits', Chénier talked. As a result of his information, an emergency meeting was held, of which Fouché gives an eyewitness account: 'Bonaparte, Cambacérès, Lebrun, Lucien, Joseph, Berthier, Réal, Regnault, and Roederer were present.

[1] Extract from a note by Siéyès (1772), quoted by Sainte-Beuve.

We discussed the possibility of a counter-project, and the line
Bonaparte should take in the plenary sessions which everyone
was anxiously awaiting.'

The General eventually decided to accept Siéyès's proposals
for the assemblies and elections, but to reject the idea of a Grand
Elector, demanding in its place the establishment of a quasi-
dictatorial power, to be vested in Bonaparte himself. He communicated his wishes, via Roederer, to Siéyès, who retaliated by
offering him the position of Grand Elector (originally earmarked
for himself); but Bonaparte flatly refused to consider this 'ridiculous role'. In a direct encounter, arranged by Talleyrand, the
discussion became heated. 'What do you want, then?', Siéyès
demanded, 'to be *king*?'

Boulay de la Meurthe now put forward a compromise, whereby
the Grand Elector would be replaced by a First Consul, assisted
(in a purely advisory capacity) by two other consuls. This solution pleased nobody, however, and on 11 Frimaire Bonaparte,
anxious to get the whole business settled, summoned Siéyès and
Ducos, together with the two *sections*, to his rooms at the Luxembourg. That day, and on the days that followed, they debated
into the small hours, with Bonaparte, naturally, taking the chair.

The exact nature of the proceedings must remain, to some
extent, shrouded in mystery. No minutes of the debate have
survived, and there are many gaps and discrepancies in the eyewitness accounts. For our present purposes, the most important
question is: did the republicans of Auteuil meekly surrender to
Bonaparte, or did they put up a show of resistance?

Bonaparte's first step was to call for the production of a 'first
draft' to serve as a basis for discussion. He entrusted this task to
Daunou, who had just been elected President of the Commission
of the Five Hundred. To the amazement of everyone, including
Bonaparte, Daunou finished the job in a single night. His draft
clearly owed a great deal to his own Constitution of Year III,
but also included some of the ideas put forward by Siéyès (who
was still hoping to have his brain-child accepted *in toto*).

There were now, in effect, two rival projects to consider –
Daunou's and Siéyès's. Discussions could now begin in earnest,
not only at meetings of the two *sections*, but also in the two
Commissions.

Bonaparte presently ordered Daunou to 'take a pen and sit down over there'. Taken aback, Daunou started to remonstrate; but the implacable General repeated the order, and Daunou did as he was told. From now on, it was Bonaparte who held the reins. As he put the successive questions to the vote, Daunou turned over the scraps of paper on which he had jotted down his original ideas, and noted on the back, at Bonaparte's dictation, the results of the voting. Of course, he also contributed to the discussion; nevertheless, it was he, Daunou, who penned in his own hand the words that were to seal the fate of France: '. . . the second and third consuls will act in a consultative capacity. They will indicate their presence by endorsing the record of proceedings, and may, if they so wish, register their personal opinions; but *the decision of the First Consul is, in the last reckoning, sufficient.*'

Did he feel the humiliation of his role, as a mere stooge in the service of autocracy? Less than two years before, he had declared to his colleagues at the Institute: 'There can be no philosophy without patriotism, no true genius except in the heart of a republican.' Where were those fine sentiments now? And as for his friends, how could they bring themselves to append their signatures to the damning clause (though for Cabanis at least, the idea of 'personal rule' held no terrors)?

Bonaparte at first maintained a conciliatory attitude, assenting readily to most of the suggested reforms, especially those of Siéyès. He approved the three 'lists' (though rejecting the automatic inclusion of the veteran revolutionaries). He raised no objection to the principle of a sixty-member Senate, nor to a tripartite legislature – Council of State (fifty members), Tribunate (a hundred members), *Corps législatif* (fifty members). A system whereby those who voted were forbidden to speak (the *Corps législatif*), and those who debated were powerless to act (the Tribunate), suited him down to the ground. As for the Senate, some of its prerogatives were curtailed, and its method of recruitment modified (the selection of its first members being reserved to the Government).

The first clash came with the discussion of the executive power: when the matter of the Grand Elector was broached, the General sprang to his feet. He laughed in Siéyès's face and poured ridicule on his 'metaphysical nonsense', describing the twofold Consulate as 'sheer anarchy', and dismissing the Grand Elector as the 'emaciated ghost of a layabout king'. When Siéyès, uncharacteristically, answered back, Bonaparte was beside himself with rage. 'Do you know of any man so despicable', he shouted, 'as to lend himself to such a tomfool role? How could you imagine, Citizen Siéyès, that any man of ability or integrity would consent to sit at Versailles like a fatted pig with a few millions to wallow in?'

There was a roar of laughter at this sally. 'Siéyès was left speechless, his Grand Elector was sunk without trace.' But comedy presently turned to drama, when the republicans launched a counter-attack against the majority, who had by now accepted the principle of a dictatorship. This episode, neglected by most historians, is vividly recalled in Fouché's memoirs:

'Despite the discomfiture of Siéyès himself, his adherents now returned to the attack. Fighting to the last ditch for his proposals, they urged the adoption of a strictly republican constitution. The other side countered by proposing a president on the United States model, with a term of ten years. . . . A second group, renegades like the first, suggested "disguising" the autocratic nature of the president's role; as a conciliatory measure, they proposed a Government consisting of three consuls, of whom two would act merely as advisers. The First Consul would thus possess plenary powers, including the right to nominate or dismiss all Government officials.

'This proposal immediately produced loud protests. Among others, Chazal, Daunou, Courtois, and Chénier drew attention to the limits imposed by the constitution, pointing out that if Bonaparte assumed the mantle of supreme Magistrate without prior election, he would be branded as a usurper, thereby confirming the view that he had engineered the coup of 18 Brumaire solely in his own interests. In a last attempt to dissuade him, they offered him the rank of Generalissimo, with authority to make war or peace, and to negotiate with foreign powers. "I want to stay in Paris," Bonaparte replied petulantly, biting his nails; "I am Consul, and I want to stay in Paris." Chénier broke the silence which followed; he spoke of freedom, of the Republic, and of the need to provide checks upon the supreme power, resolutely insisting on the Senate's right to depose and "absorb" the major officers of state. "Never!", exclaimed Bonaparte angrily, stamping his foot. "I'd rather have a blood-bath (*Il y aura plutôt du sang jusqu'aux genoux*)!" '

It was thus Chénier, characteristically, who put up the most spirited resistance at this critical moment. He had been a devoted admirer of Bonaparte; but ever since the banquet at Saint-Sulpice, he had grown increasingly suspicious. On that occasion, he had remarked to a fellow-guest: 'I feel as if I were at one of those funeral feasts the Romans used to give. But what are we burying? Is it military glory? Or is it freedom itself?'

To revert to Fouché's account, Bonaparte's final outburst reduced the whole gathering to horrified silence. Without further discussion, the majority entrusted the supreme power, not to a triumvirate (with two of the members limited to an 'advisory capacity'), but to a single man, appointed for a ten-year period – appointed, moreover, by himself.

There was nothing the republicans could do, except fight a rearguard action. Daunou in particular went on trying to introduce 'liberal' amendments into the text. It was, in the main, a losing battle, since his efforts were continually thwarted by Bonaparte; yet he can claim the credit for one or two modifications, as, for example, the proviso that 'the First Consul shall not be eligible for re-election at the expiration of his term of office'.

The work of the two *sections* had lasted almost a month. But it required only a few evenings for the two Commissions to debate the new Constitution, and, with a few final amendments, to vote its adoption. On 22 Frimaire the General proposed the final clause: 'that the present Constitution be accordingly commended to the approval of the French people.' The forty-eight delegates present gave their assent in writing.

One point remained to be settled: the election of the Consuls. The name of the first went without saying. For the second, Bonaparte was known to have chosen Cambacérès. The third presented more problems: Volney had been sounded out, but had refused, and it seemed certain that Daunou, who had been elected President of the Five Hundred on 11 Frimaire, would be the most popular choice. But Bonaparte, who had earlier agreed with Siéyès to offer him this position, had had a change of heart as a result of Daunou's attitude during the discussions.

The voting began. Standing with his back to the fire, Bonaparte watched the proceedings, which took the form of a secret ballot. Sudenly, as if sensing that the ballot-papers would not produce the desired result, he swept up all the papers, threw them on the fire, and, pointing at Siéyès, declared:

'Instead of counting the votes, let us once again demonstrate our gratitude to Citizen Siéyès. Let him have the privilege of appointing the first three magistrates of the Republic.'

Siéyès fell in with Bonaparte's wishes, and named Bonaparte, Cambacérès, and Lebrun. The three names were greeted with loud applause.

What can we say of Siéyès's abject surrender? It has been variously attributed to intimidation, flattery, and disillusionment. The *Mémorial de Sainte-Hélène* ascribes to him the cynical remark, after the first meeting of the provisional consuls: 'Gentlemen, we have a master – a man who knows everything, is capable of everything and wants to have everything.' Although he later disowned the remark, we know that, when Bonaparte urged him to accept the position of second Consul, he replied: 'Consul's don't come into the matter; and I have no desire to be your aide-de-camp.'

The *Mémorial* provides another anecdote relating to the same occasion (the meeting on 20 Brumaire). Siéyès, it alleges, drew Bonaparte's attention to a chest containing 800,000 francs – the Directory's contingency fund. 'There aren't any Directors now,' he said, 'so what's left is all ours. What shall we do with it?'

The General answered to the effect that, officially, he knew nothing about the money. 'You and Ducos, both former Directors, can share it out between you. Only hurry up, because it'll be too late tomorrow.' Without losing a second, Siéyès helped himself to the lion's share, 600,000 francs, leaving a mere 200,000 to poor Ducos.

Siéyès scornfully refused to comment on this story, which his friends dismissed as a pure fabrication; and one of his more recent biographers (Albéric Neton) treats it as a scurrilous fable. Nevertheless, there is other evidence to suggest that Siéyès could on occasion be swayed by unworthy motives. On 20 December 1799, Bonaparte, in a message to the legislative Council, praised the 'disinterested virtues' of Citizen Siéyès, and, in recognition of his services to the nation, conferred on him the property of Crosne. Siéyès accepted the gift (at the same time as the presidency of the Senate). His friends were horrified, and did their best to dissuade him; Daunou even contrived to hold back for a day the reading of the Consul's message. Siéyès's acceptance of the gift certainly did nothing to increase the prestige of the *philosophes*. Politically, the former Director now found himself more or less discredited; he still, however, had a far from negligible role to play. By making him President of the Senate, Bonaparte left him the task of selecting the first thirty-one members of the Senate, who in their turn were to choose the remaining twenty-nine. Ducos, Cambacérès, and Lebrun theoretically assisted him in his choice, but in practice Siéyès had the last word.

What manner of men were the two 'junior' Consuls? Cambacérès, a *conventionnel* and semi-regicide, was a choice calculated to placate the left; Lebrun, a representative of the *Ancien Régime* and former secretary of Maupeou, would reassure the right. Malicious tongues christened them 'the two arms of the chair'; but they were invaluable props for Bonaparte – especially Cambacérès, the past-master in the art of 'legalizing the illegal'.

The same principle governed the choice of ministers: Lucien for the Interior, Fouché for the Police, and Talleyrand for Foreign Affairs – always there was the nicely-measured dose, the calculated appeal the national unity.

On 24 Frimaire, Year VIII (16 December 1799), the *Moniteur* published the terms of the new Constitution, together with a short preamble which contained the famous words: 'Citizens! The Revolution is securely anchored to the principles which commenced it. It is finished!' On 3 Nivôse (24 December), long before the promised plebiscite had been completed (or even begun, for that matter), a law was passed giving immediate effect to the new Constitution. On the following day, the Consuls assumed their duties.

*　　*　　*

The Revolution was 'finished'; was it also abolished? Had the republicans any reason to fear as much, or the Auteuil *philosophes* to feel that they were witnessing the overthrow of their fondest ideals?

Appearances, at least, were safeguarded. The preamble to the Constitution professed that it was founded on the 'authentic principles of representative government, on the sacred rights of property, liberty, and equality', and guaranteed 'the rights of citizens' no less than those of the State.

The 'Rights of Man' were no longer solemnly invoked; but was this so necessary? The declaration of those rights in 1789, and again in 1793, had not prevented the September massacres or the Terror. In the long run, which was the more important – a declaration of principles, or the resolution of a man able and willing to put them into practice? Garat gave the answer in a speech to the Commission of the *Anciens*: the fame and prestige of General Bonaparte, he declared, would not only be 'an additional source of strength for the Government', but would also 'limit and restrain the powers of the executive. And this restraint will be all the more effective for existing, not in the written terms of a Charter, but in the heart and feelings of a great man!'

On 25 Frimaire, a long speech by Cabanis in the Commission of the Five Hundred struck the same confident note: 'The actions of 18 and 19 Brumaire were directed, not against a few individuals, but against an absurd and cruel system which was rapidly and remorselessly driving the Republic to its doom . . . . The object was not to establish the domination of a few men, or of a single party.'

Cabanis then passed on to a general discussion of man's moral and social needs: after a masterly analysis of the various forms of government (monarchy, democracy, oligarchy), with their respective advantages and drawbacks, he went on to emphasize the importance of the two great modern discoveries – the division of power, and, even more important, the representative system, which alone could guarantee public freedom while allowing the Government to rule effectively. This led on to a consideration of Siéyès's electoral scheme, which Cabanis defended, though without naming its author. Here, he claimed, was democracy in its most authentic form: every citizen enjoyed complete equality, with as much chance as anyone else to be voted on to the *listes de confiance* and to work his way up by means of the successive 'reductions'. With no rabble to rouse, and with the 'ignorant class' incapable of swaying the course of government, demagogues would cease to exist. Everything, from now on, was to be done *for* the people and *in the name of* the people; nothing *by* the people, or in response to its unpredictable whims.

All this is plain enough to need no commentary, except to explain that, in excluding the 'ignorant class' from political influence, Cabanis was not prompted by reactionary motives. Indeed, the spread of public education, even among the very lowest orders of society, was one of the main preoccupations of Cabanis's revered master, Condorcet. However, until the dream of an educated public was realized, he advocated giving the vote only to those citizens who were 'capable of expressing an intelligent opinion'.

The concluding theme of Cabanis's speech was the necessity of a strong executive, which would at the same time respect the liberties of the subject. Without specifically mentioning Bonaparte, his almost lyrical peroration appealed to all Frenchmen, whatever their class, creed, or political persuasion; to all alike he promised a future in which their liberties would be safeguarded and their deepest longings satisfied.

Cabanis and Garat were not alone in believing that a Golden Age had dawned. Volney, as we have seen, held Bonaparte in the highest esteem; and another of the group, Jean-Baptiste Say, who had his feet firmly on the ground, and was reputed to be the leading economist in France, shared the same illusions. His editorial comments, in the 10 Nivôse number of the *Décade Philosophique*, warmly endorsed Cabanis's speech, adding that 'all good citizens, all men of good will' had rightly welcomed the events of Brumaire.

In short, the *philosophes* were convinced – or persuaded themselves that they were convinced – that their hero had in no sense abandoned his ideals; and they brought all their enthusiasm and optimism into play to counter the growing feelings of uneasiness and suspicion. In particular, they took comfort from the parliamentary control envisaged by the new Constitution. Cabanis, in his speech, pinned his hopes above all to the Tribunate:

'The Tribunate . . . will be in a position to appeal continually to public opinion, to pass censure on the Government as and when it sees fit, and to denounce any measures which it regards as unconstitutional. . . . Its members will be free to say what they like, both in speech and in print, without fear of the consequences. The existence of this democratic forum, reinforced by an entirely free Press, constitutes one of the surest guarantees of public freedom.'

This confidence was, in theory, no idle dream. The effectiveness of the Tribunate would depend, of course, upon its composition; and this had been left, to all intents and purposes, in the hands of Siéyès. He began by selecting the founder-members of the Senate: alongside the dyed-in-the-wool Jacobins, veterans of the Convention and the Directory, he brought in the leading lights of the Institute, men like Monge and Berthollet, and some of our old friends the *philosophes* – Volney, Garat, Cabanis, and Destutt de Tracy. It was only natural that he should go on to select for the Tribunate friends of theirs who were especially well-qualified as parliamentarians and debaters: Chénier, Daunou, Ginguené, Andrieux, and Jean-Baptiste Say. These were to be joined by another interesting choice: Benjamin Constant.

In connection with Constant's nomination, it is worth recalling an unkind anecdote of the time. It would appear that Mme de Staël, who naturally favoured his claims, had asked one of her friends to provide him with an introduction to Bonaparte. The General, who had read Constant's works, complimented the young writer and assured him that he would be only too happy to number him among his Tribunes. Whereupon Constant replied: 'You realize that I'm on your side. I'm not one of those idealists who always want some abstract notion to decide every question. I'm all for positive action; if you nominate me, you'll be able to count on my support.'

No sooner had Constant left Bonaparte, than he went to call on Siéyès, who lived a few doors away. He begged Siéyès to support his candidature, and, to convince him of his sincerity, declared: 'You know how much I hate violence! I will never be a friend of the sword. I insist on principles, ideas, justice. If I obtain your support, you can rely on me; for I am Bonaparte's greatest enemy.'

The story is too good to be true, and most historians reject it out of hand. All we can say with certainty is that Joseph Bonaparte, at Mme de Staël's request, intervened to secure Constant's nomination.

The only remaining task was the selection of the *Corps législatif*. Its membership turned out to be, on the whole, undistinguished, with one notable exception – Henri Grégoire, the first of the 'republican priests', a man whose views foreshadowed the liberal Catholicism of Lamennais.[1] He had been the first to take the oath to the Civil Constitution of the Clergy. As a member, first of the *Assemblée Constituante*, and subsequently of the Convention, he had been among those who demanded the trial of Louis XVI, while at the same time advocating the suppression of the death-penalty. Bishop of Blois since 1791, he had made a courageous stand against the humiliating abjurations of 7 November 1793. Dressed in his episcopal robes, he had leapt to the tribune to defend his beliefs against the shouts and insults of the mob. A man of the broadest sympathies, he had been a founder-member of the Institute, the Conservatoire des Arts et Métiers, and the Bureau des Longitudes. He was also a frequent visitor to Mme Helvétius's *salon* at Auteuil, and was on excellent terms with such men as Cabanis and Daunou; to Bonaparte, this friendship between Christian and rationalists was quite incomprehensible.

The Tribunate and the *Corps législatif* opened their doors to a number of highly distinguished men who, while basically in favour of the recent *coup*, were not prepared to give their unconditional support to the new régime.

The membership of the Council of State was quite another matter. Here the First Consul, in addition to reserving the right

[1] LAMENNAIS, Felicité Robert de (1782–1854), priest; was the apologist of theocratic principles, and later became the apostle of revolutionary doctrines without abandoning Catholic orthodoxy. His major works include the *Essai sur l'indifférence en matière de la religion* and *Paroles d'un croyant* – the latter written in 1834, after he had broken with the Church. Although condemned by the Pope, he continued to write pamphlets and tracts expressing his democratic ideals. Recent Catholic theology has largely rehabilitated him, and has increasingly tended to see him as a fore-runner of the *aggiornamento*. (Translator's note).

to initiate legislation, had also insisted on personally choosing the Councillors. They were to act under his direct supervision, and he intended to give them an ever-increasing role in the reorganization of the country, to make them, in effect, his coadjutors in the conduct of the nation's affairs. Accordingly, while giving due weight to their competence and intelligence, his main criterion in selecting them was their unquestioning loyalty. The most notable among them were Cambacérès (the President), Thibaudeau, Tronchet, Réal, Boulay de la Meurthe, and Portalis.

*   *   *

According to plan, the Tribunate held its first session on 11 Nivôse (1 January 1800), with Daunou in the chair. Its first two meetings were taken up with a rather pointless discussion concerning the sky-blue uniforms *à la française* which were to replace the theatrical costumes worn hitherto by the members of the Five Hundred. The third day produced a more political topic for debate: the choice of the Palais Royal for the meetings of the Tribunate (the Senate was installed in the Luxembourg, and the *Corps législatif* in the Palais Bourbon). Some of the Tribunes protested that it was an insult to ask the representatives of the nation to meet in a place of such ill repute. But one of them, a certain Duveyrier, praised the choice, drawing attention to the glorious memories attaching to this historic site, and in particular to the memorable speech delivered there by Camille Desmoulins. Carried away by the impetus of his own rhetoric, Duveyrier indiscreetly exclaimed: 'Should anyone dare to speak of a two-week old idol in these surroundings, we would remind him that here we brought down an idol fifteen centuries old'.

The members eyed each other in consternation. What on earth could have prompted such a gratuitous insult? What would be the reaction of the General, with his notorious quickness to take offence? Would he order the immediate arrest of the imprudent Duveyrier? But no, the First Consul contented himself with issuing a discreetly-worded (and anonymous) warning in the pages of the *Moniteur*, appealing to the Tribunes to show moderation and good sense. He could rest secure in the knowledge that the public had had enough of revolutionary tirades, and was firmly attached to his cause. The extravagant utterances of a second-rate lawyer were hardly likely to make him lose any sleep; and in any case, it was not long before the wretched Duveyrier came to heel with a grovelling recantation.

An attack of a very different nature was launched on 15 Nivôse by Benjamin Constant. His target was the proposed revision of legislative procedure (known as the *formation de la loi*); and this time the matter was worthy of the protest. The projected measure threatened to muzzle the new-born Tribunate, which, only a fortnight before, had listened to Cabanis's assurance that it would be free to 'pass censure on the Government as and when it sees fit'. So far from permitting freedom of debate, the Government now claimed the right to fix the date, and to lay down a time-limit, for the Tribunate's discussion of any projected legislation; moreover, the Government would not feel obliged even to set forth in detail the reasons for its actions. These drastic restrictions were unmistakable evidence of the Executive's resolve to 'dictate' its laws to the legislative assemblies.

It was a rude awakening for the *philosophes*, with their starry-eyed confidence in the Brumaire revolution. They had not expected to be treated like children, nor did they intend to be; Constant gave very clear expression to their discontent in this, his first foray into the French political arena.

He must have cut a strange figure in the eyes of the other tribunes, this tall, ungainly young man with his red hair and ugly, freckled face, his prematurely hunched back awkwardly draped in a frock-coat several sizes too large for him, and his short-sighted eyes peering uncertainly at his audience. Yet almost at once he held them spellbound. Speaking in carefully chosen words, without undue emphasis or flights of rhetoric, he rejected the proposed legislation and demanded its modification.

In the first place, he insisted on a minimum of five days for the discussion of projected laws, and an equal period in which the Tribunate could present its views to the *Corps législatif*. In the rare cases where immediate action was imperative, the Government would have to make special *ad hoc* arrangements. He further demanded that every Bill should be accompanied by a full explanation of the Government's intentions. As for the choice of date, this should rest with the *Corps législatif*, not with the Executive. The Government, he claimed, was 'presenting its proposals to us on the wing, in the hope that we shall be unable to catch them', and he ended by saying that without a truly independent Tribunate there could be no national harmony and no Constitution: 'there will be nothing but servitude and silence – a silence which all Europe will hear and will judge.'

This, coming from a 'new boy', was strong stuff. The issues raised were of immense importance, and the whole Assembly listened to him with rapt attention. The effects of Constant's words were not confined within the four walls of the Palais Royal; the whole political world of Paris was impressed by his courage and ability. Courage indeed it was, giving the lie to the often-expressed view that Constant was nothing but an ambitious time-server, whose public conduct was as unpredictable as his private life was scandalous. It is, after all, on his actions as a politician that he should be judged; this 'contemptible adventurer', with the ink barely dry on his French citizenship, was standing up and attacking the authority to which he owed his position and prospects – hardly the behaviour of a coward or a flatterer.

On 4 January, on the eve of his speech, there was a big gathering in Mme de Staël's *salon;* everyone who was anyone was there, including Lucien and the other leading members of the Government. Constant, who was of course present, took the opportunity of whispering in his protectress's ear: 'If I make my speech tomorrow, your drawing-room will be deserted.'

'One must follow one's convictions,' she replied.

Constant's prophecy proved accurate. By five o'clock on the following afternoon, Germaine was beginning to receive notes of excuse from those she had invited. They included some of her most treasured *habitués*, but all of them pleaded their 'support for the new Government'. During the days that followed, three-quarters of her friends, Talleyrand notable among them, continued to avoid her.

On 16 Nivôse (6 January), the Government's supporters in the Tribunate staged a violent and clumsy counter-attack. Their spokesman was Riouffe, a former Girondin, who had subsequently become a zealous partisan of the Directory; he held the floor for two hours, inveighing against Constant's 'insulting' criticisms, and affirming his own complete and devoted loyalty towards 'the man who is governing the Republic'.

Two other speakers expressed their support for the Government's proposals, albeit in less fulsome terms: one was Chauvelin, the other – amazingly – Duveyrier. Ginguené followed, with an unprepared speech, which he prefaced with an apology for his lack of experience. He criticized those clauses in the projected measure which he found the least satisfactory, and concluded that, since the Tribunes were not being permitted to suggest any amendments, they should reject the whole proposal.

The final speaker was Thiessé, who expressed his opposition in more sophisticated terms, and proposed that the fixing of a time-limit for discussions in the Tribunate should be the prerogative of the *Corps législatif*. The measure was then put to the vote, with the following result: 54 in favour, 26 against (16 Nivôse – 6 January 1800). The measure was subsequently presented to the *Corps législatif*, which approved it by 203 votes to 23.

* * *

Majorities of this size – two-thirds in one Assembly, nine-tenths in the other – might have been expected to satisfy even the most exacting head of Government, given the existence of a healthy parliamentary system and of an opposition permitted to express its opinions. Not so Bonaparte. After Constant's speech, he completely lost his temper. 'It's a disgrace!', he shouted, 'This fellow means to turn everything upside down and take us back to the September massacres.' In other words, for demanding adequate debating time for the nation's representatives, Constant was to be branded with the same label as the cut-throats of the Conciergerie.

It will be remembered that, on his return from Italy in December 1797, the young General had declared in the courtyard of the Luxembourg: 'The peace which you have just concluded marks the begining of *an era of representative government*.' But two months earlier (19 September 1797), in a letter to Talleyrand from Milan, he had set out what he believed to be the proper functions of the legislative and executive: the elected representatives, he then wrote, should be excluded from the right to govern, or even to enact laws (other than 'organic' laws). It appears from this that Bonaparte's aversion to parliamentary institutions was of long standing; it could be plainly seen in his desire to confine the Assemblies to purely formal duties. One should rather say 'the Assembly', since he was quite satisfied to have only one – a 'great national council, nominated by the people', a body 'which supervises but does not act', which would control, not the actions of the Executive, but rather 'the legislation necessary for those actions (*la législation de l'exécution*)'. In short, on the morrow of the Fructidor *coup*, Bonaparte, while still favouring popular elections, did not envisage anything like a Tribunate in his legislative scheme; and his acceptance of it in Year VIII was a reluctant concession. This is not to say that his confidential letter of 1797 totally rejected democratic principles. He recognized the *sovereignty of the people* as the cornerstone of his structure; but, for him, it was the executive authority that must represent that sovereignty and embody it in action: 'The power of the Government ought to be considered as the real "representative of the nation".' The young General's views, even if inconsistent, were not necessarily insincere. After all, the Jacobins – or, to be more precise, the Montagnards – had reached similar conclusions, basing them on Rousseau's theories and Robespierre's practice: once the *will of the people* has been expressed, the nation has no further function but to obey the chosen leader who embodies that will. This was exactly Bonaparte's view.

It is possible now to see why he was so incensed at the opposition of a minority group in the Tribunate, and by the temerity of Constant's speech. Not content with branding Constant as a 'Septembrist', he actually threatened him: 'I shall know how to keep him in his place; my arm is the arm of the nation, poised ready to strike him down.' However, he took no steps to translate these threats into action. What was the reason for his forbearance?

The fact is that Constant and his friends in the Tribunate caused hardly a ripple of support in the country at large. On the contrary, the popular reaction was almost uniformly hostile. The Press hurled invective at the dissenting members of the legislature; the right-wing papers, in particular, made slashing attacks on the Tribunate – this 'Rump Parliament', which 'must be swept clean'. On the left, the *Journal des Hommes Libres*, the organ of authoritarian Jacobin opinion directed by Fouché, poured abuse upon Constant and Mme de Staël. The public mood was one of entire confidence in the First Consul; everyone pinned his hopes on the new 'experiment', and wanted to give it a fair trial, without obstacles or contentious criticism. In a word, the French people, whatever its loyalty to the Republic and to the principles of liberty, were determined to turn their backs on parliamentary democracy.

Thus, Bonaparte had no reason to be too dissatisfied with the proceedings in the Tribunate. They had allowed him to gauge the popularity of the new régime and the strength of his own position. Constant had not, after all, turned out to be dangerous; the First Consul could afford (once his anger, real or feigned, had cooled off) the luxury of treating him either with magnanimity or with indifference. Even so, some of the other Tribunates earned themselves a stormy interview with the young dictator: while Mme de Staël had her first taste of what she was to call her 'persecutions'. The episode is described in her *Ten Years of Exile*:

'The Minister of Police, Fouché, sent for me to say that the First Consul suspected me of having instigated my friend's speech in the Tribunate. I answered, as was certainly true, that M. Constant was far too intelligent a man for anyone to imagine that he had borrowed his opinion from a woman; and in any case, his speech was concerned only with the independence necessary for any Assembly, and contained nothing which could reasonably offend the First Consul. The Minister agreed with what I had said. I went on to say a few words about the respect which should be paid to Liberty in any legislative body; but I could tell that such generalizations meant nothing to him. He was already aware that, under the master he had chosen to serve, principles would cease to count, and he was prepared to adapt himself accordingly. . . . He advised me to go and stay in the country; in a few days, he assured me, the whole thing would have blown over.'

Her punishment, then, consisted of a brief withdrawal to Saint-Ouen. One may smile at such 'severity', as one may smile at the conduct of Siéyès, who 'beat a strategic retreat to his country estate at Auteuil'. Nevertheless, the danger to freedom was all too real; the General had served notice that henceforth the expression of individual opinions would be treated as a crime.

*   *   *

By 18 Pluviôse, Year VIII (7 February 1800), the plebiscite on the Constitution was completed, and the votes counted. There were 3,011,007 votes in favour, 1,562 against, with about four million abstentions. It was an overwhelming victory for the Government, even allowing for the circumstances of the poll.[1] Apart from the abstentions (notably in the provinces of the West), there was practically no opposition. Even if Bonaparte's cavalier treatment of constitutional freedoms was beginning to give the intellectuals second thoughts, his ascendancy over the public at large was growing ever stronger. Meanwhile he handled his propaganda adroitly, with shrewdly calculated concessions both to left and to right.

The Constitution had assigned the Tuileries to the Consuls as their official residence; it was arranged that they should move in on 1 Pluviôse (21 January 1800). However, Bonaparte let it be known (through an article in the royalist *Journal des Débats*) that he deprecated this choice of date, since it coincided with the anniversary of Louis XVI's death. In contrast, the *Moniteur* marked the occasion with a eulogy of Brutus the 'tyrannicide', whose bust, together with those of Alexander and Hannibal, Cato and Caesar, Condé and Turenne, Frederick II and Mirabeau, Marceau[2] and Washington, was to grace the *grande galerie* of the palace. Washington, incidentally, had died only a short time before, and Bonaparte, who had just heard the news, paid homage to his memory in an Order of the Day addressed to his armies (18 Pluviôse – the day that the plebiscite was completed).

[1] The citizens were obliged to enter their names on separate lists of 'acceptors' or 'non-acceptors', which were openly displayed in the local town halls; and the other arrangements – or lack of them – were equally prejudicial to the opposition side.

[2] MARCEAU, Francois-Philippe (1769–96): a French General who distinguished himself in the Vendée and at Fleurus. He was killed at Altenkirchen while commanding the Army of Sambre-et-Meuse. (Translator's note).

Two days later, under the dome of the Invalides, General Lannes presented the colours captured in Egypt to Berthier, the War Minister. The presentation was followed by a ceremony honouring the hero of the American Revolution, with Fontanes delivering the panegyric. This was an extraordinary composition, every phrase of which was designed to glorify the First Consul, though without once naming him. By singing the praises of the great soldier-citizen, who, after eight years at the helm of the young republic, had retired in deference to the principles of democratic government, Fontanes was clearly giving his listeners to understand that Bonaparte would follow his example. But above all, the implied parallel between the two men was drawn in such a way as to make Bonaparte appear the greater figure.

The ceremony was something of a stroke of genius. The monument to Washington made a handy plinth for Bonaparte himself; and the brilliance of the occasion further enhanced the glamour which had attached itself, in the popular imagination, to the Saint-Cloud régime. But the *sphère de lumière et de gloire* which Fontanes evoked was enough to open the eyes of the men of Auteuil, however warmly they might have supported the Brumaire revolution. Those who were members of the Senate – Garat, Volney, Destutt, and Cabanis (to say nothing of Siéyès) – were beginning to realize that their labours had not, after all, been directed towards the cause of Liberty. Fine phrases extolling the merits of 'strong leadership' did nothing to allay their anxieties. However, their disaffection – it would be too much to call it 'opposition' at this stage – was expressed discreetly; the debates in the Luxembourg were conducted, so to speak, behind closed doors. As for the minority group headed by Constant, Ginguené, Say, Andrieux, and Daunou, although its unpopularity increased in proportion to the popularity of Bonaparte, yet it was now definitely alerted to the dangers of arbitrary government and firmly resolved to resist it. Daunou in particular, who had turned down the proffered post of Councillor of State after the rejection of his constitutional draft, was soon making good use of his exceptional knowledge of administration and law, and proved himself a real thorn in Bonaparte's flesh.

By now, the First Consul, strengthened by the massive vote of confidence accorded to his Constitution, was feeling that the time had come to embark on his next project: to reorganize France under a strictly centralized system of government. The far-reaching effects of this administrative reform (known as the Law of Pluviôse) are common knowledge. The structure, or rather the hierarchy, which it called into being has lasted to this day.

The Departments and *arrondisssements* were put under the control of Prefects and Sub-prefects respectively, all appointed directly by the central Government. At the lowest level, each Commune was to have a Mayor. Hence the swollen importance of Paris, the dwindling status of the provinces, and the subservience of the *départements* – chronic evils, which subsequent generations have never ceased to attack. It is immediately apparent that in this respect the United States Constitution is much more democratic, since there each state is administered by an *elected* Governor. The authoritarian nature of Bonaparte's system has, it is true, been substantially modified by subsequent amendments. Gone, for instance, are the centralized appointments of district and municipal councillors and of mayors, which Bonaparte reserved to himself (except where he delegated them to Prefects). Yet even today, in Paris the Prefect of Police (not to mention the Prefect of the Seine), together with the Mayors of the Paris *arrondissements*, are appointed by Government nomination, not by election.

It might be argued that an authoritarian régime – even, for the time being, a dictatorship – was what the situation required, and served the public interest better than representative institutions, rendered ineffectual by too wide a 'spread' of executive powers. Certainly no one could maintain that Bonaparte's proposed administration contained an ounce of democracy, or that it fulfilled the pledges of the 1789 Constituent Assembly. On the contrary, it marked a return to the *Ancien Régime* with its *intendants*; it took over the centralized system of the monarchy and even strengthened it. The quasi-military structure that resulted did, it is true, provide order where previously there had been chaos – a chaos which the French people emphatically wanted to see ended; but Bonaparte, far from regarding these measures as provisional, was determined to make them permanent. Meanwhile, not a voice was raised in protest – except in the Tribunate.

The Councillor of State entrusted with the task of presenting the proposals to the Tribunate was Roederer, so recently on excellent terms with the Auteuil group, but now out of favour with them because of his uncritical support of Bonaparte. For their part, the Tribunes selected Daunou to examine the new law. He presented his report on 23 Pluviôse (12 February 1800).

It was a detailed and closely-reasoned critique. Daunou took issue with the scheme on several important points, notably the size and scope of the proposed administrative areas, and the levels at which local Government should be exercized. But he nowhere directly attacked the overall conception – the excessive centralization, and the concentration of power in the hands of the Executive. Paradoxically, one of his criticisms was directed against the provision that certain appointments should be made by Prefects, rather than by the First Consul; he expressed surprise at this 'deprivation', and even questioned the legitimacy of nominations so made. Yet in so far as his objection was to the *arbitrary* nature of appointments made by Prefects, he can scarcely have intended to express approval for an even more arbitrary control at the summit of power. Unable as he was to force a reconsideration of the new Constitution, of which the present measure could claim to be the logical development, he at least did his best to modify its more undemocratic features, protesting, for instance, that the *conseils généraux*, although invited to inspect the Prefects' annual 'reports', were not in fact given any power to discuss them or to take appropriate action.

Despite his criticisms, Daunou came down on the side of adopting the project – rather in the manner of a prosecuting counsel, who, after presenting a damning case, ends by asking for an acquittal. At all events, his strictures were by no means flattering to the Government.

For the Tribunes to vote for rejection would have been dangerous. All the same, when the matter was put to them, there were 25 'No's' out of a total of 96. In the *Corps législatif* there were 63 out of 280.

The next project for discussion was the reorganization of the judicial system. This immense reform produced a clear and coherent structure which has undoubtedly stood the test of time. Some of its clauses show a real concern for humane values – the creation, for example, of the *Tribunal de Cassation* (Court of Appeal), which could even, in principle, overrule sentences imposed by courts martial. On the other hand, it tended to make the judiciary subordinate to the executive. It was left to the Government to approve or promote judges, and the selection of Presiding Judges was reserved to the First Consul; moreover, the magistrates, though appointed for life, had negligible powers.

This loss of independence was attacked in scathing terms by Thiessé. He had already launched an offensive, some two months earlier, in a speech to the *Corps législatif*; his target then had been a relatively unimportant provision concerning the *Tribunal de Cassation*, but he had spoken with such force that the Assembly had rejected the point in question by a majority of 95 (it was subsequently amended before being included in the overall scheme). Thiessé also stressed the insufficient role accorded to juries, and described as 'monstrous' the powers abrogated by the Executive. Another Tribune, Ganilh, echoed Thiessé's objections; he accused the Council of State of putting its own decrees in the place of the laws, and drew attention to the 'loss of those civil liberties which have been won at such a cost of blood, tears, and sacrifices'. His speech made a deep impression. Nevertheless, the law was approved by 59 votes to 23, and – in the *Corps Législatif* – by 232 to 41 (18 March 1800).

The session of Year VIII was now drawing towards its close. Before it ended, however, several more projected measures were debated in the Palais Royal. The more liberally-minded Tribunes continued to display the same critical spirit, though without taking up a systematically hostile attitude. One last sally on the part of the minority group deserves to be recorded. Speaking about the Tribunate's right to hear petitions, Benjamin Constant urged his fellow-Tribunes to make full use of their prerogatives; 'Make yourselves the kind of body you ought to be – not a permanent Opposition, which would be both absurd and, in certain circumstances, criminal, nor an Assembly that bestows unchanging approval, which would be mere servility; but rather a body which will express approval or opposition according to the merits of what is put before it. . . .'

On 12 Germinal (1 April 1800) the session was declared closed. It had lasted three months. Had the Tribunate shown that it understood its responsibilities as stated by Constant? Certainly the majority had too often been content to act as a rubber-stamp for the Government's proposals; but there was at least a group of independents willing to swim against the tide, who defended the principles of the Republic against the now-apparent dictatorship of the Head of State, and also against the blind indifference of public opinion, which had by now lost its enthusiasm for the ideals of republicanism, preferring the glamour of strong leadership and military triumph.

The struggles of the faithful remnant became even more arduous and frustrating when, on 27 Nivôse, the First Consul virtually gagged the Press, thus ensuring that the country at large should hear no echo of what was being said in the parliamentary debates.

*   *   *

In the days following 18 Brumaire, newspapers and periodicals proliferated, thanks to the repeal of the Fructidor edict which had abolished the freedom of the Press. Most were favourably inclined towards the new régime, but some were critical and even subversive. For example, in Frimaire the *Bien Informé* published the text of the American Constitution in order to discredit, by contrast, the 'Year VIII' project.

Bonaparte lost no time in informing a small committee (Roederer, Cambacérès, and Fouché) of his intentions with regard to the Press. Some years later he described the difficulties he had to contend with:

'The freedom of the Press was regarded [by the more 'metaphysical' of his entourage] as something sacred. . . . I still remember the endless arguments I had to face before I could bring under police control the hundred-and-four newspapers that came out every morning. . . . Can you imagine the grave danger there would have been, in the circumstances of the time, if attacks on the Government had been allowed at every street-corner?'[1]

When someone pointed out that England enjoyed complete freedom of the Press without any disastrous consequences, the

[1] See further Chapter V (end).

First Consul, who was clearly expecting this objection, replied that the circumstances of the two countries were in no way comparable.[1]

Bonaparte's dislike of journalists was no new phenomenon. It dated back to the Italian campaign, during which he had written to Fabre de l'Aude: 'I cannot abide the insolence of these scribblers; I loathe the whole tribe . . . I'd like to have them all here in my army. I promise you my soldiers would deal with them in a way which would make them hold their tongues for a long time.'[2]

In the year VIII Bonaparte, well aware that he must moderate his military manner, felt inclined to save appearances by making the Senate responsible for the licensing or suppression of newspapers. But his advisers urged different solutions; and it was Fouché who came up with the suggestion which was finally acted on. On 27 Nivôse (17 January 1800), a decree of the Consuls, alleging that 'some of the Paris newspapers printed in the *département* of the Seine are instruments wielded by enemies of the Republic', suppressed sixty out of seventy-three publications.

What of the thirteen that were spared? First, there was the *Moniteur*, which, though relatively independent before 7 Nivôse, had now become the official Government organ. Contrary to what one might expect, none of the other twelve (which included the *Décade Philosophique*, the *Débats*, and the influential *Gazette de France* with its royalist bias) followed a conformist or middle-of-the-road line. But from now on a threat hung over them. The consular decree warned that any paper publishing 'articles disrespectful towards the Social Pact, towards the sovereignty of the people or towards the glory of the Armies' would incur immediate suppression.

The threat proved to be no idle one. By the end of 1800 Paris could claim no more than eight newspapers, with a total of twenty thousand subscribers. The *Décade* continued to appear, but without its 'chronicle' of political events. The freedom to inform and comment was a thing of the past. Over the months and years that followed, warnings, house arrests, deprivations of

[1] St de Girardin: *Journal et Souvenirs, III*.
[2] From Leghorn, 12 Messidor, Year IV (*Histoire secrète du Directoire, II*).

civil rights, and police intimidation grew increasingly frequent. There were endless prohibitions: no one must mention Army movements, provisions, and supplies, or matters connected with religion; no one must reveal news likely to disturb the economic situation or alarm the public; news items must not be summarized in the form of headlines. These limitations were justified, if at all, only on grounds of military necessity, and were supposedly introduced only for the duration of the war. But they were not rescinded either at the Peace of Amiens or subsequently. Furthermore, they were extended to cover the provincial Press, which was soon reduced to a single newspaper per *départment*, and that controlled, in effect, by the Prefect.

True, Bonaparte, in his anxiety to please the *'parti de l'Institut'*, continued to allow the publishing houses a certain measure of freedom under the Consulate.[1] But after 5 April 1800, he got Lucien to impose censorship on the theatre as well. It is easy to see why Aulard describes 27 Nivôse as 'the beginning of despotism'.

* * *

Yet it was against the return of despotism that the General declared himself to be fighting. It was true enough that many of the Paris newspapers were in the hands of 'enemies of the Republic', or, in other words, royalists. These royalists were by no means a spent force at the outset of the year 1800. While two Austrian Armies threatened France on the Rhine and the Var, there were still centres of insurrection in the West, and considerable pockets of Chouan resistance were holding out in Brittany, the Vendée, Normandy, and Maine. Two months after Brumaire, the defiance of these right-wing royalists constituted the only real danger within France – a much more serious danger, in Bonaparte's eyes, than the incipient liberal opposition in the Tribunate. As for the Jacobins, they had not yet recovered from their virtual eclipse.

[1] After his tirade against journalists quoted above, Bonaparte went on to say, 'What I've just said against the complete freedom of the Press applies only to newspapers, and does not extend to works in one or more volumes.'

The situation had improved in the Vendée, where General Hédouville had succeeded in negotiating a truce in the preceding November. Encouraged by rumours that Bonaparte was working towards a restoration of the monarchy, the Vendée royalists sent Fortuné d'Andigné, their Commander in the Angers district, to Paris in order to verify the facts. On his arrival in the capital, d'Andigné made contact with Hyde de Neuville, the secret agent of the Comte d'Artois and the English Government.

Hyde contrived to approach Bonaparte through an intermediary – a friend of his who was in close touch with Talleyrand. The First Consul let it be known that he was anxious to restore peace in the West, and agreed in principle to a meeting; as a first step, he would see Hyde on his own. On the appointed day, 5 Nivôse (25 December), the weather was bitterly cold. Even the empty room at the Luxembourg into which Talleyrand introduced Hyde was icy. While he waited, Hyde stood beside a huge fireplace in which a rather inadequate fire was smouldering. After a minute or two, he saw a slight figure enter the room, dressed in a green frock-coat; his head was lowered, and his thoughts seemed to be far away. Hyde took him for a servant. 'The man approached, leant his back against the chimneypiece, and raised his head. Then', writes Vandal, in a splendid phrase, 'he all at once seemed taller, amazingly taller, and the flame of his glance, suddenly flashing forth, declared the presence of Bonaparte.'[1]

We are reminded of the scene at Nice when that same glance had made Augereau and Masséna tremble. But if Hyde trembled, he none the less stood his ground, as did d'Andigné, with whom he returned to the Luxembourg on the following day. The interview was a stormy one. 'I will set fire to your towns; I will burn down your cottages,' the General threatened. On the religious issue, it is true, he showed himself eminently reasonable: 'As for religion, I mean to re-establish it, not for your sakes but for my own,' he said reassuringly, and added the memorable words: 'That's not to say that we nobles have much religion; but it's a necessity for the people, and I intend to re-establish it.' On the matter of restoring the monarchy, however, he would not give an

[1] Vandal (*op. cit.*), whose source for the episode is the *Memoirs of Hyde de Neuville*.

inch. Ordered to make up his mind, d'Andigné asked for two days' grace. 'Two days!', Bonaparte exclaimed; 'I'd never waste two days over something I could do in two hours – even if it cost me a hundred thousand men!'

The two royalists went away under no illusions. Bonaparte, they saw, would never be a Monk.[1] What was to be done? It would be difficult to reopen hostilities in the Vendée. At Paris, on the other hand, one could always hatch plots and seek to stir up public opinion. On the morning of the anniversary of Louis XVI's execution, the porch of the Madeleine was draped in black velvet, with an inscription which read: 'Victims of the Revolution, join with the brothers of Louis XVI; *déposez ici vos vengeances!*' The hangings of the catafalque were decorated with the fleur-de-lys; also displayed were the King's last testament, and a poster bearing the words '*Vive Louis XVIII!*' Royalists in deep mourning paraded ostentatiously in front of the church. The police reported similar demonstrations in several other parts of Paris. Louis's will was also posted up at St Jacques de la Boucherie, where it provoked a minor riot. The 'tree of liberty' at Fontenay-aux-Roses was cut down. Obviously Hyde de Neuville was the man behind all this; but where was the proof? The police retaliated by arresting Henri de Toustain, the Comte de Bourmont's agent,[2] in whose lodgings they discovered a quantity of weapons and seditious matter. He was immediately interrogated, tried, and condemned to death by firing-squad. But these incidents were unimportant; the emotions of Paris had not been deeply stirred by the memory of her beheaded King.

A much more serious problem facing the Government was the pacification of the West. In the Vendée, the armistice was ratified, the Chouan leaders accepting Hédouville's terms, which promised the reopening of churches, complete freedom of worship, and a free pardon for all proscribed *émigrés* who made their submission. Futhermore, on 28 December 1799, Bonaparte declared, in the context of certain measures favouring the Catholics: 'The ministers of a God of Peace will be the prime movers in bringing

[1] GEORGE MONK, Duke of Albemarle (1608–70): Cromwell's General, who subsequently re-established Charles II on the throne.

[2] Bourmont was the Commander of the rebel armies in Maine-et-Loire.

about peace and reconciliation between men. . . . Let them betake themselves to their places of worship, which are now reopening their doors for them, and there offer, along with their fellow-citizens, the sacrifice which will make atonement for the guilt and bloodshed of war.'

There were threats as well as promises. The First Consul had found Hédouville too conciliatory, and had him replaced by General Brune, who arrived at Angers on 18 January. Both Generals (as also the Commanders in Brittany and Normandy) received a stream of orders insisting on ruthless repression.

On 5 January 1800, Bonaparte wrote to Hédouville that, in the opinion of the Consuls, any of the ringleaders arrested while in possession of arms should be shot out of hand. 'The Government will give you full backing; your actions will be judged from the military point of view, and will come under the scrutiny of a man who is accustomed to taking strong and energetic measures.' He went on, 'The First Consul believes that it would be a salutary example if two or three of the villages with the worst records were burnt to the ground.'

The proclamations he addressed to the local communities were equally severe. Here is an example, from 11 January 1800:

'Article 4: any municipality giving asylum or protection to the rebels will be held guilty of treason, and any of its inhabitants found in possession of arms will be put to the sword.

'Article 5: any persons preaching revolt or advocating armed resistance will be shot immediately.'

Following the submission of the Vendée, the other provinces of the West received the full force of the Government's campaign of repression. Of the three main rebel leaders, Bourmont, Cadoudal, and Frotté, the first two were quickly forced to surrender, and were summoned to meet the First Consul on 5 March 1800. He tried to woo them with flattery, offering them rank and command in his own Armies; but they rejected his overtures. Bonaparte then threatened to 'smash Bourmont's head in' at the least sign of hostility; 'A man who governs must be ruthless,' he told him. Nevertheless, he treated him with a certain courtesy, as one gentleman to another. Not so Georges Cadoudal, whom he felt to be an even more obstinate opponent. Cadoudal was of humble origin, and Bonaparte made sure he did not forget it. He must, however, have retained some hope of winning him over, for he wrote to Brune: 'I saw Georges this morning. He looked to me like a lusty Breton who might, with luck, be made to serve the interests of the country.' Indeed, he sent for him again ten days later, alone this time, and offered him rank and money. The 'lusty Breton' refused, with barely-repressed anger. 'I ought to have grabbed the little whippersnapper and choked him,' he said to Hyde when they next met. Ever after, Cadoudal hated Bonaparte with a deadly hatred. But he decided to bide his time, and wrote a letter to Brune pretending to have been converted to the cause of peace; meanwhile, he and Hyde contrived to slip unnoticed across the Channel at the end of May 1800.

The First Consul, having once been tricked through this own over-confidence, took no such chances with Frotté, the rebel leader in Normandy, whom he regarded with good reason as his most redoubtable adversary. Not content that Frotté should be taken alive or dead, he put a price of a thousand louis on his head. Harassed and hunted, Frotté sought to come to terms. He was told that if he surrendered, 'he could count on the generosity of the Government, whose sole desire was to bury the past and reunite the whole people of France'. On the strength of a safe-conduct from General Guidal, the Commandant of Alençon, he gave himself up. Guidal received him in his own house and began negotiations, then broke off the proceedings and left the room. When the door reopened, a picket of soldiers marched in. Frotté was arrested, and on the following day he, and six of his companions, were taken off in the direction of Paris. When the convoy stopped at Verneuil, it found fresh orders from Paris awaiting it. A military court was at once convened, at which the seven prisoners were summarily condemned to death (18 February). There were not enough men in the firing squad. 'In order to finish them off, two or three volleys were necessary. Around the twitching bodies the ground grew red with blood – the generous blood of men who had the supreme honour, in those troubled times, of having always served one cause, and of dying loyal to their principles.'[1]

What exactly was the extent of Bonaparte's responsibility in this

---

[1] Vandal: *op. cit.*

affair, which has blotted his memory no less than the murder of the Duc d'Enghien? Lanfrey maintains that after sending the order to shoot the prisoners, Bonaparte sent a second message ordering a reprieve – but only when he knew that the first order had already been carried out. Vandal dismisses the reprieve story, but believes that when Bonaparte ordered Frotté's execution, he was unaware of the treacherous circumstances of his capture.

*   *   *

The elimination of the Chouans as a force to be reckoned with was no mean achievement. While victory and peace abroad still remained to be achieved, Bonaparte had at least succeeded in pacifying the West – something the Republic had been unable to do in ten years. The vast majority of the nation could think themselves fortunate in having entrusted their destiny to this young General, whose authority they were prepared to accept without question. He now had the necessary constitutional basis for wielding effective power, and might have been expected to rest content with the situation. But in political circles (even discounting the Assemblies, currently in recess) the fires of disaffection still smouldered, and there were endless rivalries and intrigues even in Bonaparte's immediate entourage. It was not enough that he had curbed parliamentary freedom, suppressed five-sixths of the newspapers and muzzled the rest, and subjected the whole country to the control of his network of Prefects and magistrates. He also needed a reorganized and enlarged police force, not so much for purposes of repression as in order to listen and inform. Fouché was the man he chose to carry out this task.

The consular régime now became, in many respects, a police state. The Ministry of Police created three new categories of official – *commissaires généraux*, *commissaires*, and *commissaires spéciaux* – whose functions supplemented those of the Prefect. The Gendarmerie, likewise reorganized and enlarged, was also put at Fouché's disposal, as was the secret police, a legacy from the *Ancien Régime* and the Revolutionary Governments; this force was now strengthened and modernized. Dubois, whom Fouché appointed Prefect of the Paris police, had, in theory, a subordinate role, but soon struck out along independent lines.

This was by no means displeasing to Bonaparte, who liked to have two strings to his bow – or indeed three, counting his own. The result was a proliferation of spies of every kind, drawn from every class of society, who were just as active in ministerial circles as among the 'upper crust' and in the poorer quarters – a motley crew who had little respect for the rights of the individual. Private correspondence was meticulously examined by Lavalette's *Cabinet Noir*. Where arrests were concerned, the unorthodox proceedings of the police were imitated by the Ministry of the Interior, which not infrequently quashed Court verdicts of 'not guilty', by virtue of administrative orders which were, to all intents and purposes, *lettres de cachet*.

*   *   *

What remained of the individual citizen's rights in the first days of Spring 1800, after three months of the new Constitution which Cabanis had hailed in such effusive terms? One must not paint the picture too black: the Government's proceedings were arbitrary, perhaps even dictatorial, but not actually oppressive. The best description of the régime would perhaps be 'an enlightened dictatorship'. The police were employed on surveillance rather than repression, and there was no sudden wave of arrests.[1] There was still an attempt at a policy of conciliation: the Prefects and magistrates selected were a nice blend of Jacobins, moderates, and men of the *Ancien Régime*.

On 9 Germinal (30 March), the Ministry of the Interior announced that the Government did not favour, and would not countenance, the existence of separate parties; in France there must be only 'Frenchmen'. Meanwhile those who had suffered exile or loss of rights as a result of the Revolution continued to be reabsorbed into the nation's life. Not only was the law of hostages repealed; many *émigrés* were allowed to return, as well as

---

[1] This was not solely a political police force. It was also the beginning of the *Police des Mœurs*. Public morals at the time of the Consulate were appalling; there were more prostitutes in Paris than in the London of Mayhew – and not only female prostitutes. Dubois's personal reports to Napoleon, as well as the memoirs of the English tourist, Henry Redhead Yorke, tell of some very odd goings-on. (Translator's note).

thirty-eight victims of the Fructidor purge (among them Carnot), some former *Constituants* (including La Fayette), and two 'men of the Terror', Barère and Vadier. Finally, on 7 Nivôse the Consuls (under conditions which will be examined later) had authorized the reopening of churches, and allowed the 'refractory' priests to resume their ministry.

The measures were just what the country wanted, and Bonaparte, confident of having public opinion solidly behind him, decided to delay no longer the installation of himself and his Government in the Tuileries. The move took place on 19 February 1800. From early morning a crowd had been gathering in the neighbourhood of the Luxembourg, but it had to wait till midday to see the weird procession which finally made its appearance. Transport had had to be hired, since there were not enough carriages for the members of the Government. Bonaparte and the two other Consuls rode in a splendid carriage drawn by six white horses, a gift from the Emperor Francis to Bonaparte after the peace of Campo Formio: the imperial splendour of the equipage was a sign of things to come, and contrasted sharply with the motley, down-at-heel appearance of the rest, among whom only the soldiers of the Republic provided a touch of distinction.

The Generals were resplendent in white breeches and a quantity of gold braid, with flamboyant tricolor plumes surmounting their two-cornered hats. Old cabs, with strips of paper pasted over their licence numbers, gave an occasional glimpse of a gleaming new uniform, or of some sleepy or bewildered dignitary, not yet accustomed to his exalted position. But the sight which most astonished the gaping crowd was Napoleon's Egyptian retinue, and his amazing Mameluke, swathed in native robes, prancing about on his diminutive horse.

The procession reached the *Quais* and crossed the Pont Royal. Here and there one might see royalists or Jacobins who failed to remove their hats; occasionally a voice shouted '*Vive le Roi!*', but mostly it was '*Ça ira*' and, of course, '*Vive la République!*' and '*Vive Bonaparte!*'. Never had the hero of Italy and Egypt been so acclaimed; the cheering swelled in a continuous crescendo all the way to the Tuileries.

The carriage drove in to the courtyard and the three Consuls alighted. Cambacérès and Lebrun entered the palace, while Bonaparte, clad in red from head to foot, mounted a horse that was standing ready, and returned to inspect his troops – the first of those reviews which were to become one of the major attractions of Paris. Then he too entered the palace. It was a gloomy building – Bonaparte told Roederer that he found it *'triste comme la grandeur'* – and still bore the scars of 1792, the bullet-holes making a sinister contrast with the elegance of the furnishings. Bonaparte's rooms were on the first floor, Josephine's on the ground floor; Lebrun was given the Pavillon de Flore, while Cambacérès preferred the seclusion of the Hotel d'Elbeuf, whose façade was flanked by the wretched hovels of the Carrousel.

As Bonaparte entered his apartments, he remarked to his secretary: 'Now, Bourrienne, it's not enough to have reached the Tuileries; we've got to stay here.' The crowd, at least, had no misgivings; they had every reason to believe that the Republic, in the person of Bonaparte, was now permanently installed in the palace which the last of the kings had abandoned to the Convention. And indeed Bonaparte, as if to prove that he was really 'at home', opened his doors to all comers. However, very few Parisians dared to take up the invitation.

From now on, military parades were held every ten days. The First Consul, on horse-back, already wearing the grey frock-coat which was to be his trade-mark, personally supervised the manoeuvres, which became more and more spectacular with each occasion. The people of Paris greeted these displays with enthusiasm; they were in bellicose mood, clamouring for a great victory which would lead to a secure peace and put an end to the danger of foreign invasion. Despite the conciliatory letter Bonaparte had written to the King of England on the morrow of 18 Brumaire (*'La guerre qui depuis huit ans ravage les quatre parties du monde doit-elle être éternelle?'*), they knew that the English would insist on the restoration of the Bourbons before making peace. Austria too had refused to negotiate; one of her armies was massed on the Rhine, another was blocking Masséna's path at Genoa.

On 5 May 1800 Bonaparte was preparing to leave for Switzerland, ostensibly to review the Reserve Army, but in reality to assume personal command and attack the Austrians in Italy from the rear. On the eve of his departure he learnt of Moreau's victory over the Austrians at Stokach. After telegraphing his congratulations ('*Gloire et trois fois gloire!*'), he set off at once in a postchaise bound for Dijon, Geneva, and the Saint Bernard.

*   *   *

Spring 1800. The century of enlightenment had burnt itself out, and in the new century now dawning, philosophy had lost its glamour. Paris, which not long before had put Voltaire on a pedestal, now acclaimed a conquering hero with the profile of a Roman emperor. Those deluded thinkers who had helped him on his way to the Capitol in the belief that he would prove to be another Marcus Aurelius, were now finding that he was, instead, a Julius Caesar. Too late, they saw that liberty was in jeopardy.

There were some among them in the Tribunate who had the courage and honesty to speak out. But their voices were drowned in the clash of arms and the clamour of popular enthusiasm. They were unwilling, or unable, to set down their discontents in writing, and the book they ought to have written came instead from their friend Germaine de Staël, in the shape of a monumental essay published in April under the title *De la littérature considerée dans ses rapports avec les institutions sociales.*

This important work, purporting to be a study of ancient and modern literature, was in fact a cogent exposition of the philosophic principles underlying the Revolution, in the light of those doctrines of progress and human perfectibility which had been formulated, notably, by Kant, Turgot, and Condorcet. Her thesis was that philosophy, reason, and eloquence must hold a place of pre-eminence in the State; that writers have a duty to exert their influence on the life of their fellow-citizens; and that thought must go hand in hand with action in the conduct of national affairs.

'Every tyrant,' she wrote, 'no matter what his policy may be, detests the intellect. . . . Man's intellectual power cannot attain its fullest development unless it attacks authority.'

In an obvious allusion to Bonaparte's liberal opponents, she praised the example of the Roman philosopher Cato, who committed suicide rather than submit to Caesar's tyranny, and spent his last night reading Plato's *Phaedo*. His death 'was more fruitful in results than the achievements of his life, for he became the enduring type of the Stoic, an example that kindled the imagination of the noblest Romans under the Empire.'

Elsewhere she wrote: '. . . the possibility of expressing liberal views and of cherishing an independent philosophy capable of judging all human institutions and opinions, is the only way to overthrow an unjust rule. . . . An excess of war-like spirit is a danger to freedom of thought. . . . Military discipline makes soldiers incapable of forming a genuine opinion.'

These were courageous words to write at a time when the crowds were jostling and overflowing in the Place du Carrousel as they enthusiastically cheered the plumes and fanfares of their parading armies. Mme de Staël went on to say: 'In this respect [the army's] *esprit de corps* is much the same as that of the priests. . . . The enthusiasm inspired by victorious generals has nothing to do with the justice of their cause. . . . Only by our readiness to speak out, by our love of art and literature, by our pursuit of philosophy, can we make a piece of land into *our own country* (*faire d'une territoire une patrie*).'

De la littérature caused a considerable stir in intellectual circles and provoked a number of articles. On one side, there was Fauriel's review in the *Décade*; his comments were on the whole favourable, though with some reservations. There was Daunou's, which so delighted Mme de Staël that she wrote from Coppet, where she had now returned, to thank him warmly for his kind remarks.

Bonaparte, preoccupied with the preparations for his Swiss journey, still found time to glance at the book. He told Lucien that he had studied it 'for at least a quarter of an hour' (it is six hundred pages long), and could not understand it. 'The Devil take me if I have been able to decipher, I won't say the words – there is no lack of them, and big words at that – but with all the concentration of my intelligence I failed to discover a meaning in any of these ideas that are reputedly so profound.'[1]

[1] I have taken the liberty of quoting Christopher Herold's translation. Of course Bonaparte was not speaking the truth. He understood her only too well. cf. J. C. Herold, *Mistress to an Age* (Hamish Hamilton, 1959). (Translator's note).

4

The Rue Saint-Nicaise

✤✤✤

THE news that Bonaparte had crossed the Alps gave rise to much anxious speculation. It was rumoured that the General's supporters were proposing to change the constitution and introduce a hereditary monarchy. Such ideas had indeed been mooted at one of the *dîners de tridi* already mentioned; the company had included Cabanis and some of his associates, who were now joined by Stanislas de Girardin and Miot, both members of Joseph's circle. There were also monthly meetings at Auteuil to commemorate the 19 Brumaire; these were patronized less by the *philosophes* than by the political allies of Siéyès, whose principal concern was to discuss what course to follow should the First Consul be killed in action. Fouché, Talleyrand, and Siéyès decided to call a meeting of fifty parliamentarians to study the question.

The 'Auteuil Conspiracy' remains, to some extent, shrouded in mystery. Even the names of those involved – with the exception of Constant and Ginguené – cannot be established with any certainty. The conspirators were united by one overriding anxiety: as republicans who had voted for the death of Louis XVI, what was to become of them if Bonaparte died? As they reflected on possible successors to Bonaparte, the names of several Generals were put forward – Masséna, Bernadotte, Brune, and Moreau (this last a strong favourite). Lucien and La Fayette were also proposed; but in the upshot it was Carnot who received the unanimous vote of the meeting.

The events of June gave the Government further cause for concern. Joseph wrote to Napoleon asking to be named as his

successor. Meanwhile rumours multiplied, to the effect that
Siéyès was now at the head of the Orleanist party; the same label
was applied without discrimination to every known dissident.
By now, news of Genoa's capitulation had reached Paris, but
nothing was known of Bonaparte himself. On 21 June public
anxiety reached fever pitch. A great battle, it was said, had been
fought and lost. On the very next day, however, a dispatch from
the First Consul announced the victory of Marengo.

The whole *monde politique* rushed to the Tuileries to hear the
bulletin of 26 Prairial – a virtuoso composition from Bonaparte's
own hand. A wave of excitement spread from the centre to the
working-class quarter where the citizens' passionate enthusiasm
for the heroic, republican spirit, as incarnated in Napoleon,
erupted in scenes of wild jubilation. Catholics, too, added their
Te Deums to the general rejoicing. Nothing like it had been seen
since the *Fête de la Fédération*: after eight years of continuous
warfare, surely peace was now assured?

However, the victory of Marengo was not to everybody's
liking. A curious letter from Lucien to Joseph, dated 24 June,
makes this clear; apropos of the Auteuil intrigues, he writes:

> . . . they have been discussing at length the pros and cons
> between C . . . [Carnot] and La F . . . [La Fayette], but I don't
> know yet if the High Priest [Talleyrand] chose either. Per-
> sonally, I think he was playing both of them off against an
> Orleanist candidate, and that your friend from Auteuil [Siéyès]
> was behind the whole business. They are now thoroughly
> dismayed by the news of Marengo. . . . As for us, [had Marengo
> been a defeat] we should all at this moment be under arrest.

On the night of 13 Messidor, Bonaparte arrived in Paris.
According to Fouché's account, he already had wind of the
intrigues, and was in a very bad temper. 'So they thought I was
finished, eh? Were they hoping to set up another Committee of
Public Safety . . . ? What do they take me for – another Louis
XVI? . . . I'm not afraid of anything; I'll grind their faces in the
dust!'

His temper was improved by the enthusiasm of Paris, which
was everything he could wish for. The people flocked to the

Tuileries, invading the gardens and compelling the hero of the hour to make a personal appearance on the palace balcony. The city was decked with flags and ablaze with lights. Nowhere was this spirit of rejoicing more evident than in the working quarter of the faubourg Antoine.

The feelings of the moment must have been of an extraordinary intensity. Over 300 miles away, at Coppet, Madame de Staël, who had so recently been hoping for Bonaparte's defeat, found herself caught up in the general enthusiasm. Replying to a letter from her philosopher friend Gerando, who had praised Moreau's victories on the Rhine, she wrote that these had been eclipsed by Marengo, the glorious news of which had turned even *her* head, and that she too had succumbed to the universal euphoria.

Among the opposition senators and Tribunes, nearly all of whom were former Brumairains, enthusiasm was tempered by apprehension: Marengo, they had hoped, was to have been a triumph for the Republic, not one to be exploited to Bonaparte's own advantage. So much was made clear in a moving speech by Daunou, who gave more credit for the victory to Desaix than to Bonaparte, whom, in fact, he never even mentioned by name.[1] Daunou extolled Desaix as an intrepid soldier, a simple and modest citizen, who had not only proved himself 'an experienced captain but an esteemed philosopher'. 'Oh, Desaix! [he concluded]

[1] Perhaps this needs some explanation. While Moreau was advancing from the Rhine, Bonaparte had ordered Berthier's army to cross from Dijon into Italy. Then the First Consul, 'leaping down the mountain side' (his own words), caught up with the army and led them into Milan. Deliberately seeking out the enemy, he most unusually allowed himself to be surprised by superior forces on an open plain. . . . On 14 June the French were routed and by early afternoon the Battle of Marengo seemed over. At about 4 p.m., Desaix returned from a mission detached the previous day, and turned the fortunes of war. Poor Desaix was killed at the end of the action by a musket ball. He was only thirty-two. The fact that he was the real victor was never mentioned in the official bulletin which concentrated instead on Bonaparte rallying his troops. 'To lie like a bulletin' was a current phrase in the army. (Translator's note cf. Maurice Hutt's: *Napoléon*. Clarendon Biographies).

Even should your other exploits[1] be forgotten, surely the memory of Marengo will remain immortal'.

Nevertheless, Daunou still hoped that this victory would guarantee peace and 'dispel a resurgence of anti-Republican ideals', and ended his speech with a lyrical peroration: 'the sublime thought of peace is present in the minds of all. . . .'

It was then Benjamin Constant's turn to mount the tribune. After he, too, had acclaimed the victory and the freedom it had brought to the peoples of Italy, Constant declared: 'Peace will guarantee the individual rights of citizens. . . . Peace will restore to us the indispensable freedom of the press. Old Europe, now regenerated, will be the proud possessor of the most perfect of free Governments. France will be able to show her young emulators beyond the seas an imposing organization of thirty million citizens and six hundred thousand heroes, and names held in national respect, like those of Franklin and Washington in America.'

These claims, made by the intellectual *élite* of France, surely reflected the deep-seated hopes and needs of the country. What, indeed, would have been the destiny of Europe, had the victorious First Consul responded to their call?

*　　*　　*

On 25 Messidor (14 July 1800) 'when the Government marched from the Tuileries to the Invalides and from the Invalides to the Champ de Mars to present the colours captured in Germany and Italy, an immense crowd surrounded the procession. Frenzied people – old men, women, and children – dashed among the horses' legs to get near the General, to touch the gilding on his saddle and kiss the hem of his uniform. . . . On the Champ de Mars people went mad again . . . they broke through the barriers. . . . The spectacle, grandoise though it was, interested them less

---

[1] '*Memories of your other exploits*'. Desaix (his full name was Louis Desaix de Veygou, 1768–1800) had distinguished himself with the Army of the Rhine when he defended Kehl against the Austrians to cover Moreau's retreat, only capitulating when his ammunition was exhausted (1796). He accompanied Bonaparte to Egypt where his greatest achievement was the conquest of Upper Egypt (1799). His own soldiers compared him to Bayard, and the Egyptians referred to him as 'the just sultan'. (Translator's note).

than the man providing it! [*Jean Robiquet: Daily Life in France under Napoleon*]. But was this really homage to the spirit of Liberty? Certainly in the Tribunate, Liberty was not yet forgotten. Here, orators paid homage to the memory of Latour d'Auvergne, who was killed on 26 June while serving with Moreau's army. His refusal to accept from Bonaparte the title of *Premier Grenadier de France* had become legendary; he personified the virtues of a citizen as much as those of a soldier. His was a courageous, but almost unique gesture, 'an island of republican spirit in an ocean of military glory'.

In the evening, after the military parades, there was a great banquet held in the Tuileries. The President of the Tribunate proposed the toast: 'To philosophy and civil rights,' while the First Consul proposed: 'To the Fourteenth of July and to the People of France, who are the rulers of us all.'

Before Marengo, the people, determined to keep up republican appearances, usually addressed each other as 'Citizen', nor had the Brumairains completely renounced the illusion that the new régime was consolidating the victory of 1789. Moreover, when expedient, the First Consul himself still made reference to Republican ideals, or, at least, made use of Republican terminology. After Marengo, however, Bonaparte's authoritarianism became more marked. He was intolerant of any independent opinion; royal usages and etiquette reappeared by degrees in the consular court. Bonaparte took into his service former *émigrés*, fortune hunters prepared to play the part of sycophantic courtiers. He flattered the clergy; he flattered the aristocracy. To the Prefect of the Vendée he wrote: 'I like good French priests, who know how to protect *la Patrie* against those *dastardly heretical English*, the eternal enemies of France.' (27 July 1800)

His ambition to found a hereditary Bonapartist dynasty was soon an open secret. Josephine, unable to give him an heir, and who already dreaded a divorce, was naturally opposed to the idea, but among his family and personal entourage there were many who encouraged him, particularly Lucien (who looked forward eventually to succeeding his brother) and their sister Elisa. Elisa maintained a reactionary neo-Catholic *salon*, whose brightest ornament was her lover, Fontanes, then preparing his *Parallèle entre César, Cromwell et Bonaparte* [purporting to be

translated from the English], the significance of which could not
have been more clear.

'We should not compare Bonaparte with a Monk or a Cromwell, but rather with a Charles Martel or a Charlemagne. To
find another man comparable to him, we must look back two
thousand years – to Caesar . . . [but] Caesar was a demagogue
. . . Bonaparte, on the contrary, has rallied round him men of
property and the educated classes, instead of frenzied masses!
. . . Oh, what discord, what disasters may be in store for us
without him! Who could replace him? The fate of thirty-
thousand men depends on one single man.'

The *Parallèle* was published anonymously (1 November 1800)
and circulated throughout all the *départements* with the help of
Lucien, the Minister of Interior. Bourrienne, who made no
attempt to disguise the fact that it revealed Bonaparte's plans
prematurely, showed it to the First Consul, who read it and threw
it on the floor in apparent disgust. The bad impression made by
this pamphlet soon became all too obvious as reports from
Préfets and the Army flowed in. Fouché, as Minister of Police,
came in for a severe reprimand; he was told by the First Consul
that his duty was to have had Lucien arrested and thrown into
prison. The fact was, however, that Fouché, as he explained to
Bourrienne with a wry smile, had indeed reprimanded Lucien,
but the latter had shown him the manuscript annotated and corrected by the First Consul himself.

Lucien was dismissed from his post and sent to Madrid. He
was replaced by Chaptal. The *Parallèle* was confiscated, but the
cat was out of the bag. Everyone now knew what to expect.
The crowd of toadies surrounding Bonaparte was more zealous
than ever in its adulation of the First Consul.

The Royalists, however, still believed that Bonaparte was
preparing to play the role of a Monk rather than a Cromwell.
Louis XVIII wrote to him on 20 February without success, and
addressed him again a month later, in a very dignified letter.
The First Consul did not reply until 7 September: '. . . Your
return is not a thing to be wished for; it could only be made over
100,000 corpses. . . .'

At the other extreme, these were the revolutionary followers of

Marat and Robespierre (Septembrists) and officers who in some way had compromised themselves; they plotted openly in taverns and drank to the downfall of the tyrant. All, however, were known, either personally or by repute, to the agents of Fouché, who kept himself informed of everything. Right up to October 1800, attempts on Bonaparte's life were being discussed, if not actually planned. All these were hushed up by the Minister of Police, whose policy it was to keep quiet about the plots of his former Terrorist friends.

There was one plot, however, which made the headlines, though it did little harm. This was the so-called Arena-Ceracchi plot. Arena, the instigator, was a Corsican and former deputy of the Five Hundred; his brother had presided at the Assembly of 18 Brumaire which had been so violently opposed to Bonaparte. Ceracchi, an exiled Italian sculptor, seems to have borne the First Consul a grudge for other reasons than merely political. There were many others implicated in the conspiracy, including a half-pay captain named Harel. Their plan was to assassinate Bonaparte during a performance at the Opéra. Harel, however, turned informer and was prepared to sell his friends, but instead of approaching Fouché, he turned to Bourrienne, the First Consul's secretary. Bonaparte gave orders that Harel should be rewarded, but that nothing should as yet be disclosed to Fouché, 'to show that he was the better policeman of the two'. When the time was ripe to inform Fouché of the conspiracy, the Minister of Police merely shrugged his shoulders and told the First Consul that he already knew all about it, but now that the matter was in other hands, he washed his hands of it. Dubois, the Prefect of Police, was therefore put in charge of the case.

On 10 October 1800, Bonaparte, accompanied by Josephine, Hortense, Duroc, Lannes, and Bourrienne, entered his box at the Opéra. The Conspirators were already at their posts, four of whom had been planted and armed by the police. During the first act, on a sign from Harel, the real conspirators were seized and bound before they even realized what was happening to them. They were taken to the Temple where they were to remain imprisoned without so much as a trial. Harel, for his pains, was made Governor of the fortress of Vincennes, where he was later to receive the Duc d'Enghien.

Historians differ concerning the seriousness of this plot. Those most critical of Napoleon take the view that the whole affair was engineered by the police with the connivance of the First Consul, who found it expedient to give the impression that he had escaped a great danger. Such was Fouché's opinion.[1]

The public, far from suspecting any trickery, was indignant. Just as Bonaparte had hoped, congratulations on his escape flowed in from every village and town in France. On 17 October, an ecstatic crowd flocked to see him at a military review held in the Place du Carrousel, while on the previous evening, the Tribunate itself congratulated the Head of State on his escape.

* * *

In the circumstances, it would have been difficult for the Tribunate to have acted otherwise, although the actions of the First Consul, both before and after Marengo, had done little to dispel the doubts and discontent felt by the *philosophes* and the Institute.

On entering Milan (2 June), on the eve of establishing the Cisalpine Republic, Bonaparte had ordered a *Te Deum* to be sung. A few days later, at a convocation of the Milanese clergy, he made pronouncements which were more to their liking than reassuring for the future liberty of conscience in France. There was a strange note of intolerance in his declaration that he would regard anyone who 'insulted our common religion . . . even in the slightest degree, as a disturber of the peace, whom I would not hesitate to punish . . . and if need be, condemn to death'. Here there was no question of voting, or recourse to the law. He, Bonaparte, would 'punish, and, if need be, condemn to death'. He was forcing religion on the State. This was the conduct of an hereditary monarch invoking theology and the Divine Right of Kings. Was this how the victor of Marengo intended to apply the constitution?

Ties which had united all liberals in a sort of permanent conspiracy before Bonaparte's departure, were all the more strengthened on his return. The parliamentary opposition, born

[1] *Les Memoires de Fouché.*

spontaneously in the year VIII, now became more united than ever. Although the opposition had no support from the people as a whole, enlightened opinion was on its side, which, now that Madame Helvétius was no more, was grouped around the persons of Germaine de Staël and the lovely Sophie de Condorcet, who, in the eyes of her friends represented the 'militant *citoyenne*, the very incarnation of the Republic and the Revolution'. Madame de Staël's circle of friends, however, was much wider than that of Sophie de Condorcet; indeed she was on familiar terms with men of all parties.[1]

The *salons* of these two ladies were the rallying point of all persons of independent minds. But behind the scenes, there was still Siéyès, who still cherished political ambitions. Having joined the party of the left in the Senate, composed of Cabanis, Tracy, Garat, Volney, and Lanjuinais (who had been elected in March), he was also highly respected in the Tribunate by such men as Chénier and Duveyrier, and was generally regarded as more or less the unofficial leader of all the disaffected parliamentarians.

Thus, when Bonaparte returned from Marengo, however confident he may have been, and however decided he was to exercise sovereign power (without any attempt at concealment), and although so many of his followers, who earlier had been only too ready to betray him, were now redoubling their zeal to regain his favour, he, nevertheless, found himself confronted by a much better organized and much more active opposition than before his departure. When the new *Corps législatif* was opened in the autumn of 1800, the minority represented a serious threat.

The Government received a considerable shock when the Tribunate severely criticized a Bill which would have given the Council of State the opportunity of passing laws virtually without debate. This Bill was rejected by the Tribunate by a majority of

[1] 'Some of the most prominent of her regular guests were drawn from the *élite* of Bonaparte's régime – his ministers, officials, and family. It was this which disquieted him. ... That his own brothers and intimate associates should become accomplices to her persiflage on the new order and its slogans was intolerable; it amounted to a chronic state of latent mutiny.' cf. J. Christopher Herold: *A Mistress to an Age*. (Translator's note.)

85 to 5, and by the Legislative Council by 209 to 58. This was most encouraging to the opposition. Benjamin Constant took the initiative of grouping all opposition members into a single body – the *Comité des Lumières* – with the result that the public benches, which had been so often empty during the preceding session, were now filled with the intellectual *élite*, who followed the debates with the greatest interest.

The next Bill on the agenda concerned the reduction in the number of J.P.s (*Juges de la Paix*), some of whose responsibilities, it was recommended, should in future be assumed by the police. Now, of all the institutions founded by the Constituent Assembly, the *Justice de la Paix* was the last vestige of a freely elected magistrature to be spared by the constitution of Year VIII. After three days of heated discussion, the Tribunate unanimously rejected the Government's proposals. Preferring retreat to defeat, an extremely irritated Bonaparte, who had, in turn, unsuccessfully cajoled and threatened many of the most influential Tribunes, withdrew the Bill altogether.

On 2 Nivôse (23 December), the police reported that a number of parliamentarians, including Benjamin Constant, were preparing with the connivance of Barras to overthrow the First Consul. Although there was nothing to support these charges, it was perfectly true that the opposition, encouraged by their success, now expressed their opinions much more freely and that the atmosphere was very strained.

On the night of 24 December, Paris was shaken by a terrible explosion.

*   *   *

On that evening, Bonaparte was due to visit the Opéra (situated in what today is the Square Louvois) to hear a performance of Haydn's *Creation*. He entered his carriage with Berthier, Lannes, and Lauriston. An escort of mounted grenadiers rode ahead. Josephine, delayed by a slight change in her toilet (Napoleon had objected to her shawl), followed a little later, accompanied by Hortense and Caroline. The night was very dark with a slight drizzle. No sooner had his carriage left the Tuileries, than the First Consul, tired out from a hard day's work, fell asleep. On reaching the rue Nicaise their passage was partly obstructed by a

stationary hooded cart which half blocked the road. Bonaparte's
coachman whipped up his horses, drove around the cart, and
continued on his way to the rue de la Loi (rue Richelieu). At that
very moment there was a tremendous explosion, followed by the
sound of splintering glass and falling stones, collapsing houses,
and screams of pain.

'Bonaparte has been attacked!' cried Josephine, and fainted.

The orchestra had played only a few bars of Haydn when the
Opéra was rocked by the explosion.

'What's the meaning of this?' Junot demanded. 'Why are they
firing cannon at this time of night? I should have been told.'

Bonaparte appeared in his box, cool and collected, and remarked drily, 'Some scoundrels tried to blow me up. Get me
a copy of the score of the Oratorio.'

The audience gave him a standing ovation. He had to signal to
the orchestra to continue playing. In fact, he stayed only a little
while before returning to the Tuileries. People rushed from all
sides in the hope of seeing him. It was already being said that a
cart containing a powder barrel was in pieces and that a little girl
had been blown to bits (later it was learnt that the girl in question
had been given twelve sous to hold the horse while the time fuse
burnt through). Five people were killed and more than twenty-
five were wounded.

When the First Consul returned to the Tuileries he was a very
different man from the imperturbable hero who had earned so
many ovations at the Opéra. He now gave free vent to his anger,
accusing Jacobins, Terrorists, and Anarchists alike of attempting
his murder. Fouché, who had been making enquiries on the spot,
arrived late. Everybody realized that it was Fouché who was the
real target of Bonaparte's invective. Unmoved, the Minister of
Police made no reply. Some of his friends tried to exonerate the
Jacobins and blame the outrage on the Chouans. This only made
the General doubly angry. 'It was Jacobins who wanted to
murder me. Nothing will make me change my mind. There were
no Chouans, émigrés, ci-devant nobles, or priests concerned in
this! I know who the authors were. I know how to reach them
and punish them as they deserve!' Imprecation followed imprecation. Some members of the Council of State protested that there
was as yet no real evidence against anybody. Fouché obviously

agreed with them, 'not in so many words but by his calm, his silence, and the almost imperceptible movement of his lips'.

'I don't have to rely on you; I make my own police', Bonaparte told him.

According to certain other accounts, including that of Fouché himself, Bonaparte addressed him directly: 'Well, d'you still insist that this was the work of Royalists?'

'Undoubtedly', answered Fouché, 'and what's more, within a week I will prove it.'

But it was clear that Bonaparte was not going to wait that long to get rid of him; Talleyrand even recommended that Fouché should be shot.

On the following day (25 December), the *Moniteur*, while denouncing the intrigues of the Jacobins, also published details of another affair – the *Affaire Chevalier*. Chevalier, a manufacturer of fireworks, had made a small bomb which had exploded by accident near the Salpetrière on 17 October (that is to say, just after the 'disclosure' of the Ceracchi-Arena plot). Arrested and accused of an attempt on the life of the First Consul, Chevalier obstinately pleaded innocent, as did his equally ardent Republican friends, who, as former Jacobins, were all labelled indiscriminately as 'Terrorists' and 'Anarchists'.

From now on, public opinion was so roused that even the President of the Tribunate informed the First Consul that the Assembly considered the present laws inadequate to cope with these crimes, whereas, only two months previously, after the Ceracchi affair, the Tribunate had tempered its assurances of loyalty with a demand that any measures taken against suspects, 'must be conducted with all due legal formality'.

Deputations from other Government department, in what had now become a sacred rite, congratulated the First Consul on his escape. The General, in reply to the President of the *Corps législatif*, first employed the happy formula that 'devoted as he was to his country, he considered it just as glorious to die in the exercise of his duties as First Consul, in support of the Republic and its Constitution, as to die on the field of battle'.

Instead of waiting to establish the identity of the unknown authors of the terrible crime of the previous evening and letting the law take its course, Bonaparte hurled the same accusation as he had previously levelled at Fouché; in short, the criminals were former Jacobins, Terrorists, and Septembrists. He told Dubois (the *Prefet de police*) that, had this bunch of brigands attacked him directly, he would have left it to ordinary courts of law to punish them, but since they had endangered the lives of the populace, their punishment 'would be as prompt as it would be exemplary'.

Not content with depriving the courts of authority, the First Consul wanted, in one blow, to strike at a hundred persons. Nevertheless, he still wanted to give an appearance of legality to what was an entirely arbitary act. Hence his attendance, with the two other consuls at a meeting of the Council of State on 26 December. The council had already prepared two additional clauses to the proposed Bill advocating the setting up of special courts (which was awaiting debate by the Tribunate). The first of these specified that the special courts should be given authority to try cases of attempted murder of members of the Government; the other empowered the consuls to expel from Paris, or even banish, any persons considered a danger to the State. Portalis, the *rapporteur*, began reading an exposé of the bill, but before he had an opportunity to mention the additional clauses, he was interrupted by Bonaparte, who declared that any trial by the courts would be too slow. A much more striking vengeance was demanded for such an atrocious crime. What was needed was blood. For every innocent victim of the explosion, he would have one of the culprits shot – 'some fifteen or twenty' – and have another two hundred deported and take advantage of the occasion to purge the Republic. This attack, he maintained, was the work of a band of scoundrels, Septembrists, whose hand was to be found in every crime of the Revolution. . . . 'In a country where bandits remain unpunished . . . the people can no longer have faith in a Government composed of worthy but timid moderates. . . .'

The metaphysicians, he went on to say, were at the root of all ills. Either one must do nothing, and grant pardons like Augustus, or take firm measures to guarantee the social order. He reminded his listeners that at the time of Catalena's plot, Cicero had had all the plotters put to death and had thus saved his country. The First Consul concluded his speech by saying that he was so convinced of the necessity of making an example of these scoundrels, that he was prepared to judge and condemn them himself.

Roederer was the first to protest: 'I do not think it is for you to act as judge. The greatest harm that could befall France, apart from the loss of your life, would be the loss . . . of her reputation for justice, which until now you have preserved undefiled.'

The only other Councillor of State with sufficient courage to attack the First Consul directly was Admiral Truguet. A dedicated, although not extreme, Republican, Truguet had been imprisoned during the Terror, but like Tracy and Daunou he had been released after Thermidor. Although the Admiral did not claim that all former Terrorists were innocent, he nevertheless pointed out that there were 'all sorts of other scoundrels', including *émigrés*, fanatical priests, and Chouans, and alluded to the revolt still smouldering in the Vendée, and also drew attention to the pamphlets which were corrupting public opinion – an obvious reference to the *Parallèle*.

This was altogether too much for Bonaparte. Nothing, he declared, would make him change his mind; he knew that it was the Septembrists who were organizing all these crimes. 'You speak of the nobility and priests', he continued. 'Do you want me to condemn them merely for what they are? What do you want me to do? Deport ten thousand priests – old men? Do you want me to persecute the ministers of a religion that is professed by the majority of Frenchmen and by two thirds of Europe?'

It was quite clear from this impassioned speech that he had plans for a Concordat and that he had decided to rely on Catholic support. For more than half an hour he continued in this vein, becoming more and more vehement. 'Citizen Truguet', he shouted at the Admiral, 'don't imagine that you are going to save your skin by saying, "It was I who stood up for the patriots in the Council of State." These same patriots would just as willingly sacrifice you as the rest of us.'[1]

[1] On leaving the Chamber, Bonaparte walked past Truguet, who wanted further words with him. Without stopping, the General interrupted the Admiral: '*Allez donc*! You can tell all this to Madame Condorcet.' The insubordinate Madame Condorcet, to whom he had said one day, 'I don't like women who meddle in politics', to which she had replied, 'I quite agree with you, General, but in a country where they chop off women's heads it is only natural that they should want to know the reason why.'

On 6 Nivôse, Bonaparte again returned to the attack in the Council of State. He still insisted on a law authorizing the Government (without the aid of courts) to banish brigands and impose the death sentence on the authors of the attempted assassinations. Most councillors were non-committal; they considered that the proposed Bill for special courts with the additional clauses, was sufficient to meet the case, and were equally positive that the Tribunate and *Corps législatif* would veto Bonaparte's Draconian proposals. This provoked a fresh outburst from the First Consul. 'What!' he exclaimed, 'were they frightened of the Tribunate? A military court could settle the matter within a week.' He already had a list of Septembrists and other plotters. This was a moment for extraordinary measures. Who, if not the Government, had the authority to impose them? Talleyrand, on being asked his advice, maintained that the First Consul indeed had the authority and should use it. When Miot asked how the Council of State could pass a law which would inevitably be rejected by the *Corps législatif*, Talleyrand replied, 'You are quite correct, but have we only a *Corps législatif* and a Council of State? What is the use of having a Senate if we don't make use of it?' The Council of State grudgingly acquiesced.

Now that this principle had been agreed, Bonaparte immediately put the machinery in motion. A list of 'brigands' was to be drawn up by the Minister of Police and submitted to the Government. A decision would be taken to deport some hundred persons overseas, after which the Council of State would discuss the means whereby this decision could be given a constitutional legal character.

While this legal farce was being concocted, Fouché continued with his inquest. He was violently attacked and accused of arranging things to suit his old Jacobin friends and even of complicity. But Fouché, imperturbable as ever, remained convinced of the guilt of the Chouans of which he was soon to have confirmation. He was careful however not to make his knowledge public, only divulging it to the First Consul and to the Councillors of State, several of whom were appalled to learn the truth, including Roederer, who wrote: 'This decree of deportation, which I am asked to prepare, direct, and authorize, is odious in the extreme; to deport men for a crime of which they are innocent seems to me the height of iniquity.'

On 11 Nivôse (1 January 1801), the Council of State and the consuls met in plenary session to hear three reports – one from an anonymous agent, one from Dubois, the *Prefet de Police*, and lastly one from Fouché. Most unexpectedly, and to everyone's astonishment, Fouché confined himself to accusing only Jacobins; '. . . These terrible men are few in number, but they are guilty of innumerable crimes; for a year now their only purpose has been to assassinate the First Consul. . . . This is an atrocious war, which can only be terminated by taking extraordinary police measures. Not all those named by the police were caught dagger in hand, but they are universally known to be capable . . . of using them. . . .' To this incredible charge – let us not forget the atrocities committed by Fouché himself during the Terror – was added a list of one hundred and thirty names.

An ominous silence followed Fouché's report, and the debate was slow to be resumed. Several councillors pointed out that there had been no mention of the 'infernal machine' (Chevalier's bomb) in the first two reports. Thibaudeau expressed indignation at the reading of the list of names and protested against any discussion which might lead to the punishment of pre-selected individuals. Roederer reproached Fouché for maintaining silence on the conspiracy of 3 Nivôse and insisted that the Minister should 'state clearly whether the authors of that plot were, or were not, of the same class of men as those it was proposed to deport. . . .'

Instead of the Minister of Police, it was the First Consul who replied. Even if the authors of the crime were of a 'different species from the rascals with whom they were here concerned,' he declared, 'it was nonetheless true that they had been plotting for a year; they were stained with every sort of crime, and were held in abhorrence by the whole of France and gave no peace to the Government. . . . They were being deported not on account of 3 Nivôse, but because of the events of 2 September, the 31 May, and the Babeuf conspiracy. The criminal outrage of 3 Nivôse was not the cause for taking this measure, but it provided the opportunity.'

In the course of the very lively discussion which followed, Cambacérès fully supported Bonaparte's point of view and accused the individuals to be deported of criminal intent. Finally the Council of State agreed to pass the measure. Only Truguet voted against it.

As was foreseen, the Senate, by-passing the *Corps législatif*, declared the measure constitutional (15 Nivôse, Year IX – 5 January 1801). Thus, the first of the decrees of the *Senatus Consultum*, which were gradually to become substitutes for genuine laws, was promulgated. There had been, however, opposition from a minority in the Council. On 10 Nivôse, Lanjuinais had raised violent objections, and other members, including Cabanis, Garat, Volney, and Lambrechts, had stressed the illegality of an act violating the Constitution. On the day the ballot was taken, Lanjuinais, Cabanis, Garat, and Volney had kept away from the Luxembourg. Siéyès's part in the affair is not so well known.

On the following day, one hundred and thirty deportees left for Nantes. Sixty-six were sent to Mahé in the Seychelles and later transferred to Anjouan – 'an intolerable and lethal torment'. By the end of 1806, thirty-seven were already dead. Of the sixty remaining, after several years spent in Ré and Oléron, nearly all were sent to Cayenne. With the exception of nine of the prisoners, who were more or less wrongly accused of being Septembrists, no justifiable reason for the sentences on the others was ever given. Of what exactly could they be openly accused? Of remaining faithful to the spirit of a Revolution to whose excesses they had subscribed – but surely no more so than Roederer, Réal, Thibaudeau, Fouché, and others? No, their real crime was to have protested against the *coup d'état* of Saint-Cloud, men like Destrem, who had shouted at Bonaparte in the Council of Five Hundred, 'Is it for this that you have conquered?'

*   *   *

When Arena, who was still imprisoned in the Temple with his friends, learnt of the attack in the rue Nicaise, he exclaimed: 'This is our death sentence.' The emotion aroused by the terrifying explosion indeed made the verdict a foregone conclusion. Indicted before a criminal court, Arena, Ceracchi, Demerville, and Topino-Lebrun were declared guilty and condemned to death – despite Ceracchi's and Demerville's protestations that their confessions were extracted by force at the Prefecture of

Police and that the whole affair had been staged by Harvel, the police *agent provocateur*.

The four men were executed on 30 January 1801. Earlier, on 11 and 19 January, other heads had rolled, including that of Chevalier, the manufacturer of the bomb in the Salpetrière. But in the meanwhile, the real authors of the attempt in the rue Nicaise were identified. Fouché was able to announce officially that it was the work of royalists, Chouans sent from Brittany by Georges Cadoudal. Carbon, Saint-Réjant, and Limoëlan were arrested and sentenced to death; the last, however, escaped and fled to the United States.

There could no longer be any doubt of the innocence of the 130 deportees. Should not Bonaparte have rehabilitated them, repatriated them, set them free? This was the course recommended by Berlier, a former *Conventionnel* and now one of the Councillors of State, who was particularly interested in the fate of Destrem, the father of twelve children. The First Consul humoured him, split hairs, maintaining that the measures taken were 'less of a punishment than a favour' to the victims. 'They did not ask for this favour', said Berlier. The General showed himself in a conciliatory mood. 'There have been good Jacobins', he said, 'there was a time when every man of spirit was a Jacobin. I was one myself, like you and thousands of other well-meaning men, but those. . . .' A fortnight later he accorded a second interview to Berlier. This time he claimed that Destrem was a royalist. When the Councillor referred to the connection between the attempted assassination of 3 Nivôse and the *Senatus Consultum* of the 15, the First Consul thrust the *Bulletin des Lois* before his eyes, where there was not even mention of the *attentat* as a reason for the deportations. Then, bursting into laughter, the General dismissed the Councillor.[1]

Destrem died in the penitentiary of Oléron in 1803.

*   *   *

In later times, the Dreyfus affair, which was certainly no more serious, produced a wave of indignation in France with which Nivôse has nothing to compare. But with the Press gagged, how

[1] Thibaudeau: *Mémoires sur le Consulat.*

was it possible to protest under the Consulate? Even the Tribunate had been powerless. The opening debate on the Bill respecting the formation of special criminal courts, however, gave the Tribunes an opportunity, if not to discuss the deportations, at least to remind the Consular Government of the elementary rights it owed to citizens. The Bill, which was placed before the Tribunate a fortnight before the *attentat*, was aimed only at repressing brigandage in certain *départements*; nevertheless it was one that might be used to suppress all subversive manifestations and frighten any opposition.

The debates lasted three weeks. Benjamin Constant, Daunou, Chénier, and Ginguené represented the opposition. Duveyrier, the *rapporteur*[1] of the Assembly, and their former ally, had been won over to the Government camp by Bonaparte, with a mixture of intimidation and blandishments.

On 25 January 1801, Constant presented a long and deeply considered criticism of Duveyrier's report on the proposed courts, demanding explanation and clarification, and raising many objections. For example, he contested Duveyrier's statement that the number of civilian officers would always be double that of military officers; further he demanded to know wheather it was a special court or an ordinary court which would try 'premeditated assassinations'. According to the *rapporteur*, a Government official could indict the 'guilty' party before either one of the other of the courts. Benjamin first seized on the word 'guilty' (*coupable*), which he maintained should read 'accused' (*prévenu*), and then went on to protest against the arbitrary powers given to a Government-nominated agent who would be in a position to deprive any citizen accused of a crime of the benefit of ordinary legal procedure and trial by jury. Was this not in itself enough, he said, to throw out the Bill?

Another unacceptable clause – perhaps, as Benjamin said, the most extraordinary of the whole Bill – concerned the protection afforded to individuals who had acquired nationalized property. 'Naturally', he said, 'no one claims constitutional guarantees more than myself ... but this clause is completely illusory, if

---

[1] The officer whose task it is to report on the findings of a parliamentary commission, or to prepare an exposé of a Bill, etc.

only because it is so vague, arbitrary, and provides such frightening latitude.

'What is one to understand by threats? How does one assess
a threat? . . .

'Having acquired national property myself, I do not want to
see owners of former national property made into a privileged
class. Privilege, sooner or later, rebounds on whosoever possesses
it: privilege is tantamount to banishment. . . .

'The proposed clause will give those who have acquired
national property a dangerous distinction; [they] will become an
object of suspicion in the eyes of other citizens and provide the
special courts with an inexhaustible source of arbitrary rulings.'

Benjamin continued to examine each clause in detail and to seek
precise definitions – what, for example, was the difference between *seditious* and *factious* individuals. As the clause stood, both
would come under the jurisdiction of special courts, but these
courts had been intended only to suppress organized bands of
pillaging brigands. 'It would be difficult', he said, 'for *Préfets* of
départements with an "extraordinary" police force at their disposal
to be content with ordinary police. . . .'

Constant further insisted on the maintenance of proper judicial
forms, 'which constitute a safeguard . . . any curtailment of such
would constitute a diminution or loss of this safeguard. To
expose an accused person to such an infraction of the law would
be to sentence him before he is tried.'

Constant was clearly referring to military courts, which were
always too ready to turn the law upside down, and to the irascible
impatience of a young General anxious for obedience at all costs.

But it is important to be fair to Bonaparte. It was essential that the activities of Chouans and brigands in certain districts
should be suppressed, and only by special measures adapted to
the occasion could this be done. Volney himself was later to
acknowledge the efficacy of the special courts. But what was
feared was that the First Consul would use them for other purposes, and his insistence on obtaining 'legal' formalities to deport
innocent persons made it necessary to curtail his powers.

It was obviously with this in mind that Constant, towards the
end of his speech, reminded the Tribunate that even before 1789,
under the monarchy, the Assemblies, whenever possible, had

raised their feeble voices to air their grievances. The whole nation had always protested against the formation of special courts differing from ordinary courts. Constant also quoted article 29 of the Magna Carta, to the effect that:

'None shall be arrested, imprisoned, deprived of his heritage, rights, children, or family. . . . Life, liberty, and property will be protected from arbitrary spoliation, and none will be condemned to forfeit these but by lawful judgement of his peers or the law of the land.'

Constant scathingly demanded if these inalienable rights, formulated by a barbarous people under feudal rule in the thirteenth century, were now to be abjured by the representatives of the French people at the beginning of the nineteenth century, twelve years after the Revolution and in the ninth year of the Republic!

Daunou, who might have been expected to speak only in his capacity as jurist and master of constitutional rights, also made a moving and eloquent speech. In the name of the victims of the Terror and as a former *conventionnel* who had been imprisoned for his love of liberty, he pleaded with the Assembly not to abandon the Rights of Man. He emphasized that it was not only with special courts that the nation was threatened, but with everything that could result from an extra-constitutional régime – the suspension of all individual rights and social guarantees, the imposition of military taxes, arbitrary arrest, indefinite detention, violation of privacy; in short, everything forbidden by the Constitution.

On the day following Daunou's speech (8 Pluviôse), it was the turn of Marie-Joseph Chénier to address the Assembly. He pointed out that, of the eight judges composing special courts, five were appointed by the First Consul. One of the principal guarantees of Liberty was the independent construction of the courts. What was the value of this guarantee, he asked, if five of the eight judges could be overruled by the Government? If the Tribunes passed this Bill, would they not be providing innumerable means whereby a suspected man, put on remand, would be immediately regarded as guilty. . . .

The remarkable thing was that this tragic poet, the author of

Charles IX and *Caius Gracchus*, was not content just to make a 'dramatic' speech, but he too based his arguments on the doctrines of the thinkers of the preceding century, Montesquieu in particular, whom he quoted. Like Constant and Daunou, Chénier did not hesitate to expose the violations to the Constitution, such as the suppression of the Court of Appeal. It was this, in particular, which led him to protest most strongly against the violation of the fundamental law, the basis of all legitimate authority which, from now on, Bonaparte was either to misunderstand or to ignore – the Social Pact.

But, despite his violent attack, perhaps one should not be surprised, knowing Chénier's character, that he should couch his peroration in almost conciliatory terms.

> 'Tribunes, I have said everything which my conscience as a free man dictates. . . . Let the Government always adhere to republican principles and institutions . . . ordinary laws will then suffice . . . the brigands who are still devastating France will be easily controlled and punished . . . and while, beyond our frontiers, the incredible success of our soldiers prepares the way for peace, within France itself, the wise, firm hand of the Government will consummate the task already begun by our victorious Armies. I vote against the proposed law.'

The incredible success of our soldiers? What soldiers? What success? Is this homage to Bonaparte? More than seven months had passed since Marengo. There was now no longer any question of Bonaparte's soldiers; battles were won by Dupont, Brune, Macdonald, and Moreau – particularly Moreau, who on 3 December had won the victory of Hohenlinden, a victory no less resounding than Marengo, and which was, in fact, even more decisive, since it had forced the Austrian Emperor Joseph to sue for peace.

On 11 Pluviôse, following Chénier, Ginguené also had no hesitation in attacking the Government. 'The friends of Liberty', he said, 'have been told that the Revolution is over . . . but it was for the right of suffrage . . . and above all to be represented, that the French people made a revolution and took to arms. *It is in the hope of achieving a representative government, instead of rule by autocracy*, that the people of France have been sustained for ten years at the cost of so much blood and glory.'

'I regard it as proven that [this bill] is arbitrary and one which deprives the innocent, confounded with the guilty, of all protection and hope. . . .'

We do not know the end of this speech. It must have been violent, because in the official account it is terminated by a row of dots, while the *Moniteur*, which had distorted the speeches of Daunou and Chénier, only gave the briefest of résumés of Guingené's contribution.

It was clear that the Executive was beginning to show its claws, but this did not intimidate the opposition; quite the contrary. Almost half the Tribunate voted against the bill (44 to 49), while in the *Corps législatif* – although here the opposition was not so strong – the 'no's' reached the comparatively high figure of 88 to 192.

In an audience which Bonaparte gave to a delegation from the Senate on the day following Ginguené's speech, he let fly: 'Guingené has been gratuitously insulting. There are a handful of "metaphysicians" who are only fit for the scrapheap. They are like fleas on my coat. . . . Don't imagine I am going to allow myself to be treated like Louis XVI.'[1] It is obvious that he still remembered vividly that June day, when with Bourrienne he had been the witness of the sorry picture of a King mocked by the mob and forced to wear the *bonnet rouge*, a King, who through his own weakness was destined for the scaffold.

His hatred of 'metaphysicians' is confirmed by another account of the same audience. 'I am not a king', he is reported to have said, 'and am not going to be insulted like a king . . . can I be likened to a Louis XVI? True, I listen to everybody, but I am guided only by my own head. There exists a group of men who for the last ten years have done more harm to France than the most rabid revolutionaries. They are phrase makers and "ideologues" . . . who have always rebelled against existing authority, who have always refused the necessary powers to put down revolutions; false and empty-minded, these men would have done better to take a few lessons in geometry. . . .'[2]

[1] Thibaudeau: *Mémoires sur le Consulat.*
[2] *The Papers of Lagarde*, secretary general to the Consuls, quoted by A. Vandal. According to Saint-Beuve, Bonaparte expressed himself

Bonaparte, who did not want to be compared with a King, wished to be obeyed better than a King. But if he multiplied his sarcasms against the Republican intellectuals, whom he had so flattered on his return from Egypt, they in turn, or at least some of them, showed increasing resentment at his behaviour. However much he might threaten Ginguené, the latter regarded himself as being far from beaten, and in turn uttered warning threats: 'There are Generals who will not see this in a favourable light [he said]; we have friends in the Armies. . . .'

The opposition was both disappointed and stimulated by the vote of 14 Pluviôse. More determined than ever to exercise its right to examine all Bills presented, it adopted a generally hostile attitude during the last weeks of the legislature. The proposed Bill to determine taxation for Year X was merely a repeat of the previous year and presented without estimates of public expenditure. In other words, the Government dispensed with presenting a budget. The Tribunate gave its approval on condition that this was only a provisional measure, a provisional measure which was to last until the end of the Empire! But another project, relative to the national debt, was vigorously opposed, particularly by Benjamin Constant, and was vetoed by a majority of 26. The result of the ballot was greeted by cries of *Vive la République*, something which had not happened for a long time. The public galleries had to be cleared.

Finally on 27 Ventôse (18 March 1801) the Government received a final set-back. The Palais Bourbon rejected a Bill relative to the procedure of the Court of Appeal, which had been strongly attacked earlier in the Palais Royal.

Thus ended the parliamentary session of Year IX, which deserves more than honourable mention in the history of the fight for democracy. A fight conducted under conditions no less difficult than that of the preceding year and without the support of the nation. If the Tribunate did not overtly condemn the iniquity of the deportations following the crime in the rue

---

in similar terms, still in connection with the debates in the Tribunate, to Laplace, Monge, and Roederer: 'I am a soldier, a child of the Revolution, sprung from the bosom of the people. . . . I won't allow them to insult me as they would a King.'

Saint-Nicaise, at least one must recognize its courageous stand against the 'special courts'. All in all, the legislature had maintained its prerogatives as the nation's representative and had defended the rights of the individual with firmness. What little power was still left to it had been used to full advantage. Too much so, in fact, for the liking of the angry General, who considered it was merely quibbling over trivialities and matters of principle. But by the end of 1800 he had not yet altogether given up the idea of winning back to the fold the 'metaphysicians' and 'idealogues' of Auteuil.

After Brumaire, Daunou had refused to be nominated a Councillor of State, preferring to enter the Tribunate (which brought him in only a very small salary). After Marengo, Bonaparte had once more returned to the attack. He invited Daunou to dine and begged him to leave the Tribunate for the Council of State. Daunou again refused. Such was Bonaparte's anger (according to Saint-Beuve) that Daunou suddenly took fright and slipped out of the room when the First Consul's back was turned. Another version of the story runs that the First Consul, irritated by his guest's consistent refusal, shouted at him: 'It's not because I am fond of you that I offer you this post, but because I need you. For me, men are like tools; to use as I please. There are perhaps only two or three people I love – my mother, my wife, and my brother Joseph.'

'For my part', Daunou replied calmly, 'I love the Republic', and left the room.

Not all historic words have actually been pronounced; nevertheless it is seldom that they do not express the truth of a given situation.

5

The Idéophobe

✦✦✦

WHILE the defenders of liberty were playing their difficult game in Paris, the fate of France was being decided between the Rhine and the Danube. The war dragged on through 1800, until the decisive defeat of the Austrians at Hohenlinden. On the same day as the explosion in the rue Saint-Nicaise, the Archduke Charles asked Moreau for an armistice, and while the Tribunes were fighting tooth and nail over the Pluviôse measures, Joseph was negotiating terms with Cobentzl at Lunéville.

The treaty signed on 9 February 1801 gave back to France all the territories she had acquired by the treaty of Campo Formio; and peace with England, now left isolated, could be expected to follow in due course. This success abroad still further consolidated the consular régime, already greatly strengthened by the victory of Marengo. Had Bonaparte been a true republican at heart, it might have been reasonably assumed that the restoration of civil rights would now be his first concern. Instead, he turned his attention to negotiating a Concordat.

Certainly, freedom of worship – and not just a 'paper' freedom – was a matter of the highest priority. By the civil constitution of the clergy, the Revolution had severely tried the conscience of many Catholics. Under the Terror, an inverted fanaticism had outlawed all worship, and persecution of the faithful had gone to hideous lengths. But is it true to say that it was Bonaparte who 'reopened the churches'?

The Constitution of Year III had already marked a return to normality, despite Chénier's advocacy of an almost atheistic republican cult. On 30 May 1794, the churches were thrown open to Catholics, provided they conformed to the laws of the Republic. This was confirmed by the Directory (law of 7 Vendémiaire, Year IV [1 October 1795]), and resulted in a great religious revival between 1795 and 1797. But Fructidor was the signal for fresh persecutions. Nearly two thousand priests were deported, mostly to French Guiana, while, at the same time, attempts were made to enforce strict observance of the Republican Calendar. These measures, however, were badly applied and unpopular. They exasperated the faithful, who were divided into some half-dozen different sects, including 'non-submitting' Catholics and confirmed royalists; these now found themselves obliged to share churches with theophilanthropists and congregations of the *culte décadaire*. It is difficult to get a clear picture of what was really happening. According to Grégoire,[1] 32,000 parishes were once again being served on the eve of the Consulate, but there is other evidence of 'Christians deprived of priests, and abandoned churches'.

Even if it is allowed that Bonaparte did not actually reopen the churches, the credit should not be begrudged him for clearing up a very unhealthy situation by restoring complete freedom of worship in place of the rather precarious freedom that had previously existed. In his decree of 7 Nivôse (28 December 1799), he insisted on only one condition: that every priest should swear allegiance to the new Constitution. Despite the intransigence of a few, who refused to swear, in general the renaissance of Catholic practice was so spectacular that even Bonaparte was taken by surprise.

What more could be desired, except, perhaps, the suppression of the *promesse de fidélité* demanded of the clergy? It would be difficult to find fault with Mme de Staël's statement that the nation wanted only three things: 'that all persecution of the clergy should cease forthwith; that they should not be obliged to swear any kind of oath; and finally, that there should be no interference whatsoever with people's religious opinions.'[2]

Such just and sensible principles would, in the modern age,

---

[1] Op. cit.
[2] *Considérations sur la Révolution française*, IV.

commend themselves to all civilized communities. But at that time they would have satisfied neither the Church nor Bonaparte: the Church, because she rejected freedom of conscience, and was determined to regain all her former dominance; Bonaparte, because he too, for different reasons, set little store by freedom of conscience, and saw the restoration of the Church as a weapon for mobilizing the consciences of his subjects to his own advantage.

Bonaparte was himself no believer, though he never completely lost respect for religion. The extent of his scepticism may have escaped some people, misled, perhaps, by the edifying tale of his first communion – 'the most beautiful day in my life', as he is supposed to have remarked. Yet there is abundant evidence of his true feelings: for the present, we need only recall two of his official pronouncements on the subject.

On 10 December 1797, speaking in the courtyard of the Luxembourg after returning from his first campaign in Italy, he had, in effect, denounced 'religion, feudalism, and monarchy' as the three 'prejudices' which had had to be conquered in order to achieve, after eighteen centuries, a constitution founded on Reason.

On 2 July 1798, in his proclamation to the people of Egypt, he had declared that he had 'even more respect than the Mamelukes for Allah, his Prophet, and the Koran', and added: 'Was it not we who destroyed the Pope? . . . Was it not we who destroyed the Knights of Malta?'

The Bonaparte who saw fit, in 1801, to 're-erect the altars', after having, in the preceding year, denounced 'those wicked heretics, the English', can hardly be described as a Catholic, anxious to serve truth, his God, and his faith, nor even as a disciple of the *philosophes*, inspired by a spirit of tolerance. On the contrary, he was a dictator determined to secure possession of a matchless instrument for dominating the minds of his subjects. A national church, however powerful, was not enough; it smelt too strongly of heresy. Rather than some Gallican compromise, he wanted the real thing – the Catholic Church in its entirety, with the whole army of the faithful ranged in its time-honoured ranks under its authentic head, and all at his, Bonaparte's, disposal. He told Thiers:

S.O.T.E.—5*

'I must have the real Pope – the Roman, Catholic, and apostolic Pope who resides at the Vatican. With my Armies behind me, and the occasional bit of flattery, I shall always be able to keep him in his place. As soon as I reopen the churches, give my protection to the clergy, and *cosset* them [*nourrirai*], and treat them as ministers of religion should be treated in every country, [the Pope] will do whatever I ask, for the sake of peace and quiet. He will put the minds of the people at rest, round up the scattered flocks, and hand them over into my keeping.'

Has there ever been such a cynical attitude towards the Papacy? Of course, bargains have always been struck between the temporal and spiritual powers. Far from finding such bargains shocking, Bonaparte saw them as positively good. He remarked to Molé in 1806: 'Men have always been swayed by two forces – the material force wielded by armies, and the moral force wielded by priests. Since the days of the Roman empire, all monarchies have rested on the same foundation, namely, on the power of the clergy.'

So much for the political aspect. But the Church also had its social uses, as Bonaparte was quick to realize. The cynicism of some of his remarks makes Marx's famous aphorism about religion being the 'opium of the people' pale into insignificance. 'Society', he said, 'cannot exist without inequality, and inequality cannot exist without religion. When a man is dying of hunger and sees his neighbour gorging himself, he can never reconcile himself to the situation unless there is some authority which tells him, "This is God's will".'

Bonaparte had other, and even more pressing, reasons for wanting to negotiate a Concordat. He had to disarm the Catholic and royalist malcontents, and win them over to his side. He showed characteristic astuteness in his choice of a representative for the negotiations – the Abbé Bernier, sometime *curé* of Saint Laud d'Angers and a fanatical Vendean of long standing. A full account of Bernier's lengthy discussions with the Papal legate falls outside the scope of this book; but something must be said about the terms which were eventually settled.

The Pope certainly made major concessions. He accepted the loss of ecclesiastical properties expropriated and sold by the nation – these were to remain in the hands of the purchasers; he accepted a reduction in the number of bishoprics and agreed that the incumbents of the sixty dioceses remaining should be appointed by the Government, and that the clergy should swear loyalty to the Head of State. One of the great victories of the Revolution and of the *philosophie des lumières* was abandoned – the principle that religion was a matter of personal conscience. Just as though Voltaire and Condorcet had never existed, it was now declared that 'the Government of the French Republic recognizes that the Catholic religion is the religion of the vast majority of French citizens and the Government itself professes it'. This was almost tantamount to recognizing Catholicism as the State religion.

The news of the signing of the Concordat (15 July 1801[1]) was on the whole well received. It meant the end of the *décadi*, which was unpopular in the provinces, and the re-establishment of Sundays and the ringing of church bells. It conferred religious peace in the West and put an end to quarrels between constitutional and non-juring clergy. Naturally it was warmly welcomed by the neo-Catholic movement and the *antiphilosophes* led by Fontanes. But on the extreme right, among the bishops of the *Ancien Régime* and partisans of the Bourbons, whether *émigrés* or not, there was much resentment, for with the restoration of the Church, the Bourbon cause now seemed lost; religion conferred a scandalous prestige on the usurper, and the pacification of the West meant the end of royalist hopes.

This hardly worried Bonaparte at all; on the contrary, it was a proof of his success. On the left, on the other hand, the signing of the Concordat exacerbated two currents of dissident opinion and united them – the Army and parliamentarians, liberals and republicans.

The irritation expressed by many officers at the time of the Concordat was perhaps not altogether inspired by profound philosophic considerations, nor by devotion to the cause of Liberty. Some were simply jealous of Bonaparte and were

[1] Actually 16 July, at 2 a.m., in Joseph's house, between Joseph, Crétet, and Bernier, on the one hand, and Cardinals Consalvi, Spira, and Caselli on the other. (Translator's note).

disappointed that after Brumaire they too had not been promoted
for services rendered. As Soldiers of the Revolution who had
fought kings and priests, they were only too ready to denounce a
policy which threatened to make 'monks' of them all. Macdonald, Brune, Lannes, Bernadotte, Moreau, and many others
did not hesitate to voice their discontent publicly. How this
military resistance showed itself, and how Bonaparte was able
to coax back these former fighters for Liberty, will be seen later.
For the moment we will confine ourselves to Moreau. He was a
staunch republican; his own self-sacrifices and those of his
officers are well known, and his Army of the Rhine was always
animated by the legendary virtues of 1792 and faithful to revolutionary ideals. This glorious Army, inactive since the victory of
Hohenlinden, represented a menace to Bonaparte. It was, however, difficult for the First Consul to attack the victor of Hohenlinden directly, or dispose of him by giving him a subaltern
command. But at least he could get rid of his soldiers by sending
them overseas. Hence the expedition to San Domingo, a subject
on which many historians prefer not to dwell.

*   *   *

San Domingo (Haiti) was the richest of the French colonies
now that France had lost Canada and India. Since the western
half had been ceded by Spain under the Treaty of Bâle (1795), the
whole of the island belonged to France. Its prosperity, like that
of the other West Indian islands and the Southern States of
America, depended on slavery. Many great fortunes had been
made in the Western ports of France from the slave trade.
Naturally, it was the *parti philosophique* which had first denounced
this abominable traffic. It was Brissot who, with Mirabeau, La
Fayette, Condorcet, and the Abbé Grégoire, had founded the
Société des Amis des Noirs. Grégoire, who all his life defended the
cause of the 'Blacks', was hanged in effigy by the furious colonists
of San Domingo, while at Nantes a subscription was raised to
murder him. Even Robespierre, in 1791, made an impassioned
plea for the abolition of slavery.

It was not until 5 February 1794, however, that the Convention
voted the decree abolishing slavery in all French colonies. This

came too late to spare San Domingo the convulsions of a civil war, a war made all the more complicated by foreign intervention, in which a confused mixture of whites, mulattos, negroes, French, English, and Spaniards were involved. One astonishing figure was to arise to save the situation, the negro Toussaint-Louverture, who proclaimed himself Governor in the name of France. Bonaparte, whose acumen in the circumstances can hardly be applauded, did not take advantage of the situation. He did not appreciate that the interests of the French nation could accord with the spirit of justice expressed by the *Amis des Noirs* or, at least, with the application of the progressive Rights of Man. It was not until he was imprisoned on St Helena that he realized the advantages he would have gained by granting autonomy to the richest of French colonies.

Toussaint showed abundant proof of his loyalty and ability in fighting and driving out the English and Spaniards. In 1797 the Convention made him General of Division and, a little later, Commander of the Army of San Domingo. The Consulate confirmed his appointment. He restored order and prosperity to the island, recalled the *émigrés*, and abolished slavery. On 9 May 1801, he proclaimed an almost autonomous constitution, but qualified the island as 'a colony forming part of the French Empire [sic]'. To show, however, that this was not an act of secession, he sent a copy of the constitution to the First Consul on 16 July for his approval.

Bonaparte did not reply until November, in a civil enough letter, in which he praised Toussaint's activities ('If the flag of France flies over San Domingo, it is thanks to you and your brave blacks'), but at the same time he criticized his constitution and invited him to recognize the sovereignty of France. He once again guaranteed 'the sacred principle of liberty and equality of coloured peoples', which had been promulgated to the citizens of San Domingo by the new constitution on 25 December 1799.

But unfortunately, five days before writing this conciliatory letter to Toussaint, Bonaparte had already directed Talleyrand to obtain consent from the English for an expedition 'to destroy the black Government', because 'if once the liberty of the blacks in San Domingo is recognized by the Government, it could always be a rallying point for a republic in the New World. . . . The sceptre of the New World would sooner or later fall into the hands of blacks ... the consequence of which would be of incalculable harm to England. . . .'[1]

It is difficult to conceive greater duplicity. While addressing the negroes in diplomatic language, he posed to the English as a protector of the colonial system and of slavery – which indeed he was. In the autumn of 1801 Bonaparte called a meeting of concillors, ministers, and other important functionaries to discuss the question of San Domingo. Most were in favour of resorting to force to reimpose French rule. Grégoire remained silent; Volney predicted disaster.

But why these questions, this pretence at consultation, since a punitive expedition had already been decided upon and organized? Moreover, it was essential at all costs to remove Moreau's republican soldiers to a safe distance.

On 11 December 1801, a fleet set out from Brest with 3,000 men, nearly all of whom were drawn from the Rhine Army, commanded by General Leclerc, the husband of Pauline Bonaparte. Large reinforcements were to treble the size of this expeditionary force. Leclerc was the bearer of the First Consul's letter of the 18 November; he also had instructions directing him 'to destroy Toussaint . . . and the principal brigands'.

No sooner had they disembarked than the French undertook the reconquest of the island. None of the French soldiers guessed that they were fighting for the re-establishment of slavery; all thought naïvely that they were fighting a revolutionary war. Although Toussaint offered to come to terms with Leclerc, he was treacherously arrested and deported to France (5 May 1802), where he was imprisoned in Fort Joux. Here, dressed as a convict, he suffered terrible privations from cold and hunger. In vain he wrote to the First Consul demanding a trial, considering himself always as 'a son of the one and indivisible Republic'. He was found dead, after months of suffering, on 7 April 1803.

The war, however, did not end with his arrest. On 20 May 1802, the *Corps législatif* voted for the re-establishment of slavery

[1] To Citizen Talleyrand, Min. of Foreign Affairs, Paris, 22 Brumaire Year X (13 November 1801).

in the colonies. Richepanse, the brilliant second-in-command to
Moreau, was sent with an expeditionary force to Martinique and
La Guadeloupe. The negroes rose in revolt; hardly a Frenchman
returned to tell the tale. Richepanse died of yellow fever on
3 September. Ten days later there was a general rising in San
Domingo. A terrible and interminable guerilla war ensued,
which with the help of the lethal climate exterminated the expeditionary force. Leclerc himself fell a victim to it and died 2 November 1802. Rochambeau was sent to replace him, but was incapable
of redressing the situation. The whole of San Domingo was
recaptured by the negroes and mulattos. Rochambeau capitulated
on 19 November 1803. Of 33,000 men sent there, only a few
thousands returned alive. The white colonists disappeared; the
negro population was reduced by half.

*   *   *

To return to the autumn of 1801: Bonaparte had viewed with
relief the departure for San Domingo of the republican soldiers
of the Army of the Rhine, men who were hostile to his ambitions
and were disgusted by the Concordat. What he needed, now that
the Concordat was signed, was its ratification. But the circumstances were unfavourable. At the opening of the session of the
Year X, the opposition in the Assemblies, encouraged by the
intellectual *élite*, proved even more serious than in the preceding
year.

The former Auteuil circle continued to meet in Paris itself
under the roof of Sophie de Condorcet, who was living in the
Grande-Rue-Verte (today the rue de Penthièvre), not far from
Lucien and not far from the former dancer, Julie Talma. Divorced
from the great actor since 1797 and complaisant mistress of
Benjamin Constant, the gentle and witty Julie was attached by
the strongest ties of friendship to the impetuous Sophie. Both
shared the same convictions and the same admiration for the
philosophes who had contributed so much to the foundation of the
Republic. For some years now, Julie Talma had also delighted in
entertaining intelligent men like Cabanis and Fauriel.

Madame de Condorcet had once again resumed her *salons* as of old, when her home in the Hotel de la Monnaie was known as the *foyer de la République*. It was now in the Grande-Rue-Verte that she welcomed the intelligentsia and where foreigners came to meet the opposition members of the Tribunate and Institute. Fauriel, who had happily replaced Mailla-Garat in her life, was always at her side; he had for some time been employed in the Ministry of Police and as secretary to Fouché, but had now resigned his post and was working in the Museum, where Sophie met him.

Fauriel was also a great friend of Madame de Staël, who was back in Paris in the November of 1801, and who once again cherished illusions concerning Bonaparte. She still hoped to force her attentions on him by her talent and the success of her forthcoming book, *Delphine*. But she was still activated by the same ideal – to convert the First Consul and restore him to the cause of liberty.

On 1 Frumaire, Year X (22 November 1801), Parliament was opened at the Palais Bourbon with unusual ceremony, with salvos of artillery, and graced by the presence of the Minister of the Interior. But Bonaparte obviously did not want to enhance the prestige of the Assemblies or to give the impression that he was submitting to their control; he still expected a solemn approbation of his past and future policy, and of the Concordat in particular. On the following day, in the *Corps législatif*, Thibaudeau read the *Exposé de la situation de la République*, an imposing picture of the results already obtained under the Consulate, of treaties concluded and laws in course of preparation. It was without doubt a most impressive balance-sheet. The internal security of France was now established; the brigands who infested the highways had been completely eliminated. Twenty main roads, which after ten years of civil war had fallen into ruin, had been repaired. Four new routes had been opened over the Alps. Canals were being dug; bridges had been built across the Seine; industry was flourishing in Lyons, Lille, St Quentin, and Rouen; vast land reclamations were in hand; the new administrative organization was producing good results – although the condition of hospitals was worse than ever and no provision was as yet made for foundlings. Abroad, the situation was even more favourable. The peace preliminaries, signed in London on 1

October, promised results surpassing even those of the Treaty of
Lunéville. Russia had hastily concluded peace on 8 October,
whilst the Porte, Portugal, and others followed suit. All this
combined to make the preliminary arrangements in London the
precursor of a general European peace.

But in the eyes of the opposition it was clear that Bonaparte
intended to exploit all these successes only to accentuate the
dictatorial character of his régime and to ratify new reactionary
measures, beginning with the Concordat.

The first sign of protest was the election of Dupuis to the
presidency of the *Corps législatif*. Dupuis was an erudite rationalist,
on familiar terms with the Auteuil circle; he was, moreover, the
author of the *Origine de tous les cultes*, a frankly hostile book on
religions, the very antithesis of Chateaubriand's *Génie du Christianisme*. It was also significant that the Assembly of the Palais
Bourbon chose Grégoire to be the spokesman of the deputation
sent to thank the Consuls for the *Exposé* of the previous day.
Grégoire did not confine himself merely to congratulatory
platitudes, but in a forceful speech he urged the Government to
finish with war once and for all. Nor did this courageous republican priest[1] hesitate to remind his listeners that 'the trustees of
Government existed by will of the people for the people'. But this
was the last Assembly of the Senate to have the right of criticism;
there was to follow a year of enforced silence, during which only
the Tribunate was able to carry on the struggle.

However, the left wing of the Tribunate did not engage in the
systematic opposition of which Thiers has accused it, any more
than it had done in the last session. In fact, it almost unanimously
approved all the recently signed peace treaties (United States,
the Two Sicilies, Bavaria, and Portugal) with the exception of
the treaty signed with Russia, in which it was stipulated that 'the
two contractual parties promise not to allow any of their *subjects*
to maintain any correspondence whatsoever with the internal
enemies of the present Governments of the two states. . . . Any
subject contravening this interdiction will be banished. . . .'

The word 'subject' was pounced on with a great show of

---

[1] Grégoire was deprived of his episcopal dignity by order of the
Pope on 12 October.

indignation. 'For ten years', exclaimed Marie-Joseph Chénier, 'our Armies have fought to make us citizens, and now we are subjects again!' This was nothing but a deliberate quibble, obviously intended to wreck the whole proceedings. But the Assembly burst into vociferous applause, and the treaty, instead of being accepted unanimously, was passed by 88 votes to 14. During an audience granted to the Tribune Stanislas de Girardin, Bonaparte referred to the above incident relating to the Franco-Russian Treaty in violently abusive terms; but, basically, it was the hostility of the two legislative assemblies to the Concordat which alarmed him. Girardin tried to persuade the First Consul to adopt a conciliatory attitude to the Tribunate, but Bonaparte refused. 'They are curs ... I meet curs wherever I go; they are constantly putting a spoke in my wheel ... I long for the day when they will be deprived of power. ...'

The critical moment awaited by the First Consul was at hand, when the first clauses of the Civil Code were debated. Not that Bonaparte attached extreme importance to the points under discussion, but his *amour propre* was deeply wounded inasmuch as he was obliged to subject his own masterpiece to the criticism of the Tribunes.

To what extent was Bonaparte the sole begetter of the Civil Code? According to some, he not only ordered, and hustled on, the realization of this great task, but also made frequent personal interventions, all very much to the point. 'Thus, it is not merely flattery, but a just homage to its principal architect, that the Code has been entitled the *Code Napoléon*, the name under which it has passed down to posterity' [L. Madelin, *Le Consulat*]. The opposite contention is that this great legal monument, which replaced the complicated legislation of the *Ancien Régime*, was successively compiled by the Constituency, the Legislative, and the Convention, and that it was already far advanced under the Directory, and that 'it only remained for the new Government to pick up the threads and finish a work which was already nearly complete'.

No one, however, can deny the vigorous *élan* which the First Consul gave to the Council of State, nor the good sense and penetration he brought to bear on the compilation of the Code. Everyone, too, recognizes that in the realization of civil equality (*égalité civile*) he accomplished what the Revolution had set out to do. But his adversaries stress the fact that he would not have put such fervour into this unless it was to abolish the other victory of 1789, *la Liberté*. 'It was thus, that formerly, under the Roman Caesars, one observes civil rights developing inversely to political rights.'[1]

While, on the whole, the Code did not conflict with the principles of the Assemblies, they nevertheless considered it their duty to examine each Clause in detail. This was a delicate job. The Constitution did not allow the Tribunate to make the slightest modification in proposed laws: either it approved them or vetoed them *in toto*; what was often merely criticism appeared, therefore, as deliberate obstruction.

This is precisely what happened when the preliminary Clause[2] was debated (3 December 1801). Andrieux, a highly cultivated man and brilliant dramatist, who with Ginguené and Say had been one of the founders and editors of the *Décade*, and who, moreover, had been a lawyer, jurist, and vice-president of the Court of Appeal before becoming a member of the Five Hundred, was eminently qualified to discuss the preamble in question. He criticized it severely, and concluded by saying: '. . . we find that this Bill is, in general, incoherent, ill-considered, and out of place at the head of the Civil Code and unworthy of being placed there. . . .' Chazal, Thiessé, and Mailla-Garat expressed similar opinions and, despite the efforts of Portalis and Boulay de la Meurthe, the Bill was vetoed by 65 votes to 13, and was next rejected by the *Corps législatif* by a majority of three.

The first clause of the Code was even more severely criticized. The debates, which began on 17 December and ended on 1 January, were interrupted to examine Clause II (*Des Actes de l'état civil*). Apart from some criticisms from Benjamin Constant, this last was, on the whole, favourably received; indeed it was accepted by a considerable majority (28 December). But the acceptance of Clause II, which in effect deprived the clergy of one of their essential social attributes, was not enough to soothe Bonaparte's irritation; it showed only too well the feelings of the Tribunes towards the Concordat. A few days later, the Assembly

---

[1] Jules Barni: *Napoleon 1er et son historien, M. Thiers.*
[2] *De la publication, des effets et de l'application des lois.*

in the Palais Royal once again showed its hostility to the consular régime by rejecting Clause I[1] by a majority of thirty.

The Assembly then proceeded to vote on another matter of no less importance – the choice of a candidate for a vacant seat in the Senate. It will be recollected that under the terms of the Constitution it was necessary for three candidates to be put up for election to the Senate, one to be chosen by the First Consul, one by the *Corps législatif*, and the third by the Tribunate.

A few days earlier, the Senate had filled a vacancy by electing the constitutional bishop, Grégoire, in preference to Generals Jourdan and Desmeuniers (the respective candidates of the First Consul and the Tribunate). The significance of Grégoire's election to the Tribunate was clear; it was an act of defiance to the Concordat.

On 1 January, the Tribunate had once again to choose a candidate for the Senate. This time Daunou was elected, Daunou, the avowed enemy of Rome. He was elected by 48 to 39 votes, in preference to General Lamartillière, the protégé of Bonaparte. But even more significant was the fact that two days previously the *Corps législatif*, too, had chosen Daunou in preference to the General, by 39 votes to 25.

As Cambacérès fully realized, what had hitherto been merely opposition now amounted to insurrection. Daunou's election must be considered as an act of war against the First Consul. It was not long before the Head of State himself gave vent to his feelings. He expressed his astonishment that the Senate had failed to elect the generals and accused Siéyès and others of intriguing with the Duke of Orleans. 'Citizens', he said, 'I warn you that I regard the nomination of Daunou . . . as a personal insult.' The Senate, whose task it was to safeguard the Constitution, was duly cowed.

---

[1] This clause (*De la jouissance et de la privation des droits civils*) was scarcely likely to appeal to men faithful to the principles of 1789, since two of its articles re-established practices of the *Ancien Régime* – *Droit d'aubaine*, (by which, on the death of a non-naturalized foreigner, his inheritance reverted to the State), and *La mort civile*, by which a criminal's goods were confiscated to the deprivation of his children. Furthermore, the consular Government wished to reintroduce the branding of certain classes of criminal, which had been abolished in 1791.

Another example of Bonaparte's lack of respect for the Senate occurred in the spring of 1801 when, apropos of the Concordat, he had a violent scene with Volney. According to some accounts, he even went so far as to kick his old friend in the stomach. Other accounts only mention that there was a bitter discussion and complete disagreement between the two men. But even at the time, the story of the kick was current gossip, as we know from Stendhal's *Journal*. Whatever the case may be, this quarrel did not lead to an immediate rupture between Volney and Bonaparte. Despite their growing differences, they still continued to meet; indeed, Bonaparte would have welcomed a man of his intelligence in his Government and went so far as to offer him the post of Minister of the Interior. Volney's reply to the person who brought him this offer was: 'Tell the First Consul that he is too good a coachman for me to be harnessed to his carriage. He drives too quickly for me, and one stubborn horse can upset all the rest – coachman, horses, carriage too.' Although, together with Monge and Laplace, he still remained a familiar figure at Malmaison long after Brumaire, there was no *Idéologue* more disappointed than he to see the soldier-philosopher turn military despot.

But it was in the Tribunate rather than the Senate that the main opposition was to be found. Bonaparte was determined to crush it. Cambacérès recommended caution; he would find a solution. When Clause III of the Code had again been thrown out by the Tribunate, all the contentious Bills presented were suddenly withdrawn. A Consular announcement on 3 January (in the semi-official *Messager*) read: 'The Government finds itself obliged to postpone to some future occasion the laws awaited with so much interest. . . . It is convinced that the time has not yet come when these weighty discussions can be conducted with the requisite calmness and unity of purpose.'

Thus the two Assemblies found themselves paralysed and temporarily silenced, though not yet subjugated for good and all. But the First Consul continued to threaten the Tribunate. On 2 Nivôse he told his Council of State that 'of all the Assemblies, this was the most despicable' and demanded that it should be reorganized in such a way that it 'could no longer insult the Government in public'. In 1800 he had already complained to

Roederer that an assembly consisting of a hundred members, which cost the country four millions, was both ridiculous and useless when things went well and nothing but a hindrance when things went badly. He wanted it to be reduced to thirty members, with no public sittings. He again brought the matter up on the 17 and 18 Nivôse at a meeting of the Council of State. He impatiently dismissed the example of England. 'There is a great deal of difference,' he said, 'between a country which has enjoyed a constitution for a long while and a country which has not . . . *I repeat that here there must be no opposition.* In England the opposition is not seditious – all *they* want is to be bought off by the Crown – here, it is quite a different matter!' In other words, since the Tribunate could not be bought, it must be eliminated. There was no provision, however, in the Constitution for such a measure. Bonaparte gave Cambacérès a free hand to find the solution.

Now, according to the Constitution, one-fifth of the Assemblies would shortly have to be re-elected. Constitutionally, it was the Senate which was entrusted with the task of replacing, or re-electing, the outgoing members. But were out-going members selected by lot, or by the Senate? Cambacérès decided in favour of the latter interpretation of the law and undertook to instruct the Upper House on which members should be retired. Only fifteen senators, including Cabanis, Destutt de Tracy, Grégoire, and Lambrechts, voted against this dishonourable act. In all, by this measure, twenty tribunes and sixty deputies of the *Corps législatif* were removed, including all those who belonged to the Auteuil group – Benjamin Constant, Andrieux, Ginguené, Mailla-Garat, Laromiguière, Chénier, Chazal, Bailleul, and Ganilh, as well as Jean-Baptiste Say, former editor of the *Décade*, who had made the fatal mistake of criticizing Bonaparte's financial policy. They were replaced by docile men, drawn mostly from the Civil Service or the Army. But, in order that the operation should not appear to be too much of a political manoeuvre, Carnot, who a short time previously had been dismissed from the Ministry of War, was appointed to the *Corps législatif*, while Daru (Intendant-General of the Army) and Lucien, recalled from Madrid, were re-elected to the Tribunate.

Lucien was quick to make good his blunder over the *Parallèle* by re-organizing the Tribunate, which in future was to hold all its sessions in camera, thus becoming completely powerless. The Council of State, to all intents and purposes, was deprived of any say in the drawing up of laws; instead, a cabinet, presided over by the First Consul, would be responsible for the principal legislation. The small group of liberal-minded men who still remained in the Council of State were soon to have no influence. Siéyès, who had abstained from voting for the 'purge', was not seen again in the Luxembourg; 'the first of the Revolutionary thinkers' stepped quietly out of the pages of history.

The First Consul's attack on national representation caused no wave of popular indignation; on the contrary, never had Bonaparte been more popular. What a harvest of magnificent peace-bringing victories he had secured for France! Peace with Austria and Russia; peace with Spain; the creation of an Italian Republic (of which he had 'accepted' the Presidency at the *Consulta* of Lyons, early in January); and finally, on 25 March, there had been signed the Treaty of Amiens, which restored peace with England.

The Treaty of Amiens was certainly a great moment in France's history. It confirmed the territorial conquests of the Revolution; the Republic of France was recognized by the rulers of Europe, and it finally brought an end to ten years of upheavals, wars, and threats of invasion, and seemed to offer prospects of an unbelievable prosperity. How many Frenchmen at that time were capable of reading beyond appearances, or would have dared to say that the seeds of disaster were already present in this triumph? Are we not ourselves inclined to criticize Madame de Staël for delaying her departure from Switzerland in order to avoid the peace celebrations? But, as subsequent events were to show, Madame de Staël and her friends were right.

It was the 'purging' of the Assemblies – the 'skimming', as she put it – that made Madame de Staël the implacable enemy of Bonaparte. She watched the last bulwarks against despotism thrust aside. The most reactionary measures were being introduced, beginning with the ratification of the Concordat. Of course she and her friends would have welcomed the Peace of Amiens had it represented a victory for liberty, but they could not whole-heartedly rejoice in the triumph of the General whom they had once hailed as the 'philosopher commander', but who now openly despised all 'idéologues' and ideology.

Napoleon's aversion to 'idéologues' and ideology was perhaps never more candidly expressed than in a conversation he had with his brothers, Joseph and Lucien, one morning at Malmaison, when they called on him unexpectedly at breakfast time.

But let Lucien tell the story:

'. . . He asked us several questions relating to the theatre and society, then suddenly turning to Joseph he said: "A propos, my dear brother, what has happened to your very great and intimate friend, Madame de Staël? My enemy, I'm told."

JOSEPH: (first very calm, but growing increasingly animated). "My friend, yes, but my 'great' friend – that's an exaggeration. As for being my intimate friend, well, we hardly see enough of each other for that to be true. As for being your enemy, that is a lie."

THE CONSUL: "Peste! How you do go on! Là, là, là, so it's a lie, is it? So much the better. . . . What about Lucien? Does he think she's not my enemy? He ought to know, as he is so attached to her."

LUCIEN: "I don't know exactly what you mean by 'attached to her', but the truth is, Citizen Consul, I am honoured to claim the friendship of this illustrious lady. I would not be her friend if I believed her to be your enemy."

THE CONSUL: "Very courteous indeed. You reduce me to silence. Well then, there's nothing more to be said."

LUCIEN: "May I be allowed to add that, if you would only show her a little more consideration, she would worship you instead of just admiring you. . . ."

THE CONSUL: "O come! That's going too far altogether. I don't care for that sort of worship – she's far too ugly!"

The conversation continued, but no longer on a note of gay persiflage. Napoleon spoke of the evil influence exercised by his brother's 'illustrious lady friend'.

THE CONSUL: "I know her for what she is – an intriguing woman, accustomed to defying Governments. First of all in the *salons* of M. Necker, where the trial of Louis XVI was initiated, for, mark you, it was M. Necker who was the first executioner of that unfortunate king. Then, after Thermidor, she was again intriguing and playing an underhand part in the orgies of the Directory, and finally, and quite recently, lording it over the Tribunate, so that I was obliged to purge it of her friends, or 'skim' it, as she so impertinently put it. Tell her not to interfere with any of my plans – otherwise I'll break her, I'll smash her. But how stupid I am to get all worked up like this. Tell her just to keep quiet; that's the best way."

Lucien, in an attempt to provide a diversion, praised Madame de Staël's conversation, her writings, so highly esteemed by the metaphysicians, and her novels.

THE CONSUL: "Yes, I know, but first of all I haven't read a novel in years, and as for her metaphysical works, I must admit to my shame that, thumbing through them, I found nothing to make me want to continue reading them, for the very good reason, alas, that I couldn't make head or tail of them."

One might well ask if Napoleon was not just playing the clown. Was it possible that he, who had read Plato, Machiavelli, Montesquieu, and Rousseau, should find Mme de Staël so obscure? Lucien tactfully replied that Madame de Staël, for her part, would be incapable of solving a trigonometry problem.

THE CONSUL: "By that you imply I know nothing of metaphysics. Well, you are quite right. Metaphysicians are my pet aversion. I class all of them under the heading of *idéologues*, which is a particularly suitable term. They are idea seekers and, as a rule, their ideas are worthless. The term 'idéologues', which is so apt, has rendered them more ridiculous than I ever dared to expect. The name has stuck – probably because it came from me. There is no harm in it. There will be less ideology around. 'Ideology', that's the right word – the science of ideas. Apart from everything else – and I have given the matter a lot of thought – these wretched scholars don't even understand what they are talking about themselves. ... How could I ever come to terms with such men, who are always interfering in my policies? They talk, talk, talk.

I don't care who knows it, but my aversion for these *idéologues* almost amounts to hatred."

JOSEPH: "Then you in turn won't be surprised to know that they call you an *idéophobe*."

THE CONSUL: (astonished and indignant) "So that's what they call me, is it? I am glad to hear it. I'll give them tit for tat. . . . *Idéophobe* indeed! Why not hydrophobe?" '

Bonaparte's reaction needs no comment, except to draw attention to the fact that he flattered himself on having coined the word *Idéologue*, derived from 'ideology', or at least for having put it into circulation in a pejorative sense. An *idéologue*, like a *metaphysician*, connoted in his language an intellectual dreamer opposed to everything he stood for.

But the word 'ideology' was in fact coined by Destutt de Tracy; it had not the same meaning, however, for him as it has for us today. It corresponded to 'an analysis of sensations and ideas' or to 'psychology' rather than to a doctrinal or Utopian politico-social system.

*   *   *

Now that the Tribunate had been 'purged', the ratification of the Concordat could proceed without much difficulty. Certain Organic articles had been added, which deprived the Papacy of some of its privileges and marked a return to the Gallican church of 1682. *The Régime of the Catholic Church in its relations with the Rights and Police of the State* (8 April 1802) provided that there should be only one liturgy and one catechism for all Catholic Churches in France [Article 39]; all ecclesiastics were to be dressed in French fashion and in black [Article 43]; no decrees by councils . . . and no bulls, briefs, etc. were to be received, published . . . or otherwise put into effect without the authorization of the Government [Articles 1 and 3]. No religious processions were to be held without Government authority.

Deaf to the protests of the Cardinal legate, the First Consul, moreover, insisted on the inclusion of the twelve constitutional bishops in the episcopal body. Finally, the Protestant religion was officially recognized and endowed. These tolerant measures, inspired by Fouché and Talleyrand, would in their opinion overcome the last public and parliamentary resistance to the signing of the Convention. But even after the 'purging' there was still some opposition in the Tribunate, which was summoned to an extraordinary session on 5 April, when 7 out of 85 tribunes voted against the Concordat and Organic articles, while in the *Corps législatif*, which at this juncture had merely been 'renewed', only 228 out of 300 members voted in favour, 21 voting against and 51 abstaining.

On 15 April 1802, the Concordat became law. Three days later the Restoration of Public Worship was celebrated with a display of pomp and ceremony altogether new. The great bell of Notre Dame, which had been silent for years, rang out a full peal. Salvos of cannon thundered in chorus as Bonaparte left the Tuileries to take his place with the other consuls in a carriage drawn by eight horses, led by Mamelukes of the guard. Coaches bearing Ministers of State, ambassadors, and ladies of the court, accompanied by lackeys dressed in the costume of the *Ancien Régime*, followed in a sumptuous procession, escorted by prancing cavalry. Through streets lined with gaping spectators, the colourful cortège wound its way to the Cathedral, where, beneath the portico, thirty bishops, with the nonogenarian Archbishop Belloy at their head, were awaiting the arrival of the First Consul. Bonaparte, dressed in red, took his place on a dais to the accompaniment of martial music and the peal of the organ. Slowly and majestically the ceremony unfolded until the moment of the elevation of the Host, when the words of the service were drowned by the rattle of muskets coming to the present and the roll of drums, a tumultuous homage to the man who had come in all humility to announce the reign of Almighty God, whose Kingdom is not of this world and who adjured men to sheath their swords. But to be fair, the Te Deum was also a celebration of peace.

But what of the congregation? What were they thinking? Talleyrand and Fouché stood and knelt as required, and if occassionally they exchanged a sly wink, they kept straight faces and refrained from nudging each other. The members of the Senate, *Corps législatif*, and Tribunate also behaved respectfully. But behind them and in the aisles, a crowd of irreverent, noisy general officers, whom Berthier had almost forced to attend, conducted themselves in a scandalous and insolent fashion. However, there was one General who was conspicuous by his absence – Moreau, who during the service might have been seen walking up and down the terrace of the Tuileries with a cigar between his lips.

Another well-known figure kept away: Madame de Staël, 'I remained inside my house,' she wrote, 'to avoid seeing this odious spectacle; but I heard the salvos of cannon celebrating the servitude of the people of France. . . .'

*   *   *

Neither the grumblings of soldiers nor the silent indignation of the liberals at this 'skilful rehearsal for a coronation', as Madame de Staël wittily put it, worried Bonaparte overmuch. Not only had he the support of the majority of Frenchman, particularly in the provinces, but he had also acquired the support of a far from negligible section of public opinion among Royalists, who were happy to see the restoration of religion and a quasi-monarchic régime, which compensated to some extent for the loss of the Bourbons.

These feelings were expressed fully in Chateaubriand's *Génie du Christianisme*, published a little while earlier. No book could have served the dictator's designs better. It was not only a Christian apologia, but it also had a political purpose and was a direct and provocative attack on Bonaparte's opponents. Chateaubriand's purpose was to refute and check the irresistible philosophic movement which had given birth to the Revolution. But the *Idéologues* were not so easily routed. Ginguené launched an eloquent and vigorous counter-attack in three articles which appeared in the *Décade* between 19 June and 10 July 1802.

If one was to believe Chateaubriand, the glorious victories of the Republican Armies had been won by Christian peasants and gallant officers, who all their lives had practised their Christian duties, while the so-called *grands esprits* had kept away from the battlefields. Returning blow for blow, Ginguené replied that at least the *grands esprits* had not deserted their country 'to dream and write romances in the Appalachian mountains or on the banks of the Meschacebé [a reference to Chateaubriand's romantic novel

Atala]', and, recalling his Girondist friends and Condorcet, that the terrible persecution to which they had been subjected 'reaped a far greater harvest than any reaped by Austrian or Russian bayonets'.

Ten days after the Te Deum at Notre Dame an amnesty was granted to all *émigrés* who agreed to swear an oath of loyalty to the Constitution.

This led to their return *en masse* and a consequent reinforcement of the right wing. Although the amnesty in itself was a humane act, and one which contributed to internal peace and general cohesion of the country, nevertheless it was as unconstitutional as the acts which authorized the Nivôse deportations and the 'purging' of the Tribunate, and which, like the Bills relating to the re-organization of education and the institution of the Legion of Honour, were passed by a *Senatus Consultum*, without reference to the *Corps législatif* (1 and 19 May 1802). Although the public education act of Year X did not as yet embrace the system conceived by Bonaparte (to which we will refer later), it gave an indication of what he had in mind – to sacrifice primary education, and even senior education, in favour of secondary education, which would eventually produce a disciplined coherent society. This was in contradistinction to the vast projects conceived by Condorcet and others during the Revolution; it meant also the abandonment of the plans inspired by the *Idéologues* during the Directory. Central schools were to be replaced by Lycées, in which the teaching of history, philosophy, and other 'subversive' subjects was to be abolished. The *Gazette de France* of 28 April 1802 wrote that in future teachers would instruct without being distracted by *politics*. But not everyone agreed. Roederer, addressing the *Corps législatif*, emphasized the political aspect of the Bill.

The intellectual degradation of the 'skimmed' assemblies is apparent in the very considerable majority which approved this 'reform', which allowed the people to fall back into illiteracy, at the same time as it lowered the educational standards of the *bourgeoisie*. The days of 'victory over ignorance' were long past.

But the creation of the Legion of Honour, on the other hand, was met with violent opposition, even in the Council of State, where the Bill was passed by only a majority of four. In the

Tribunate there was a majority of only 18, and in the *Corps législatif* 56 out of 276. So many 'No's', however, were not indicative of hostility to the régime, but can be explained by the anxiety of former revolutionaries, who, although they had renounced the principles of 'liberty' propounded in 1789, were still loath to abandon the principle of equality. The creation of honorary distinctions, the existence of a hierarchy through the establishment of this new 'Order', would pave the way, they declared, to the restoration of an aristocratic class.[1]

In bestowing the red ribbon[2] in recognition of services rendered to the nation, Bonaparte was, in fact, creating a legion of servants entirely dependent on himself. True, the statutes of the Legion stipulated that its members must swear 'to devote themselves to the service of the Republic and to combat . . . any tendency towards the re-establishment of a feudal régime . . . and *to contribute to the maintenance of liberty and equality*'.

This was its official justification, but some of the Council of State saw it in another light. In reply to criticism of the incorrigible Admiral Truguet, the First Consul exclaimed: 'You call this a bauble! Very well, it is with baubles that one leads men. I wouldn't admit this to a tribune, but [here] I can say anything. *I do not believe that the French people care a jot for liberty and equality*. They have not changed in ten years of revolution. . . . Look how they fawn in the presence of foreign gewgaws!' [*crachats*, i.e. showy decorations].

*　　*　　*

On 20 May, the day following the voting on the Legion of Honour, the law re-establishing slavery was passed. There is no point in returning to the subject, except to specify Articles 1 and 2 :

> *Article 1.* The laws and regulations to which the blacks were subject before 1789 shall remain in force in the colonies returned to France by the Treaty of Amiens of 6 Germinal, Year X.

[1] Cf. Madelin: *Le Consulat*.
[2] The law creating the decoration was only published two years later (3 June 1804); in its first form it bestowed only the rank of legionary. (Translator's note).

Article 2. The same will apply to the other French colonies beyond the Cape of Good Hope. . . .

It is easy to understand the silence on this point of historians who elsewhere extol the constructive genius of Napoleon and the new France he created based on the famous 'blocks of granite'.[1]

When on 16 Floréal (6 May 1802) the Councillors of State laid the Treaty of Amiens before the Tribunate, Chabot de l'Allier, the President, proposed a motion to invite the Senate to give the Consuls a proof of the nation's gratitude. The motion was carried and forthwith communicated to the Luxembourg; it was further decided to send a deputation of Tribunes to the Tuileries in the hope that Bonaparte might reveal his intentions. But he did nothing of the kind, and pretending not to understand, declared 'he desired no reward beyond the gratitude of his fellow citizens. Death itself would lose its sting if with his dying eyes he could see the happiness of the Republic as irrevocably assured as its glory.' He pretended to a similar detachment when he received the delegation from the Senate, which had already been informed by Cambacérès that what he really wanted was to be made Consul for life. In the ensuing debate in the Senate on 18 Floréal, some Republican members expressed disgust at Bonaparte's pretensions – Lanjuinais in particular, who was said to have declared: 'How can any Frenchman be so craven as to accept as a master a foreigner from a nation which the Romans did not even want for slaves.' But it was Garat's speech which proved decisive. He protested strongly against the proposal of a life consulship and adroitly succeeded in obtaining a unanimous vote in favour of a compromise solution – that of prolonging the First Consul's tenure of office by ten years. Garat received unexpected support

---

[1] This reference is to Bonaparte's speech to the Council of State prior to the introduction of the two Bills on Education and the Legion of Honour: 'As long as I am here [he said] I can answer for the Republic, but we must think of the future. Do you imagine that the Republic is definitely established? . . . We have the power to establish it, but we have not yet done so, and we shall never succeed unless we *hurl a few blocks of granite on French soil.*' (cf. Louis Madelin's *Consulate and Empire*). (Translator's note).

from the lawyer Tronchet, who had formerly been a staunch
supporter of Bonaparte for his part in drawing up the Civil
Code.[1]

After forty-eight hours' deliberation, Garat's proposal was
accepted by 60 votes to 1, the exception being that of the irrepres-
sible Lanjuinais. The majority considered they had done well; the
liberals believed that they had put a check on Bonaparte.

He was in fact furious; he would refuse to accept. But Cambacérès suggested a more skilful rejoinder. The First Consul was
to reply by saying that he would accept an extension of his term of
office only after the matter had been referred to the people.[2]

On 20 Floréal (10 May 1802), the Council of State prepared two
questions to be put to the vote.

    1. Was Napoleon Bonaparte to be made Consul for life?
    2. Should he be granted the right of appointing his own
       successor?

Bonaparte angrily deleted the second (suggested by Roederer[3]);
only the first question appeared on the following day in the
Moniteur, together with a notice that polls would be opened in all
town halls, registrars' and lawyers' offices. As in the Year VIII,
it was to be a plebiscite in which it would be impossible to vote
'against' without exposing oneself to reprisals from those in

[1] According to Fauriel, it was Tronchet who, when the Senate met
to debate the Tribunate's proposal, was the first to speak and gave it as
his opinion 'that of all the ways in which the desire of the Tribunes
might be interpreted and accomplished, the most proper and effectual
would be the conferring of the First Consulship on Bonaparte for life'.

[2] In a message to the Senate (19 Floréal, Year X) the First Consul
wrote:

'The honourable proof of esteem contained in your resolution of
18 Floréal will ever be graven on my heart. The suffrage of the people
has invested me with the supreme magistracy. I should not think
myself assured of their confidence if the act which retained me there
was not again sanctioned by their suffrage. . . .

You deem that I owe to the people a new sacrifice: I will make it if
the wish of the people commands what your suffrage authorizes.

                           Signed BONAPARTE'
                          (Translator's note).

[3] At the instigation of Joseph. (Translator's note).

authority. There was scarcely any pressure brought to bear if one
is to believe Aulard: it would have been superfluous. The people
were far from regarding Bonaparte as a tyrant. The polling took
three months. On 2 August 1802, it was the Senate which,
entrusted with the task of collecting the votes, announced the
results in the form of a *Senatus Consultum*: 'The French people
nominates and the Senate proclaims Napoleon Bonaparte First
Consul for life.' There had been 3,568,885 'Yeas'; only 8,374
Frenchmen had openly dared to vote 'No'.

Two of these bore illustrious names – Carnot and La Fayette.
Carnot wrote in the margin of the register of the Tribunate:
'Nothing can make me hide my feelings even if it means signing
my own arrest.' La Fayette wrote: 'I cannot vote for such a
magistrature until public liberty is sufficiently guaranteed; only
then will I give my vote to Napoleon Bonaparte.' Furthermore,
he took the trouble to write a long letter to the First Consul
expressing his reasons for refusing him his vote, a letter which he
delivered personally.

Although the role played by La Fayette in 1792 cannot be said
to have contributed greatly to his reputation, he at least remained
faithful to his own conception of liberty. When Bonaparte
returned from Egypt, La Fayette, no longer a prisoner of the
Austrians, but still banished, wrote to congratulate him, but
received no reply. In 1800, tired of his exile, he wrote again to
inform Bonaparte that he was returning home. The First Consul
chose to disregard him; he even forbade Fontanes to mention his
name in his speech in praise of Washington. Did Bonaparte
consider his own greatness threatened by a reminder of one of the
noblest gestures in the history of France? After Marengo, Lebrun
[the third Consul] introduced La Fayette to the Tuileries; this
time Bonaparte decided to be friendly. The two men met again at
Joseph's residence at Mortefontaine. 'You must have found the
French very coldly disposed to liberty,' said Bonaparte, 'the
Parisian shopkeepers no longer want it.' La Fayette replied that,
on the contrary, they were ready to receive it and were expecting
it of him.

Nevertheless, the First Consul hoped to enlist his support by
offering him a seat in the Senate. Cabanis, who at that time had
not yet broken with Bonaparte and evidently hoped to reinforce

the small liberal group in the Luxembourg, undertook to speak to him. 'The first proposition I received,' La Fayette recounts, 'was honourable and attractive. M. Cabanis, whose superior intellect and ardent republicanism impressed me greatly, was not yet an intimate friend.' La Fayette, however, declined the proposal: if he were to accept, he would assume an attitude which the Government would regard as an act of 'insurrection' and which would cause embarrassment to his friends. 'M. Cabanis listened to me with a respect and understanding which contributed in no small measure to our close relationship. . . .'

La Fayette retired to his château of La Grange in Brie, a rural retreat hidden among trees, and abstained from any further political activities, though he did not hestitate to criticize the consular Government to friends who came to visit him. From time to time, however, he went to see Bonaparte to ask him to delete names from the list of proscribed *émigrés*. One day the First Consul spoke to him of his project for the Concordat: 'Admit,' La Fayette answered, 'that the only reason for this is to have a little phial broken over your head' [*que cela n'a d'autre objet que de vous faire casser la petite fiole sur la tête.*] After the Treaty of Amiens, they had a long conversation:

'Lord Cornwallis claims that you are still incorrigible.'

'How so?' the Hero of Two Worlds answered sharply, 'For loving freedom?' The discussion became heated. For the second time, Bonaparte vainly offered him a seat in the Senate and reproached him for his obstinacy in not supporting him.

'What more can I do?' said La Fayette. 'I live a retired life in the country and avoid all opportunities of speaking publicly, but if ever someone asks me if your régime conforms with my ideas of freedom, I must answer "No"; after all, General, I want to be prudent, but I don't want to be a renegade.'

He kept his word. Until 1814 he stayed at La Grange without ever interfering in politics or soliciting anything of the Government. After casting his negative vote for the Consulate for life, he broke off all personal relations with Bonaparte. In his Memoirs he explains his reasons and has something to say about the attitude of the Army, which is not without interest:

'Among the troops, whose opinion was purported to be consulted, those who refused to vote in favour were quickly

punished by deprivation of rank and sent on the fatal expedition
to San Domingo. . . .'

La Fayette's letter, written to Bonaparte at the time, and
happily rescued from oblivion, is a fine example of dignity and
civic sense:

'. . . the 18 Brumaire saved France. . . . Since then we have seen
the consular régime re-establish a dictatorship, which under the
auspices of your genius has succeeded in many great things, but
none so great as the restoration of liberty. It is impossible, *mon
Général*, that you could wish for nothing better than an arbitrary
régime for the world and yourself, as the only result of such a
revolution, so many victories, so much bloodshed and misery,
and prodigies of valour. The people of France know their rights
too well to forget them for ever.'

La Fayette's veto awoke no great echoes, but his example was
followed by his former lieutenant, Latour-Maubourg, who
demanded freedom of the Press as a first condition of his adherence
to the First Consul.

*   *   *

On 15 Thermidor, Year X (3 August 1802), the whole Assembly
repaired in a body to the Tuileries to inform the Consul of the
result of the plebiscite and present the text of the *Senatus Consultum*. The deputation arrived, as though by coincidence, in the
middle of a full meeting of the diplomatic corps [it thus came
about that it was in the presence of the whole of Europe that the
Consul was informed of the will of the people].

Bonaparte made an appropriately 'modest' reply to the effect
that the life of every citizen was dedicated to his country; since
the people of France had placed their confidence in him in per-
petuity, he accepted their decision and pledged himself to uphold
the laws of the country based on a far-sighted policy.

The docile servant of the French people did not lose a minute
in setting about this task. On the following day, he obtained
approval from the Council of State to confirm by a *Senatus
Consultum* the modifications to the Constitution of the Year VIII
on which he had already set his mind, the most important of
which was the right to appoint his own successor. The other
innovations introduced into this new Constitution of Year X

eliminated the very last traces of democracy in the Republic. Electoral colleges, whose presidents, drawn from Paris, were appointed by the First Consul himself, took the place of the provincial 'lists of notabilities'; the Tribunate was reduced to fifty members and divided into three sections, and was in future to hold its debates *in camera*. The responsibilities of the Council of State were also reduced; peace terms were to be discussed by a privy council in place of the legislative assemblies; the Senate was to have much greater powers and, on the initiative of the Government, could, by a *Senatus Consultum*, alter the Constitution, suspend or dissolve the Tribunate and the *Corps législatif* and annul any decisions made by the Tribunes. Finally, the First Consul was to have the right to nominate sixty new senators, bringing their number up to one hundred and twenty. A few months later he created an *élite*, known as the *senatories*, who, because they received rich emoluments, national estates, and residences, could be counted on to set an example of devotion to the Government in the Luxembourg.[1]

Henceforth no parliamentary protest was possible and the overwhelming results of the plebiscite had broken the back of what little opposition still existed in the Senate. Nonetheless, there were still some signs of opposition: Garat, Lanjuinais, and Lambrechts voted against the measures; Siéyès, Volney, Cabanis, and Destutt de Tracy abstained. Always the same names. Of the Councillors of State who had voted for the Consulate for life, Thibaudeau and Roederer,[2] among others, had hoped for a truly republican consulate, providing constitutional controls and guarantees. Such ideological concepts, however, were now out of the question. ... In 1802 Bonaparte had placed Roederer in charge of the *Direction de l'esprit public*, i.e. Minister of Education and Comptroller of Theatres. In September, however, Roederer

---

[1] The First Consul ... can appoint to the Senate, *without previous presentation by the departmental electoral colleges*, citizens distinguished by their services and talents, on condition, nevertheless, that they shall be of the age required by the Constitution and that the numbers of Senators shall in no case exceed one hundred and twenty. [*Senatus Consultum* 16 Thermidor Year X Duvergier *Lois* XIII 262–267]. (Translator's note).

[2] Octave Aubry, Preface to the *Mémoires* of Roederer.

was retired from this post as well as from his presidency of the section of the Council of State. He was appointed a Senator by way of compensation.

Thanks to the faulty system of literary censorship, criticism of this autocratic régime of the summer of 1802 was not, as one might have expected, confined to a few timid protests, but appeared overtly in the form of books.

The first was the *Vrai sens du vote national sur le Consulat à vie*, published anonymously, but which was known to be by Camille Jordan, a former deputy of the Five Hundred, banished at the time of Fructidor, who had returned after Brumaire. Jordan paid homage to the genius of Bonaparte; true, he had also voted for the Consulate for life; but so far and no further. He was filled with indignation at the powers given to the dictator and rejected violently the principle of hereditary rule. He refused 'to bind himself to an unknown successor of Bonaparte, who would lead them into insensate wars and spread the darkness of super-stition and despotism over the land. . . . Ah! one's blood boils at the horrible thought. . . .'

He protested equally vehemently against the adoption of the title of Emperor, which was apparently already being mooted. He demanded the reinstitution of the freedom of the Press, universal suffrage in the legislative assemblies, independent law courts, limitation of the authority of the clergy – in a word, all the guarantees proclaimed in the Constitution of 1789 and willingly accorded by the English monarchy. In support of his remon-strance, he quoted the lofty traditions of Spain (the Cortes) and a discreet reference to England under Charles I allowed him to remind his readers that sometimes one must consider the will of the people.

Printed in July, this brochure was naturally immediately impounded. The revindication of the freedom of the Press in-furiated Bonaparte. He told the Council of State, 'La Fayette and Latour-Maubourg wrote to me to say that they would say "Yes" if the freedom of the Press were re-established. What can one expect of men who are always insisting [*à cheval*] on the meta-physics of 1789.'

A reprint and clandestine distribution, however, prevented the little book from passing unnoticed. Benjamin Constant wrote to

Fauriel that it was being distributed throughout Paris. Madame de Staël, who in the first place had urged Jordan to write it, relied on it to prepare the way for a much more important work, the *Dernières vues de politique et de finance de M. Necker*, also inspired by her, which appeared in the first fortnight of August.

Louis XVI's former Director General of Finance, persuaded by his daughter, still thought himself sufficiently important to have the ear of France and of Bonaparte himself. Beginning with what was now the almost ritual homage to the 'indispensable man', Necker went on to criticize severely the Constitution of Year VIII, the importance of the Assemblies and the omnipotence of the First Consul. He once again brought forward the arguments propounded in *De la Littérature* concerning military despotism, calling into question the very existence of a Republic, and demanded a new Constitution, '*parfaite pour l'ordre, et bonne aussi pour la liberté*, and poured scorn on the idea of a Bonaparte dynasty and the, as yet, secret ambitions of the dictator.

However, few people read this little book. But then, mid-August was now celebrated as a national fête in honour of Bonaparte's birthday. With all the spontaneous congratulatory messages flooding into Paris from all parts of France, how could this old Minister expect his work to be heeded? However, it did have one result. Bonaparte exclaimed on reading it: 'Necker's daughter will never return to Paris. . . .'[1] This ban was repeated in December when the publication of *Delphine* once again roused Bonaparte to anger.

When Mme de Staël began her first great novel, she had promised herself that it would not be political. The action of her plot was placed in the recent past (1792) and not in the immediate present. But *Delphine* is in fact a social criticism and manifestly anti-conformist in content, and makes a violent attack on the rigid hypocrisy of the moral status imposed on women, and the state of subordination and inferiority to which Bonaparte wished to subject them after the licentiousness of the Directory.

Hence Bonaparte's exasperation when the book had such

---

[1] Naïvely, Necker had sent a copy to Lebrun, the third Consul, to present to Bonaparte, whose reaction can be well imagined.

success in France and abroad. Only eight months after the ratification of the Concordat, this devilish *femme de lettres* was compli-
cating and spoiling everything. This novel (which Bonaparte
described as *vagabondage d'imagination, désordre d'esprit, métaphysique du sentiment*) encouraged free thought, admired the
English, and advocated divorce – which alone was enough to
rouse the spleen of the virtuous General who had forbidden
Josephine to meet such women as Mme Tallien and Mme Grant.
In Lebensei (one of the principal characters of the novel), a
Protestant gentleman, educated at Cambridge, it was easy to
recognize Benjamin Constant, who expresses anti-Catholic sentiments. Above all, the book preached the ideals of the 'Age of
Enlightenment'. This was altogether too much. Bonaparte himself wrote (anonymously) wounding, brutal, and even vulgar
criticisms in the *Débats* and other papers and forbade the sale
of *Delphine* at the Leipzig fair. As for its author, he said: 'I hope
her friends will advise her not to return to Paris; if she did, I
would be obliged to send her back to the frontier with a police
escort.'

Having forbidden Germaine de Staël to return to Paris, it is
difficult to see what more Bonaparte, the *Idéophobe*, had to fear
from the *'chevaliers de la métaphysique'*, the former circle of Auteuil
and *Idéologues*. Only a handful were left in the Luxembourg;
their voices were stifled and their votes counted for nothing.
Those who had been in the Palais Royal were now expelled. In
neither Assembly could they speak from the rostrum or publish
their works, or even exchange independent views.

But these representatives of an enlightened, but silent, France
still had a foothold in the Institute – or, to be more precise, in the
Second Class thereof: Moral Science and Politics. It was the last
stronghold of philosophy and the ultimate refuge of free thought
and liberalism in France. It was to this class of the Institute that
the country owed the foundation of the Museum, the School of
Oriental Studies, the Polytechnique, and Central schools. But
even this was to be abolished.

On 3 Pluviôse, Year XI (23 January 1803), Bonaparte closed the
second class of the Institute and 'deported', or should one say
'dispersed', its members among other classes.

The hall where the greatest brains of France had held their

sessions was closed. The light of the eighteenth century was hidden under a bushel. . . . No word, no thought would again be raised against arbitrary rule, against impulsive and excessive actions, or the use of violence.

6

Caesar and Pompey

❖❖❖❖❖❖❖❖❖❖❖❖❖❖❖❖❖❖❖❖❖❖❖❖❖❖❖❖❖❖❖❖❖❖❖❖❖

THE Institute was now rendered harmless, the Assemblies were purged, newspaper opinion was suppressed. The police, who were everywhere, saw everything, heard everything, were able to report optimistically on the loyalty of the good people of France. Bishops and priests, who were just as much part of the vast Government machinery as Prefects and gendarmes, zealously encouraged hero-worship of the First Consul. In March 1803 it was established by law that all coins would in future bear the old royal device 'God protects France' and the effigy of Napoleon Bonaparte. Was there nothing left now but to bow one's head and submit in silence to the enslavement of the Republic by the very men who had been elected to preserve it? What hope was there for liberty betrayed, except to have recourse to military insurrection? But were there still any Republican soldiers left in the Year X?

At an early date relations had been established between the opposition members of the Assembly and malcontents of the Army. When the 'Special Courts' were being debated, Ginguené and Chénier had made contact with some of the Generals. Although most of Bonaparte's comrades in arms had warmly approved of his action in 'sweeping away the rule of lawyers', they had been antagonized by his rise to supreme power, and, in particular, the haughty and distant attitude he had assumed towards them. Peace had increased the number of unemployed Generals, who ranted against 'Sultan Bonaparte'. The Concordat fed their disaffection even further. At the beginning of 1801, the

First Consul had made a rigorous purge of the Army, and by dispatching – or perhaps we should say deporting – strong contingents of the Army of the Rhine to San Domingo he had avoided the danger of a revolt. Nevertheless the *malaise* persisted. In 1802 it took the form of a widespread movement, known as the 'Generals' plot', which was at first confined to officers of more or less junior rank. On 25 April, General Oudinot gave a dinner at his villa to which he invited Generals Marmont, Dupont, and Delmas (who a week previously had expressed their disapproval of Bonaparte) as well as several junior officers, including a Colonel Fournier (Sarlorèze), a hot-headed, dashing hussar, who had completed the rout of the Austrians at Marengo and who was, moreover, a crack pistol shot. There was much drinking, loud talk, and bragging. Anxiously Oudinot begged Delmas to be more prudent. 'You'll get yourself deported', he said. 'In that case,' Fournier shouted, 'I take it on myself to shoot down Bonaparte at fifty paces.' A police informer, who was mingling with the guests, did not lose a crumb of this conversation.

The police were also aware of a plot to murder the tyrant that was being hatched by some junior officers under the leadership of Donnadieu, a cavalry major (*chef d'escadrons*). Two attempts at assassination were to be made, one on 4 May at the Théâtre des Arts, and the other on 5 May at a military parade in the Carrousel. Fournier and the First Consul were both at the theatre: their glances met. Fournier was immediately, but quietly, arrested and taken to the Temple, where he found Delmas already a prisoner. Soon both were removed from Paris and placed under house arrest. Donnadieu was arrested on 3 May, but released on condition that he acted as a police informer (reporting on *émigrés* in England).

But disaffection was not limited to these rather trivial incidents. The future Emperor was much more concerned with the intransigent attitude of the High Command. In order to break up this body he sent them abroad on various honorific missions, playing on their fears and vanities. One of the most difficult of his generals was Lannes, the son of an ostler and one-time apprentice dyer, now Commandant of the Consular Guard, who regarded himself as indispensable and who continued to address Bonaparte with the familiar 'tu'. Bonaparte got rid of him by appointing him Ambassador to Lisbon. Another 'loud mouth' was Augereau, who was easy to handle as he was guilty of vast embezzlements.

The 'glorious' Jourdan might have proved a more difficult customer. As a member of the Five Hundred, he had rebelled against the *coup d'état* of Brumaire. Exiled and then pardoned, he had accepted the post of Ambassador to the Cisalpine Republic. This former Commander of the Army of *Sambre et Meuse* sacrificed his Republican principles to military discipline and now transferred his devotion to liberty to the person of Napoleon.

The same cannot be said of Lazare Carnot. On the repeated insistence of Lebrun, he had finally agreed to accept the Ministry of War. The First Consul, however, had nominated him to this post, for which he was eminently suitable,[1] only to cover him with insult and injury, so that he was finally obliged to resign. 'I won't be here for long,' said Carnot one evening, after a particularly stormy interview, 'this man needs Ministers as a matter of form; he wants to use them for his own ends, not for France.' The first time he proffered his resignation it was refused; on the second occasion (8 October 1800) it was accepted. He was replaced by Berthier, who wanted to appoint Carnot G.O.C. of the Corps of Engineers.[2]

The First Consul's reply to this recommendation was: *Carnot ne doit être rien dans une république* (!) In other words, he was an officer unfit to serve under a dictatorship.

Carnot has been blamed for remaining in the Tribunate after the purging, but he was always in disagreement with his fello

---

[1] It will be recollected that, during the early wars of the Revolution, Carnot was known as the 'organizer of victory'. The Committee of Public Safety had entrusted him with the organization of the Armies of the Revolution, in which he had displayed marvellous energy and ability. He raised fourteen armies and drew up a plan of campaign by which the forces of reaction were driven back from the frontier. His energy, skill, and fertility of administrative resource also helped to achieve the brilliant results of the Italian and Rhenish campaigns of 1800. (Translator's note).

[2] Carnot had been a major in the Engineers and was a brilliant mathematician. Of his numerous writings, the best known is *Réflexions sur la Métaphysique du Calcul Infinitésimal* (1797). (Translator's note).

members. He voted against the establishment of the Legion of Honour and against the Consulship for Life, and, was later alone in voting against the Empire.

Although an opponent of Bonaparte, Carnot was neither an intriguer nor a rival. Bonaparte's real rival, and, for a time, the most embarrassing of all, was Bernadotte. This colourful, attractive, extrovert, and extremely ambitious one-time Gascon sergeant (nicknamed Belle-Jambe) was always the centre of numerous intrigues, from which he always managed adroitly to disengage himself at the last moment. He had refused to become implicated in the *coup d'état* of 18 Fructidor, and later, he withdrew from Jourdan's proposal to join with the Jacobins in overthrowing Siéyès – but not too soon to lose the portfolio of Minister of War. He had, however, suggested to the Jacobins, after Saint-Cloud, that he should share power with Bonaparte. Barras had said to him one day: 'It would be enough if, at a review, twenty Generals were to draw their swords and plunge them into the heart of the First Consul.'

'Sublime, ineffable, worthy of the antique', replied Bernadotte. But he would never have had the courage to implement such a plan; on the other hand, he did have the courage to confront Bonaparte, with whom he often had violent quarrels, as for example during the first Army 'purges'. But, as brother-in-law of Joseph and very popular at the time, it would have been difficult to have had him shot, or 'eliminated'. Although Bonaparte knew that Bernadotte was involved in the Ceracchi plot, he pretended to believe his protestations of innocence and, on the advice of Fouché, sent him to Rennes in command of the Army of the West – an unemployed, discontented, undisciplined Army, in which Bernadotte played an equivocal role. He often returned to Paris, and was finally recalled in December 1801.

It was his presence in the capital that brought the 'Generals' plot' to a head. These Generals were senior in rank to the Fourniers and Delmas; less braggart and more secretive; moreover they tried to co-operate with the political opposition. But there has always been some mystery concerning this conspiracy. In 1808, Napoleon told Chaptal that the Generals, jealous of his success, had several times attempted to overthrow him or share in the Government. Twelve Generals, he said, had devised a plan to divide France into twelve provinces. 'Very generously, they had left me Paris and the suburbs,' he said. Masséna had been appointed to present the Generals' manifesto (signed at Reuil) to Bonaparte, but he refused, saying that if he left the Tuileries alive it would be only to be shot by Bonaparte's guard. 'That fellow knew me well. . . .' was Bonaparte's comment.

On 4 May 1802, Bonaparte felt obliged, in view of these conspiracies, to make an anti-militarist speech to the Council of State: '. . . military rule could never take root in France, unless the nation were stultified by fifty years of ignorance . . . a soldier knows no law but force, he looks only to his own needs, he sees no further than himself . . . I unhesitatingly believe that the civilian, on the contrary, sees only the common good.' Bernadotte's role in the conspiracy is described by Madame de Staël as follows: 'A group of Generals and senators wanted to know if Bernadotte had some plan to prevent Bonaparte's usurpation of power. Bernadotte made various proposals, all based on some sort of legislation; any other method was contrary to his principles. But, for such a measure to be taken, at least several senators would have to be involved, and none of them dared to subscribe to such an act. . . .'

It was obviously unreasonable for Bernadotte to expect the few senators whom he met (Garat, Grégoire, Destutt, Lambrechts, Lanjuinais) to propose a bill to remove the First Consul. They had arrived at an impasse. Is this why more violent measures were proposed as a solution? According to Savary, Bernadotte often attended meetings of officers to discuss means of getting rid of Bonaparte, but, although the majority were in favour of assassination, Bernadotte recommended that he should be 'kidnapped by main force'.

While the 'Generals' plot' was gradually losing impetus in the capital, a dangerous revolt was developing among the garrison of Rennes, where Bernadotte had left his Chief of Staff, General Simon. Simon dispatched secretly the most virulent 'libels' on Bonaparte to all corners of France.

'Brave brothers in arms! . . . the Republic, which you have helped to found with such constancy and courage, is now no more than an idle word. Soon a Bourbon will be on the throne,

or Bonaparte himself will proclaim himself Emperor or
King. . . .'

'A tyrant has assumed power; and who is this tyrant?
Bonaparte!'

Simon, who was soon identified as the author of these 'libels'
was arrested, together with other officers, on 24 June. Because
some of this seditious literature had been sent to a Captain
Rapatel, a frequent visitor to the Château de Grosbois (Moreau's
residence), Bonaparte over-hastily concluded that Moreau himself
was the *deus ex machina* of the whole affair. He ordered Fouché to
demand an explanation. Moreau dismissed the whole business in
an off-hand manner; it was nothing more, he said, than a *conspira-
tion de pots de beurre* [the 'libels' had been found hidden in earthen-
ware crocks]. This was altogether too much for the First Consul,
whose reaction was violent and astonishing. 'This contest must be
finished once and for all,' he said to Fouché. 'Tell him [Moreau]
to be in the Bois de Boulogne at four o'clock tomorrow morning.
His sabre and mine will decide the issue. Don't fail to execute my
order.'

The most sensational duel in history, however, was not to be
fought. Fouché arranged a reconciliation. Moreau agreed to
present himself at the Tuileries, where Bonaparte apparently gave
him a cordial welcome and all seemed to pass off smoothly.

It was soon established by Dubois, the Prefect of Police, that
the real instigator of this Rennes conspiracy was in fact none
other than Bernadotte. But the obscure General Simon nobly and
determinedly accepted full responsibility. It was in the interest
of both Fouché and Bonaparte to accept this version. If Bernadotte had been arrested on the eve of the plebiscite, it would have
led to a mutiny in the Army; it was enough to send him on sick
leave to take the waters at Plombières, with a promise of being
made either Governor of Louisiana or Ambassador to Washington – a flattering offer which Bernadotte refused. As for Simon,
after a term of imprisonment in the Temple, he was deported to
Guiana; the garrison of Rennes was disbanded, and one of the
regiments was sent to San Domingo to join the remnants of the
Army of the Rhine. In their quarters at Rennes were found

inscriptions reading: 'Vive la République! Vive Moreau! Death to the First Consul!'

Now there only remained Moreau. There was no question of buying *him* off with an embassy.

*   *   *

The hero of Hohenlinden combined the virtues of a Republican soldier with those of a civilian. Moreau was the son of a Breton lawyer and he himself had studied law. On the outbreak of the Revolution he was chosen to command the National Militia of Rennes; he served under Dumouriez in 1793 and showed such military talent that in 1794 he was made a General of Division. He combined noble disinterestedness and sang-froid with physical and moral probity. At the end of 1796, on orders from the Directory, he willingly sacrificed two divisions of his Rhine-Moselle army to support Bonaparte. It was not until 30 Vendé-miaire, Year VIII (22 October 1799) that Moreau met Bonaparte for the first time, when Gohier invited both Generals to the Luxembourg.

Like many another, Moreau believed that the *coup d'état* of 18 Brumaire was the saving of the Republic. On 7 Nivôse, Year VIII, when he assumed command of the Army of the Rhine at Zürich, he announced to his troops that 'the legislative Commissions and the Consuls of the Republic are at this moment giving us proof of their devotion to the sacred cause of liberty and are hastening to give the people of France a constitution which will guarantee their rights in full.'

This speech was no ordinary official formality. It was essential to give this solemn assurance to his Army, in which the flame of the Year II still burnt so strongly, an Army which remained unshaken in its belief in the principles of the Revolution – very different from the Army of Italy. Bonaparte's soldiers, electrified by his promises, fought for glory, promotion, and booty. Moreau's troops, on the other hand, were honest and poor. There were even some, like Latour d'Auvergne, who refused promotion. These republican soldiers treated the inhabitants of the countries they invaded as brothers whom they were liberating. Their leader set an example in moderation and justice. He exacted obedience without brutality.

He also set an example of discipline by agreeing, for a second time, to send a considerable proportion (a quarter) of his forces to reinforce Bonaparte on the eve of the latter's passage of the Saint Bernard. Good relations continued to exist between the two Generals. Moreau's loyalty was a precious asset to the First Consul: he was obliged to recognize his merit, for he knew that the name of Moreau had been put forward to replace him during the Marengo campaign.

In the autumn of 1800, during the weeks that Moreau spent in Paris, overtures were made to him from all sides. But Moreau encouraged none, and his relations with the First Consul remained cordial.

In November he was back with his Army. On 3 December, the great, decisive Battle of Hohenlinden was fought and won. This time it brought true fame to the victor. Concerted praise, more or less disinterested, was lavished on the 'Second General of the Republic'. 'Thanks to his experience [wrote Thiers] his ability to command and his high reputation, he was, after General Bonaparte, the only man capable of commanding a hundred thousand men.' But the 'First General of the Republic' took umbrage at Moreau's success, and signs of Bonaparte's ill-humour were to become increasingly manifest. Promotions and punishments advocated by Moreau's H.Q. were disregarded by Paris, and when Madame Moreau visited Malmaison, Bonaparte asked no news of her husband. Tendentious articles were published in the *Moniteur*, accusing Moreau of mis-appropriation of Army funds. Moreau protested in a letter to Berthier, Minister of War. This letter is headed *Army of the Rhine. Liberty. Equality. H.Q. at Strasbourg, 29 Floréal, Year IX of the French Republic, one and indivisible*, [it is given in full as an appendix to Fauriel's posthumous memoirs. *Translator's note*] but this was never published.

In 1801 Moreau returned to Paris. When he visited Bonaparte on 25 May he wore civilian dress. The meeting was frigid. He was conspicuous by his absence at a great reception given at the Tuileries a little while later – either he was not invited or perhaps he preferred not to attend.

But Moreau's attitude may be explained by his own personal resentment and the jealousy and petty spite shown by his wife and mother-in-law (Mme Hulot) to Josephine. This is a theory which

Napoleon himself maintains in his Memoirs of St Helena, and one which is supported by many serious historians.

Moreau's greatest fault at the time seems to have been the raising of false hopes first in one party and then in another. This is not to cast doubt on the sincerity of his convictions. While resolute on the field of battle and showing a coolness of mind proportionate to the dangers surrounding him, he showed himself in politics, for which he had no aptitude, weak and vacillating. In fact, Bonaparte's return from Egypt had relieved him of a great responsibility. 'Here is your man', he had said to Siéyès, who had considered him as the figure-head for the *coup d'état* of Brumaire. Moreau neither discouraged, nor encouraged, anyone. That is why, finally, Mme de Staël placed all her hopes on Bernadotte. But once Bernadotte was out of the picture, all the hopes of the opposition were focussed on Moreau – indeed the eyes of all Fouché's myrmidons were on him too.

Even before this, rumour had hinted at some shadowy conspiracy between Moreau and the Auteuil group, though without, of course, specifying a date for the supposed intrigue. The story was that Moreau had been seeing a great deal of Daunou, and also of Jacquemont, the *chef du bureau des sciences* at the Ministry of the Interior and a member of the Institute. Jacquemont, a suspected royalist, did not hide his desire to see Bonaparte overthrown; his was the master hand behind the whole affair. Among the others involved, the principal names were Ginguené, Garat, Volney, Destutt, Chénier, and Cabanis (Cabanis, who had by now lost all his illusions, being among the most zealous). The conspirators met at Daunou's house and at the Diners du Tridi already mentioned; later, after a warning hint from Fouché, they transferred their meetings to Destutt's house at Auteuil, and to the houses of Mesdames de Condorcet and de Staël.

According to Fauriel, who was a friend of the Auteuil group, Moreau was in political sympathy with only five or six men who belonged to the minority group in the Senate, but neither he, nor then they, were agreed on any definite plan to thwart Bonaparte's ambitions.

In any case, it was not so much Moreau's association with the *idéologues* that gave offence to Bonaparte as his increasing display of contempt for the régime. No wonder Bonaparte was furious and had reacted to Moreau's insolent reply to Fouché by challenging him to a duel. For example, he had chosen not to attend the *Te Deum*; he had refused the Legion of Honour but had decorated instead his cook, after a banquet, with a 'Casserole d'honneur'. No wonder Bonaparte was furious, and after Moreau's mocking reply to Fouché we can well understand that he had been prepared to fight him with sabres. Although after their meeting at the Tuileries the two Generals seemed to have settled their differences, Moreau continued to show his independence, and when bidden to a reception given by the Minister of War in December, arrived wearing sober civilian dress and sporting a *chapeau rond*: very much out of keeping with the multi-coloured splendour of the costumes of the other guests, which were *de rigeur* with the new régime.

In 1803 he came out of his shell. He now adopted a style of living so magnificent that a royalist reported to London that he was trying to rival the Court of Saint-Cloud. He was now a constant visitor to Madame Récamier's *salons*. During the short while that Moreau continued to appear in public, it was considered necessary to prohibit all meetings and even to close the theatres.

On 31 January Moreau gave a brilliant ball, which was distinguished by the fact that no member of the Government nor any of the Bonaparte family was invited. What was Moreau up to? The police imputed all sorts of plots to him. Did he want to become leader of the Republican party? Or did he want to re-establish the Bourbons? Or was he simply practising a form of blackmail?

Henceforth the General was followed, spied on, his correspondence was strictly scrutinized. What was the significance of the inscriptions, which appeared in March, scrawled in huge letters on the doors of taverns (to which nobody paid any attention) – 'Long live General Moreau, to hell with the Government!'?

*　　*　　*

25 March 1802 – The Treaty of Amiens.

17 May 1803 – Rupture of the Treaty of Amiens.

In 1802 Bonaparte, thanks to the peace, became absolute master of France. When war was declared again in 1803, he hoped to become master of the World.

Who was responsible for the breaking of the Peace? Was it Bonaparte or England? Opinion is divided. What we are concerned with here is the fact that the Cabinet in London again lent its support to the subversive activities of the *émigrés* surrounding the Comte d'Artois, and in particular to the most daring of all, Georges Cadoudal.

It will be remembered that it was Georges who had come to Brittany to organize the *attentat* in the rue Saint-Nicaise. At the end of 1801 he had returned to England when he realized nothing more could be expected from the West. Now that peace had been broken, however, he was once again able to engage in fresh plots, assured of the help of the English. On 21 August 1803, a British frigate quietly landed Georges and four companions beneath the cliffs of Biville, between Tréport and Dieppe, from where he made his way to Paris where a hiding place had been prepared for him.

The presence of this most dangerous of Chouans in the capital, unsuspected by the police, was the result of a plot devised by the police themselves. A certain Mehée de la Touche, a former Septembrist, condemned to be deported in Nivôse, had 'escaped' to England with the connivance of Réal, deputy of the Grand Judge Régnier, who had now replaced Fouché as head of police. Mehée's instructions[1] had been to convince the British Cabinet that collusion existed between Revolutionaries and Royalists and that the only means of overthrowing Bonaparte was to strengthen the alliance between the two parties. By introducing an agent every plot hatched in Paris would be known in London. Mehée succeeded in his mission so well that the British Government and the Comte d'Artois decided to win over the malcontent Generals, beginning with Moreau. It was for this reason that Cadoudal was landed in France, although unbeknown to Mehée.

[1] Received from Fouché and Réal. It should be pointed out that, although Fouché had been dismissed as head of police, and the police department was now attached to the Ministry of Justice, Fouché was still very much involved. This is an extremely simplified version of one of the most complicated plots and counterplots that has surely ever existed. Fauriel, in his posthumous *Last Days of the Consulate* (published 1886), gives a long account of the affair. Mehée also wrote his memoirs (probably quite untrustworthy) but which nevertheless show what a tangled web of intrigue was woven. (Translator's note).

How could London possibly belive that such an irreproachable Republican General as Moreau would ever agree to work for the King of France? In fact, this was because a certain *agent provocateur*, an unemployed General, Lajolais, had told Pichegru (who had now joined the ranks of the Royalists and had been living in England for some years) that he had seen Moreau (which was true) and that the latter had made it clear that he was prepared to save the cause of the Bourbons (which was not true).

As a result of Lajolais's false information, more conspirators were landed at Biville at the end of December 1803 and in mid January 1804, including Pichegru, Lajolais, the Marquis de Rivière, and the two brothers Polignac. Their purpose was to contact Moreau. Once an arrangement had been reached between them, the third phase of the operation was to take place – the landing of the 'princes' – the Comte d'Artois, the Duc de Berry, and other illustrious noblemen, who at the head of an insurrectionary Republican Army would march triumphantly into the good city of Paris.

Is it possible to believe that the arrival of Pichegru and his companions, their clandestine comings and goings in the capital, and the inevitable ferment in the royalist camp were completely unknown to Bonaparte and his police?

Before 15 January 1804 [when the *Corps législatif* was informed that 'the British Government will endeavour to cast on our shores, and perhaps has already done so, some of those monsters which it has nourished in its bosom only to destroy the land of their birth'] only a few arrests had been made. The First Consul had even written to Régnier 'not to be in too much of a hurry' to make any arrests. But after this date the police became extremely active indeed. Bouvet de Lozier, one of Cadoudal's lieutenants, was arrested on 10 February. He was taken to the Temple and seemed to have been left there forgotten for three days. But at dawn on the fourth day he was found hanging half-strangled in an attempt at suicide. When he was cut down he insisted on being brought before the Grand Judge, Régnier, and Councillor Réal, to whom, he said, he wished to make an important statement, one of the strangest ever made by a man in a situation like his. His words were taken down in writing.

'A man who comes forth from the gates of the grave' (thus he began), 'who is still overcast by the shadow of death, calls for vengeance upon those whose treachery has flung him and his party into the abyss in which they lie.' The rest of the declaration was a plain and full 'revelation' of the plans of the conspirators. Pichegru, he said, had been in Paris for some weeks and, accompanied by Cadoudal, had met Moreau in the Boulevard de la Madeleine. Moreau had promised to ally himself with the cause of the Bourbons, but had later retracted, and had proposed instead that, with the help of the conspirators, he should be made dictator. Bouvet, however, admitted that he only had half-proofs to support his accusations. The promises he put into Moreau's mouth were based on the fallacious assurances given by Lajolais in London.

In the early morning of 14 February, Réal hurried to the Tuileries to impart these sensational tidings to a half-awake Bonaparte. A secret council was held, which lasted all day and all night. On the following day a detachment of gendarmes was sent to Grosbois. It met Moreau on the bridge of Charenton; he was arrested and taken to the Temple.

On 17 February, in the presence of an astounded Tribunate, Regnault de Saint-Jean d'Angély read the report of the Grand Judge on the conspiracy in general and of Moreau's guilt in particular. Only one Tribune protested – Moreau's brother – who declared that the victor of Hohenlinden was 'innocent of the atrocious crimes' imputed to him, and demanded that he should be judged by his *juges naturels*, but the jury of the Department of the Seine was replaced by a *Senatus Consultum*. For weeks, even months, a vast number of letters signed by officers of the Army, Church, and State were published, stigmatizing 'the traitor Moreau, the instigator of the Royalist plot'. To read contemporary copies of the *Moniteur* is to remind one irresistibly of the spontaneous indignation shown by the Soviet masses at the height of the Moscow and other trials.[1]

[1] Bonaparte hastened to inform the Generals in command of the different corps of Moreau's arrest. On 29 Pluviôse he wrote to General Soult that Moreau 'had decided on making Pichegru come to Paris where he had seen him four times and also Georges'. These four visits are reduced to two in a letter written on the same day to Davoust [*Correspondence de Napoléon 1*, Vol. IX, pp. 305–321]. Every word

This was all very well, but neither Pichegru nor Cadoudal had yet been arrested. On 28 February the *Corps législatif* proposed a law by which 'any individual harbouring Georges, Pichegru, or his sixty accomplices . . . would be punished by death. Anyone seeing them, who did not denounce them, would be punished by six years in irons. . . .' Murat was made Governor of Paris and police precautions were doubled. 'No one was allowed to leave the city limits (*barrières*) and patrols were ordered to fire on sight at anyone attempting escape' (Thiers). These measures, reminiscent of the worst days of the Terror, proved efficacious. The person providing asylum to Pichegru denounced him, the brothers Polignac and the Marquis de Rivière were arrested, and finally, on 9 March, Georges Cadoudal was apprehended near the present Odéon, after an exciting chase. Pichegru was interrogated by Réal and Dubois and, although tortured, remained obdurately silent. Cadoudal, on the contrary, admitted that he had come to abduct the First Consul, but not to assassinate him. He had intended to attack his escort 'on equal terms'; as for the date, he was awaiting the arrival of 'a French prince'.

There was nothing surprising about this admission. From the cliff-top of Biville, Savary had been on the look-out for 'this prince' for a month past. But why did Bonaparte suddenly decide that the leader awaited by the conspirators was no longer the Comte d'Artois from London, but the Duc d'Enghien, living a few kilometres from the French frontier near Strasbourg? Did he really believe the reports of the gendarme, ordered to spy on the Duke, who reported that he had quite recently been joined by the 'traitor' Dumouriez [at Ettenheim]?

For a century and a half the whole world has considered the execution of the Duc d'Enghien as an indelible blot on the career of Napoleon. Any further censure would be superfluous; it is sufficient to here consider only the main facts of the case. No proof was ever produced that the young Duke was involved in Cadoudal's

---

was a lie. Moreau knew nothing of Pichegru's return and was so little known to Georges that, when they were confined in the Temple, the latter begged a gendarme to point out the General to him (cf. M. L. Lalanne's introduction to Fauriel's *Last Day of the Consulate*). (Translator's note).

plot; Bonaparte's outbursts of anger were probably simulated and, in any case, unjustifiable ('Am I a dog to be slaughtered with impunity by the first comer?'). Nevertheless, the Duke had taken up arms against the Republic and was ready to do so again.

Legally this was basis enough to condemn him to death, provided always that the verdict was obtained by a regular trial. But to have abducted the Duke from foreign soil was already a violation of the rights of man. What more can be said? It was the mere pretence of a trial, limited to an interrogation by Hulin without witnesses, with no counsel for defence, and with no members of the public present; the sentence was read beside a grave already dug some hours previously in front of a firing squad already alerted, by the light of a lantern hung over the heart of the victim.

The crime, as we know from the memoirs of O'Meara and Las Cases, and also from Savary, was to weigh heavily on Napoleon's conscience. It did little good to his cause, and although it had the effect of rallying fanatical Jacobins and was noisily approved of by Bonapartists of the left who still claimed to be faithful to the spirit of the Convention, it antagonized Chateaubriand and furnished a pretext to the European powers to form the third coalition, and, according to Thiers, was the principal cause of the third war.

French Catholics reacted cautiously. On 21 March, the *Moniteur* devoted its first column to a brief from Pope Pius VII addressed to 'his dear child in Jesus Christ, Napoleon Bonaparte', begging him to intercede on behalf of the German churches.[1] A little further on, a discreet reference was made to the discovery 'of an *émigré* plot on the right bank of the Rhine, directed by a Bourbon prince'. On the following day, 22 March, the leading article was devoted to an account of the solemn mass and *Te Deum* which had just been celebrated at Saint-Roch. The Bishop of Coutance, who was officiating, apostrophized his congregation in noble words: 'Soldiers! Never forget that the God worshipped by the victor of

[1] Article VII of the Treaty of Lunéville, having stipulated that the hereditary [German] princes whose possessions were included in the cession to France . . . should be indemnified, it had been recognized that, in conformity with the Congress of Rastadt, this indemnification should be carried out by secularization. (Translator's note).

Marengo, the God before whom he bowed his laurel-wreathed head in the Cathedral of Milan ... is not a God of cowards. Today I come to offer at the throne of the supreme arbiter of life and death the nation's prayers of love and loyalty for its chosen leader.'

This piece of holy eloquence served to gloss over the sentence passed on the said Louis-Antoine-Henri de Bourbon, Duc d'Enghien. It is ironic to think that only a few days previously (8 March) Roederer had told Bonaparte that he had grave doubts concerning the loyalty of the clergy. 'They regard your Government [he had said] as merely an interim expedient. The most devoted of them declare that after your death, should it be the will of God to raise up a Bourbon, they would swear fealty to him. That's what the Bishop of Coutance told me recently, and he is the most loyal of all the clergy; it is his great ambition to be your private chaplain.'

If the *Moniteur* was discreet in its references to the end of the Duc d'Enghien, it went into the greatest detail concerning the death of Pichegru, who was found strangled in his prison on the morning of 6 April. The strangulation was effected by a strongly knotted black silk cravat, through which a baton, measuring 45 centimetres in length by 5 centimetres in circumference, had been passed; this had served as a tourniquet, with which the cravat had been tightened. The doctors and surgeons appointed to examine the corpse concluded their autopsy by 'estimating' that 'the individual in question had strangled himself'.

In other circumstances this verdict of suicide would have met with incredulity, but Pichegru's reputation had been so defamed in the eyes of the nation that his assassin (supposed or real) had nothing to fear. Even today we cannot know for sure whether it was murder or not; certainly, there is no evidence that Bonaparte was personally responsible. But the First Consul's innocence is in no way proved by the fact that he allowed Moreau, a much more dangerous adversary, to leave his prison safe and sound. If Moreau had been found strangled, there would no doubt have been violent reactions of incalculable danger to the Government.

Moreau was instead brought to trial.

Between the deaths of the Duc d'Enghien and Pichegru the Empire was instituted. Napoleon himself admitted that the death

of the Prince and the trial of Moreau had served to accomplish
the task on which he had set his heart for a long while now. He
used the plot as a springboard to achieve hereditary rule.

Ever since the end of February the columns of the *Moniteur*
had been filled with loyal addresses. They began by expressing
no more than indignation at conspiracies, and loyalty. But, after
the events in question, hereditary rule was being advocated as the
only means to ruin the hopes of the conspirators. These articles
were always signed by Government officials – magistrates,
bishops, or municipal councils. They were even supported by
Masséna, Bernadotte, and other Generals on behalf of the Army.

Fouché, anxious to return to favour, made every effort to
influence the Senate in this respect. As a result of evidence confirming that English agents in Germany had participated in the
Cadoudal plot, the Senate decided that there was 'room for
modification in the instructions', and on 6 Germinal (27 March)
presented the First Consul with the address he had so long
awaited. 'Defer no longer, great man, achieve your work and
make it as immortal as your glory.'[1]

Pretending to consider the matter, Bonaparte urged his Prefects
and Generals to stage more 'spontaneous' demonstrations, while
consulting the Council of State. Despite a few objections and a
forceful protest from Berlier ('Those who made the Revolution
will become a laughing-stock if they re-erect the edifice they have
overthrown'), the Council opted for hereditary rule.

A month after the Senate's address to the First Consul, he gave
his reply (6 Floréal):

'. . . I want us to be able to say to the people of France on
14 July of this year: Fifteen years ago, in a spontaneous movement, you ran to take up arms in the cause of liberty, equality,
and glory. Today, these benefits are definitely assured, sheltered from all storms; these gifts are yours and those of your
children for ever.'

[1] However, neither the word *monarchy* nor *Empire* was ever mentioned and it was left to the First Consul to choose for himself the form
in which the wishes of the Senate should find expression. (Translator's
note).

Only fifteen years after the capture of the Bastille! And now the people of France were being invited to vote for a hereditary dictatorship, the better to preserve their conquests of 1789!

The Tribunate (reduced and purged), however, was more representative of Republican France than the Senate, and it was its vote that Bonaparte required. Fabre de l'Aude, President of the Tribunate and friend of all the Bonaparte family, offered his help. He had discovered the ideal man to present the required Bill. This was the tribune Curée, an ex-*conventionnel*, who boasted of being 'a tried Republican'. Curée duly prepared a Bill proposing that Napoleon Bonaparte be proclaimed Emperor of the French and that the Imperial dignity should be hereditary within his family.

On 10 Floréal, Year XII (30 April 1804) the Bill was debated in the Palais Royal. Carnot, alone, opposed it. He rendered sober tribute to the distinguished services of the First Consul '. . . but reason dictates that there are limits to the expressions of national gratitude. . . . *If this citizen has restored public liberty, if he has achieved the salvation of our country, will it be a recompense to offer him the sacrifice of this same liberty?*'

Carnot did not hesitate to expose Bonaparte's premeditation and lack of faith; ever since the Consulate for life had been established, it was only too easy to see that he had an *arrière-pensée* and ulterior ends. 'I voted against the Consulate for life,' he said. 'I will also vote against the re-establishment of a monarchy, as I feel obliged to do in my capacity of Tribune.'

Carnot then went on to say that he would nevertheless abide by the will of the people should the need arise. He ended his brief, but well-considered, speech by declaring his loyalty to his country, threatened by the world-wide ambitions of England. His was the only independent voice in an assembly of lickspittles. All those who had an opportunity of speaking in defence of Curée's motion outbid each other in denigrating the Revolution and placed the new monarch on a level with a Capet or a Charlemagne, or even higher.

On the following day the motion was taken to the Senate, where, in view of the Tribunes' vote of confidence, it was not unnaturally passed with almost equal approbation. The Commission appointed to examine the First Consul's reply to the

Senate of 6 Floréal had sent a circular to all senators, asking each one individually to give his honest opinion in writing on what improvements might be made in the institutions of the Republic. All but three – Grégoire, Lambrechts, and, apparently, Volney – replied by agreeing with the findings of the Tribunate.

Two blank papers were returned, attributed to Siéyès and Garat. 'Some made no reply; these were the so-called Auteuil Society, Cabanis, Praslin, etc.'[1] This small minority was still further reduced when the new constitutional Act, the last formality in establishing the rule of Bonaparte, was presented. The only senator to speak against it and make alternative proposals was Grégoire, who demanded (but was naturally refused) that his statement should be included in the official report of the proceedings. Lambrechts and Garat (and perhaps Volney) voted against it.

Opposition from the *Idéologues* in the Senate was further reduced when Cabanis asked for leave of absence on 1 Floréal, and Lanjuinais also absented himself for reasons of health. Destutt de Tracy, as far as we know, never made any protest nor even refrained from voting. ... Thinkers rather than fighters, they were no doubt resigned to a *fait accompli*.

An exception must be made of Volney, who would have preferred a Louis XVIII guaranteeing certain liberties to a Napoleon who suppressed all. He was, however, very perplexed. On 8 Floréal he wrote to Jefferson: 'Would you have preferred the vote of the Army?' Since the accession of the new sovereign was inevitable, was it not better that the authority conferred on him should be granted by civilians rather than by the Army, which was becoming increasingly impatient. Had not Murat, the Governor of Paris, claimed that he would be unable to 'restrain' his troops much longer? This argument, methodically propagated, achieved its purpose and, as we have seen, even influenced Volney. But not for long. Volney tendered his resignation. This, however, was refused, and by decree of the Senate its members henceforth were forbidden to resign.

His action had not been a signal for resistance (as Napoleon had thought) so much as the action of a man who had decided to

[1] Thibaudeau: *Le Consulat et l'Empire.*

remain stubbornly silent. Slow to lose his illusions concerning his young friend from Corsica, he felt more deeply than anyone else the outcome of the Brumairian adventure. But now he had another grudge against Bonaparte – the Moreau scandal. Volney and Moreau had been comrades at Rennes before the Revolution and had fought side by side, the former as a journalist, the latter as a law student. They had not lost touch with each other, and it was Volney who had praised Moreau's qualities to his friends in Auteuil and had thus contributed in no small measure to the hopes which the *Idéologues* had placed in him at the time of the *tridi* dinners.

Moreau's alleged part in the Cadoudal conspiracy was made public on 18 May 1804, the same day as the Senate voted the 'Organic *Senatus Consultum* of 28 Floréal, Year XII', instituting the Empire. Without losing a minute, the Senate had repaired to Saint-Cloud, where its President, Second Consul Cambacérès, saluted the First Consul with the title of 'Imperial Majesty', to which Napoleon replied:

'I accept the title which you believe to be beneficial to the glory of the nation. I submit the law of heredity to the sanction of the people.'

By this it was inferred that a plebiscite would be held, the results of which were a foregone conclusion.

What were the principal articles of this constitution of the Year XII? It entrusted the Government of the French Republic to an hereditary emperor, Napoleon Bonaparte, and determined the principles of the succession. In default of a natural, or adopted, heir, succession was to be bestowed on Joseph and his natural legitimate descendants [to the perpetual exclusion of women and their descendants], and in default of Joseph, on Louis, and his male descendants. There was scarcely any change in the administrative services (*pouvoirs publiques*).

The Senate, it will be recollected, had originally hoped to introduce a vote of veto into the constitution, which would safeguard individual liberties, and have the right to debate any *Senatus Consultum* referred to it. Bonaparte, however, had called this a 'monstrous pretension'. Two Commissions, one on personal liberty, the other on the freedom of the Press, were appointed, but their functions were severely restricted. The first, which was designed to receive petitions from persons who believed themselves to be unjustly detained, or from the families of such persons, could 'invite the Senate to refer the affair to the *Haute-cour impériale*', while the powers accorded to the second were even more derisory. As for the *Corps législatif* and Tribunate, their feeble margin of activity was even further reduced.

The most remarkable innovation was the creation of new titles of an ostensibly aggressive monarchic character. Promoted to the rank of Prince (like all other members of the Bonaparte family, excepting Lucien and Jerome), Joseph and Louis now found themselves addressed by the title of 'Imperial Highness'. Joseph was made Grand Elector, and Louis, Grand Constable. Cambacérès was made Arch-Chancellor; Lebrun, Arch-Treasurer.[1] There were other new posts created, such as Grand Almoner, Grand Marshal of the Palace, Grand Master of the Hunt, Grand Master of Ceremonies, and a Grand Chamberlain (Talleyrand), together with Chamberlains and Almoners-in-ordinary (including two bishops), two masters of the horse (*écuyers cavalcadours*), and pages and heralds-at-arms. The same sort of anachronisms and *Ancien Régime* household were created on behalf of the Empress and Madame Mère. A new Versailles, in fact, was conjured up, where regicides and *sans-culottes*, desperate to become aristocrats, rubbed shoulders with the survivors of La Vieille France, who, in turn, were anxious to reaffirm their status as *gentilshommes* by becoming lackeys, and what is more, lackeys to a usurper.

* * *

The new régime, proclaimed to the sound of trumpets, provoked no particular reaction in Paris. On the other hand, the great trial which had just begun was discussed with passionate interest by all.

On 28 May 1804, the former Commander of the Army of the Rhine was arraigned before the Special Court of Criminal Justice of the Seine, together with Georges Cadoudal and forty-five other persons. But, as Thibaudeau wrote: 'Pichegru had

[1] Murat, the cavalry officer, was made Grand Admiral! (Translator's note).

sentenced himself, Georges had admitted his guilt; only Moreau remained. Strictly speaking he alone was on trial – a trial more serious than the conspiracy itself. *It was a trial between Bonaparte and Moreau, between Caesar and Pompey.*'

The court, although especially convened for the purpose, was not a military court. This nicety for legal formality, however, did not prevent the prosecution from attempting to corrupt witnesses and extract confessions by the most crude methods. Réal, for example, offered one of Moreau's aides-de-camp the rank of General of Division and 100,000 *écus* to denounce his master. The offer was refused. Several of the accused were tortured, including Cadoudal's servant, Picot.[1]

From the evidence extracted, it was obvious that the royalists in London had been completely misled by Lajolais and that Moreau had never made any promises; on the contrary, he had obstinately refused to participate in any conspiracy.

The first time Moreau was interrogated in the Temple, he had made statements which the President of the Court claimed, justifiably, were untenable. Moreau had claimed that he had seen neither Georges nor Pichegru and was even unaware of their presence in Paris. When questioned on this point, he had replied: 'I regarded this interrogation as a police interrogation . . . I did not want a single word of mine to be the cause of Pichegru's arrest.' He had wanted, he said, to reserve his statements for the First Consul only. In fact, on 9 March he wrote to Napoleon explaining his relations with Pichegru: 'I rejected some proposals he made to me, telling him that in my opinion they were the most arrant nonsense.'

It should be said that Moreau had already earned the disapproval of the Directory by his indulgent attitude towards his

[1] '. . . Picot, with a passionate gesture of a man driven beyond restraint, declared to the President of the Court that . . . he had been garotted, scorched by fire, and his fingers crushed in a gunlock. . . . He stretched out his hands towards the judges and the public, crying in a terrible voice, "Look at the marks!". There were on his hands only too surely the marks of the torture he had undergone three months previously.' (Quoted by Fauriel from the shorthand report of the trial, *Procès recueilli par les sténographes*, Vol. IV, p. 335 (1804)). (Translator's note).

former Commander of the Army of the North. Although already aware of Pichegru's treasonable activities on 18 Fructidor, he had not notified Paris of the fact until the 19th. This had earned him a year's disgrace. But in the spring of 1799, when he replaced Scherer, and later Joubert, as Army Commander in Italy, he once again gave brilliant proof of his loyalty to the Republic.

Now he was accused of meetings with Pichegru, who had been determined to kill the First Consul. Several witnesses, however, maintained that as a result of these meetings Pichegru had been so discouraged that he had decided to quit France. But, asked the prosecution, could he deny that he had not broken off relations with the traitor? Moreau, no longer vacillating as he did in politics, but displaying the courage he had shown on the battle-field, replied that there were many traitors, and that '*there were many Republicans who were no longer worthy of the name*'.

On 5 June the courtroom, even more crowded than usual, was suffocatingly hot. All present, among whom Moreau recognized some of his old comrades in arms, notably the courageous Lecourbe[1], were waiting to hear the counsel for the defence. Suddenly Moreau rose to his feet and asked permission to speak first.

'At the beginning of this revolution, which was to have given freedom to the French people, my life was dedicated to the law. The revolution changed my destiny; instead, I devoted my life to arms. It was not ambition that led me to enter the ranks of the soldiers of liberty; I embraced a military career out of respect for the rights of the nation: I became a soldier because first and foremost I was a citizen, and it was as a citizen I served under the flag of freedom, and a citizen I have always remained. The more I loved liberty, the more I was subject to discipline. . . .'

Moreau went on to remind the court that Siéyès had invited him to make a *coup* similar to that of 18 Brumaire, but that he had refused, and of the part he had played on that day, and of his

---

[1] LECOURBE (Claude), 1759–1815. General. Distinguished himself against Souvoroff in the Saint Gothard Pass and assured Moreau's victory at Zürich.

devotion to Bonaparte. Was it not absurd, he said, to accuse him of conspiracy, when his only thought, when peace was made, had been to demobilize his Army of 100,000 men, an Army which had so often been triumphant?

'... Since the victory of Hohenlinden until my arrest, my enemies have never been able to find or accuse of me of any criminal activity on my part other than my freely spoken speeches (*liberté de mes discours*).

'My speeches ... were often in favour of the Government's actions – but sometimes not. *Am I to believe that freedom of speech is regarded as a crime among a people who have so often advocated freedom of thought and freedom of the Press and who even, to a considerable degree, enjoyed these rights under our kings?* If I had really desired to organize, or enter into, a conspiracy, would I have hidden my thoughts? Would I not have solicited a position which would have put power within my grasp? Despite my lack of political acumen – something I have never possessed – I had only to follow examples known to the whole world; examples all the more impressive because they were successful. I knew that Monk was still with the Armies when he decided to plan [the Restoration of Charles II] and that Cassius and Brutus gained Caesar's confidence the better to stab him.'

This magnificent peroration roused the audience to the highest pitch of enthusiasm; the floor shook with stamping feet. Throughout the whole trial the atmosphere had been electric. Fauriel recounts one incident told to him by Bourrienne: 'I can still see General Lecourbe's ... unexpected arrival in court with a young child. Taking him in his arms, he held him aloft and shouted in a voice charged with emotion, "Behold the son of your General". ... All the soldiers present stood up spontaneously and saluted, while a murmur of sympathy ran through the audience. If Moreau had said a word at that moment, the court would have been overthrown and the prisoners freed. It is said that Georges said on this occasion, "If I were Moreau, I would be sleeping tonight in the Tuileries".' But Moreau was not Georges Cadoudal and remained silent.

The trial made a profound impression in the capital, particularly in intellectual circles and among the *bourgeoisie*. Madame

Récamier wrote '. . . At the close of the trial all business was closed down, the whole population was out of doors . . . on the night before sentence was passed, the approaches to the Palais de Justice were crowded with anxious people; there was universal consternation.'

This might be thought to be exaggeration, but her words are confirmed by Chaptal, the Minister of the Interior. The reaction in the theatres to any passages applicable to the Moreau case was such that every day the police were obliged to remove one or two plays from the repertory. 'Even *Phèdre* would have been banned and the Théâtre Français closed, had the trial continued longer.'[1]

It goes without saying that the *Idéologues* were not indifferent to the proceedings. The Auteuil circle considered the idea of helping Moreau to escape; Garat offered to defend him, but to prevent this the *Senatus Consultum*, which had already suspended the jury, also stipulated that the accused should be defended by lawyers.[2] The lawyer appointed to defend Moreau, a man by the name of Bonnet, made an effective speech, but not one to excite the public. Even if Moreau had been imprudent [he argued], he had never been the accomplice of Pichegru and Cadoudal. At the close of the examinations, even the court was convinced of this.

Napoleon knew it too. Through the mediation of Réal and Cambacérès, who were installed in premises next to the Council Chamber, he had exercised constant pressure to obtain the death sentence. On 9 June, when the twelve judges met to decide on the sentence, the one who had prepared the charges, a former 'Montagnard' named Thuriot, stated that the Emperor desired them to pass sentence of death in order that he might then pardon Moreau. 'But who is going to pardon us, if we bring in such an infamous verdict?' exclaimed another judge, Clavier, the Greek scholar. They voted, seven to five, in favour of acquittal.

There remained nothing now but to make known the verdict, as Lecourbe (the general's brother) demanded. The President, Hémart, refused. The Emperor, learning of the vote, had in-

---

[1] Chaptal, *Mes Souvenirs sur Napoléon.*

[2] Nevertheless, according to Bourrienne (*Mémoires* Vol. VI), Moreau's speech was composed by Garat, who was not afraid of antagonizing Bonaparte.

structed him to resume discussions on the basis of new charges and new confessions obtained from the accused. He demanded, through Cambacérès, 'a sentence more in keeping with justice and the interests of the State'. Lecourbe returned to the attack in the defence of justice. Other judges weakened, impressed by Thuriot, who argued that an acquittal would be exploited by the foreign powers, that it would provoke a civil war and force the Government into a *coup d'état*, altogether a picture so menacing that one of the judges (Granger) declared that, sooner than that, it would be better to condemn even an innocent man. A compromise was finally reached; by a majority of eight to four, Moreau was sentenced to two years' imprisonment.

'This is the height of horror and infamy', wrote Moreau on hearing the verdict; 'if it were proven that I had taken part in the conspiracy, I ought to have been condemned to death as a leader. Nobody could believe that I would have played a subordinate role.' Napoleon was furious. Moreau had been given a sentence barely adequate for a pickpocket, he said. As an alternative, Fouché proposed that he should be exiled. Moreau and his wife left for the United States.

At dawn on 10 June 1804, sentence was passed, not only on Moreau, but on all the other accused. Twenty were condemned to death, others to imprisonment, some were acquitted. On the intercession of Josephine, Napoleon commuted eight capital punishments to banishment. Bouver de Lozier was one to benefit from the Imperial clemency. It is significant that the twelve men who were not pardoned were all of plebeian origin.

On 25 June they were taken from the Conciergerie to the Place de Grève, where the guillotine was erected. Georges demanded to be the first to mount the scaffold, and, like a second Danton, asked the executioner to show his head to the crowd. He made his confession, received the blessing of the Church, embraced his friends, and just had time to cry *Vive le Roi!* twice before the blade fell.

During the course of the trial, this lusty, great-hearted Breton had given proof of great courage. He had refused to give any information concerning his arrival in France, or of his stay in Paris, or of whom he had met there. His replies were contemptuous, sarcastic, and brief. But he declared quite frankly that he had wanted to re-install the Bourbons and, if need be, dispose of the First Consul. But he never let drop a word which might compromise his companions, and in particular stressed Moreau's refusal to be implicated in the plot – which was the truth, a truth which in public opinion did no good to Bonaparte.

Such fortitude commands respect, but it does not imply that Cadoudal's cause was necessarily a worthy one. What would have happened to the liberty of France in the powerful hands of a victorious Cadoudal? Had not Bara, the little drummer boy, in the Vendée, when called on to shout *Vive le Roi*, been killed for shouting *Vive la République* instead?[1] The purpose, here, is not to decide between the different sides, but to distinguish between those who remained steadfast to their ideals (whether of the right or the left) and those who cravenly submitted. There were few of the former in the France of 1804. Anyone who sacrificed his life, career, comfort, or who even placed honour before vanity should be remembered. Without claiming him in any way as a hero, let us at least recognize Chateaubriand as one of the latter.

Chateaubriand, who had never wavered in his loyalty to royalist institutions, had however admitted in his *Essai sur les Révolutions* (1797) that the future belonged to democracy. A little later, seeing the First Consul putting an end to chaos and devoting himself to reconciling all Frenchmen, he wrote (as we know) the *Génie du Christianisme*, a valuable piece of propaganda for the new régime. In his preface he wrote: '. . . Every writer who hopes to have a few readers renders a service to society by trying to rally the minds of men to the cause of religion; and should he lose his reputation as a writer, he must devote his energies, small as they may be, to helping the great man who has plucked us from the abyss.'

Bonaparte openly expressed his satisfaction. Meeting the author for the first time at a reception given by Lucien, the First Consul singled him out and engaged him in conversation. Thus *distingué* (as they used to say of royal favours at Versailles), Chateaubriand was able to realize his ambition. In May 1803 he was appointed secretary to the French legation in Rome. In February

[1] Carrier, the Republican Commissioner in the Vendée, on the other hand, drowned and killed some 10,000 men, women and children for not crying *Vive la République*. (Translator's note).

of the following year he was made Minister to the newly created Swiss Republic of Valais, with the promise of an embassy. Before taking up his post he went to the Tuileries to take leave of the First Consul (whom he had not seen since Lucien's reception). But the audience room was crowded and the two did not have an opportunity to meet. Chateaubriand, however, found something sinister about Bonaparte. The following day he realized what it was, in a flash of understanding which he was never to forget. Returning from the Boulevard des Invalides, where he had gone 'to take his farewell' of a cypress planted there by Mme de Beaumont, he crossed the Pont Louis XVI and the garden of the Tuileries. Near the Pavillion de Marsan he heard town criers announcing to 'petrified' passers-by the news of the sentence of death and execution of 'the man named Louis-Antoine-Henri de Bourbon, born 2 August 1772, at Chantilly'.

'It was as though I was struck by lightning. It changed my life, just as it changed that of Napoleon. I returned home and said to Mme de Chateaubriand, "The Duc d'Enghien has just been shot." I sat down at a table and began to write my letter of resignation. Mme de Chateaubriand made no protest and watched me write with the greatest fortitude. She did not hide from herself the dangers I was running. The trial of Moreau and Georges Cadoudal was in progress; the lion had tasted blood and this was not the moment to irritate him. . . .'

Chateaubriand was well aware of the dangers, but on the advice of a friend, he deleted 'angry remarks', and tendered his resignation for reasons of his wife's ill-health. Nevertheless he begged Talleyrand, to whom the letter was officially addressed, to inform the First Consul of the real '*douloureux motifs*' for resigning. Chateaubriand has recounted[1] that his immediate entourage feared the worst. Fontanes, he says, was almost crazy with fear – which is not hard to believe. For several days and almost hourly, his other friends called at his porter's lodge in fear and trembling lest he should have already been arrested.

[1] *Mémoires d'Outre Tombe.*

But the sympathy they had first shown him began to wane. 'Those who had most applauded my action, now avoid me. My presence was a reproach to them.'

The master of France was approaching the steps of the throne. Everyone stepped aside to make room for him; the whole country hailed him.[1] Any feelings aroused in Paris by the Moreau trial were now stifled by the popular acclaim.

[1] The result of the plebiscite, which strictly speaking was concerned with hereditary rule rather than the institution of the Empire, was announced on 6 November: 2,579 *No's*; 3,572,329 *Ayes*, including abstentions.

7

The Iron Sceptre

✢✢✢

PARIS certainly presented a magnificent spectacle on 2 December 1804. The Cathedral of Notre Dame was transformed. The doors were masked by a triumphal arch bearing the arms of the Emperor and ornamented with pyramids; the vaulting was boxed in. As soon as the sovereigns made their appearance, two gigantic orchestras, drowned by the roar of cannon, struck up martial music. The ceremony, so patiently awaited for two whole hours by Pope Pius VII, was about to begin. The actors took their places.

In David's picture of the *Sacre*, one of the most famous in the world, the artist has represented neither the consecration nor the crowning of Napoleon, but the coronation of Josephine, who kneels before a grave and handsome, laurel-wreathed Napoleon, who, very much at ease, in the posture of an operatic Roman Emperor, is about to place the crown on the head of his spouse. Seated in a box beneath that of the painter's own family, we see Madame Mère, the epitome of happiness, watching her Nabulio. But, in fact, Madame Mère was not present. In order not to be a spectator of the triumph of the 'widow Beauharnais', whom she insisted on referring to as 'that woman', she had retired to Italy to stay with Lucien, first in Rome and then at Frascati. Napoleon was already dividing up Europe between his family. But he was furious with Lucien for having married a plebeian, the beautiful Alexandrine Jouberton, whose late husband had been a broker; he was equally furious with Jerome, who was also absent from the coronation, for marrying the simple Miss Patterson. But for posterity, *la mamma* must be shown to be presiding exultant, and the clan solidly united.

We will pass over the details of the service, the liberties taken with the liturgy, the fact that the Emperor crowned himself before crowning the Empress. ... It will suffice to recall one incident, when Napoleon, finding himself for a moment beside his brother, murmured, 'Joseph, if only our father could see us now!'

Everything had been perfectly arranged by the Master of Ceremonies, Louis-Philippe, Comte de Ségur. Fontanes had welcomed His Holiness with a few well chosen words and had succeeded in persuading His Majesty to accept the ritual emblems of the Capet – and indeed of the Carolingian – monarchy: the sceptre, the orb, the hand of justice. Napoleon needed no persuasion. At Aix-la-Chapelle he had bowed before the true, or supposedly true, relics of the great Charlemagne, by whom he was more and more obsessed. The first time that Cambacérès had addressed him as Sire, he had been unable to disguise his joy. How much less now when the Pontiff of Rome pronounced the solemn words: VIVAT IMPERATOR IN AETERNUM!

In the years to come, the reactionary, antiquated, and despotic character of the régime became increasingly marked. On 1 March 1808, Napoleon instituted the Imperial nobility. Conferred in recognition of services rendered, this nobility, although hereditary, did not have the privileges extant before 1789; but its institution was a violation of the principles of equality, inasmuch as elder sons benefited to the detriment of the younger.

Divorced from Josephine and then married to Marie-Louise of Austria (1810), thus becoming the nephew by marriage of Marie-Antoinette and Louis XVI, the Emperor of the French imposed the strict etiquette of the *Ancien Régime* on his courtiers. The court grew even larger. In 1812 it possessed as many as eighty-five Chamberlains and was dominated by the old aristocracy; Madame de Montesquieu, formerly governess to the royal children of France, was appointed lady-in-waiting to the Empress.

This mentality, which one is tempted to qualify as ultra-royalist, not only permeated the court, but also the Government. Thus in the *Mémoires* of Grégoire we find a very curious reference to the election of *muets* [i.e. non-speaking, but voting, members] to the *Corps législatif* by the Senate.

'The selections were made in advance and lists of names were circulated. . . . In default of merit, the following sort of reasons for the choice of candidates were shamelessly put forward: "Genealogy, very old family – one of his ancestors served under Henri IV – extremely rich. Suitable therefore to be a legislator." Other reasons: "Four uncles, Knights of Saint Louis. Parents, Knights of Malta – Decorated with the order of Cincinnatus. *Ergo* legal ability. . . ." "Host to Her Majesty the Empress – attended the coronation – attended the christening of the King of Rome – Qualified".'

This then was the spirit governing the Senate at the height of the Empire and how the *Corps législatif* was henceforth to be recruited. The Senate no longer debated, its only purpose was to vote the decrees presented to it by a *Senatus Consultum*, which had now taken the place of laws. What was left of the Tribunate was dissolved in 1807. The Council of State was purely administrative.

The year of the Austrian marriage was also the year of the establishment of an arbitrary monarch. A decree of 15 March 1810 re-established *State Prisons*, in which suspected persons were confined without trial.[1] There were some twenty of these Imperial Bastilles (including the Temple, Mont Saint-Michel, Vincennes, and the Chateau d'If). In 1814 it was estimated that there were some 2,500 'detainees' – not an astronomical figure perhaps – but there were means other than imprisonment for disposing of embarrassing individuals; some were sent to 'sanatoria', others placed under house arrest, others banished to island prisons.

Not an exorbitant number of arrests, but why any at all? Although Napoleon's popularity was on the wane after the opening of the war in Spain, he was never obliged to subdue any insurrection at home. It would be an exaggeration to say that he employed terror as a method of Government, but he certainly

---

[1] 'The power which [this decree] vests in the Minister to keep persons in confinement without bringing them to trial is so likely to alarm the citizens that I wish to afford them some guarantee against abuses of this power. For example, the decision of the Privy Council may be transmitted to the Attorney General, and this officer should be required to visit the prisoners once a year.' *Napoleon to the Council of State.* (Translator's note).

used fear. The limitless power of his police was terrifying. The year 1810 also saw Savary back as Minister of Police in place of Fouché (who after being reinstated in 1804 was again dismissed for being 'too indulgent' and for having relations with enemies of the régime). More than ever, Napoleon insisted on being kept informed of all that was going on and of what people were thinking, from the humblest classes to his own entourage and his own family. Spying and informing were essential to his Government. Although 'intelligence' was one of the main activities of the police, their powers were greatly increased and 'administrative detention' often replaced the verdicts even of civil courts. Moreover, the magistrature had been drastically purged; the choice of juries was left to prefects. Special courts of an entirely military nature were set up; the rights of accused persons were reduced to practically nil by the *code d'instruction criminelle* and the penal code. The latter re-established the most reactionary punishments; for example, the hand of a parricide was amputated before he was decapitated; branding, the ball and chain, and iron collars were re-introduced for convicts – measures against which Chénier and his friends had fought so ardently in the Year X.

Napoleon was not cruel, but neither was he easily moved to pity. His philosophy of autocracy repudiated the spirit of enlightenment and invoked the shades of the Middle Ages. Had he not gone to the most extravagant lengths to rediscover the historic emblems of the coronation rites, the sceptre, the hands of justice, and the rest? The sceptre however had not been genuine: its staff was made only of silver gilt covered with velvet. What he required was a sceptre of iron.

In 1811 he even instituted a catechism to be used in all the churches of France, which contained the following:

Q. What must one think of those who fail in their duty to our Emperor?
A. According to Saint Paul the Apostle, they would be acting contrary to the order established by God himself and render themselves *worthy of eternal damnation*.

This catechism even imposed military service as a Christian duty, and bishops personally intervened to ensure the success of conscription. If their pastoral letters were too few and insufficiently loyal in tone, the Imperial Government called the episcopate to order. ... The clergy was assured of the constant protection of the Government. A certain prefect was obliged to order his mayors to attend high mass regularly (1808); another was reprimanded for not following a Holy Day procession (1806); Lalande, the astronomer, who had defended atheism in one of his works, was directed 'to print nothing more'. But who could still print under the Empire?

Under the Consulate, books could only be published with the consent of a *commission de révision* under the presidency of the Grand Judge. In 1805 Fouché re-organized the control of all writings by creating the *Bureau de presse*, later to be known as the *Bureau des journaux, des pièces de théâtre, d'imprimerie et de la librairie*. Napoleon was particularly sensitive where the theatre was concerned. Attentive to the reactions of the public and concerned with the effect of political allusions on the stage, he closed down all but eight theatres in 1808. The number of printing houses was also reduced to sixty in Paris, and all printers were registered and sworn. Some weeks previously, the Emperor had, in theory, lifted the censorship on books. A publisher could print what he liked, but at his own risk; so much the worse for him if the police decided later that the work was subversive and seized it.[1]

It was not until 5 February 1810 that censorship was properly instituted and regularized [and entrusted to a Director General of Printing 'charged under our Minister of the Interior with everything that relates to printing and book-selling'].

The policy of the Emperor towards the Press was no less tyrannical, but more complex. Aware of the power of the Press, he wanted to make use of it. On 22 April 1805, he wrote to Fouché: 'Restrain the newspapers a little; get them to insert some good articles. Give the editors of the *Journal des Débats* and the *Publiciste* to understand that the time is not far off when, if I see they are no longer of use to me, I will suppress them and all the others, and only retain one. . . .'

He did not carry out his threat completely. True, of the thirteen papers authorized in Nivôse, Year VIII, only three or four

[1] E. d'Hauterive: *Napoléon et son Police*.

worthy of the name (excluding the official *Moniteur*) remained at
the beginning of the Empire: the *Débats* and the *Gazette de France*
(discreetly royalist in tone); the *Publiciste* (which belonged to
Suard); and the *Décade*. Their circulation was, however, very
limited: *Débats* 1,850; *Publiciste* 2,850; *Moniteur* 2,450; *Décade*
660 (figures for 1803).

The *Décade*, directed by J.-B. Say, was the last refuge of
Republicanism at the beginning of the Empire. It never discussed
political matters, at least not directly, which in itself was a form of
opposition. This organ of the *Idéologues* disappeared in 1807.

Following the death of the Duc d'Enghien and the Moreau
trial, Suard of the *Publiciste* showed great courage – a courage in
great contrast to his behaviour ten years previously, when he had
failed to shelter the fugitive Condorcet. Napoleon had written
asking him to 'guide back' public opinion, which had been 'led
astray' by these two events. 'I am seventy-three years old,' Suard
replied, 'and my character is not so flexible as my limbs. . . .'
He was 'profoundly distressed' he wrote, by 'this act of
violence' and quite understood the dissatisfaction of the people
with 'the Government's interference in a judicial matter submitted to a court of justice'. This reply was not made public; it
seemed wiser to confiscate the newspaper and appoint a new
editor. The *Publiciste* was thus able to survive until 1810, when it
was incorporated with the *Gazette de France*.

On 10 May 1805, Napoleon instructed Fouché to appoint a
censor to the *Débats*, whose salary (12,000 francs) would be paid
by the proprietors of the newspaper. This form of censorship was
later extended to the remainder of the Press, but not always
altogether successfully. Abandoning the idea of using the Press to
his own ends, Napoleon reduced the number of newspapers to
four (September 1811). Up to that date, particularly between 1805
and 1810, Napoleon had frequently given verbal or written instructions concerning what articles should be inserted. He himself
read the daily papers and ordered an analysis of all books, bro-
chures, public notices, speeches, and even sermons, to be submitted to him every ten days. His main preoccupation, though,
was military: to disclose as little of his plans as possible and mislead the enemy; to impress the coalition powers and to damage
England's interests. For example, he had instituted a Press

campaign denouncing the atrocities committed against Catholics in Ireland. In short, war propaganda. As far as internal policy was concerned, he forbade the publication of anything which might cause alarm or despondency. Neither religion nor philosophy were to be attacked – nothing in fact which might revive old Revolutionary scores. He dreaded anything which might make his court or entourage look ridiculous, or impute them with extravagance.

To direct public opinion, maintain and develop confidence, enthusiasm, and zeal, that is what he expected of journalists and writers. But, in the long run, first and foremost, he placed his faith in educationalists. In the field of education, Napoleon in 1811 realized the project, the foundations of which he had laid in the Year X, with the definitive organization of the Imperial University. The 'grand master' of this University, which had the exclusive monopoly of instruction throughout the Empire, was Fontanes (his 'brother-in-law' on the distaff side), who carried out his mission to perfection. 'Produce me men who believe in God', the Emperor had commanded him. The lycées were filled with prayers, devotional exercises, and practices. This was excellent; Catholic teaching was just what was needed. But there had also to be instruction in the classics and literature – Corneille and Bossuet, for example. This too was 'grand and sublime, but *subordinate*', said Napoleon. Scant attention, however, was paid to science, and none to philosophy. But there had to be military discipline; the Imperial lycées were more like barracks than seminaries. Students wore uniform; study sessions, recreation, and examinations were all accompanied by the roll of a drum.

And what of the *Écoles normales*? In the school where Ville-main[1] taught as a young man in 1811, there were only forty students and three or four masters. And what of primary schools? These were in the care of the *Frères des Écoles Chrétiennes*, for, as Napoleon said, he preferred to see village children in the hands of a monk, who knew no more than his catechism, than in the hands of half a dozen savants with no guiding principles or moral opinions.

[1] VILLEMAIN (François), 1790–1870. Professor at the Sorbonne. Minister of Education 1839–44. Liberal historian and Member of the Académie française. (Translator's note).

It was, above all, secondary education that Napoleon wished to organize. What he demanded of his University was that it should develop an aptitude to direct and command, but first and foremost to *obey*, and *obey him*. The aim of the teaching given should be to mould citizens in conformity with the spirit of the institution itself. The colleges and the lycées were to cast the raw material of the nation, the future citizens, in this mould.

*   *   *

The power of the Government was now much stronger than in the days of the Consulate. The Army no longer presented any danger, and open political opposition was unthinkable. In the circumstances, what were the *Idéologues* of Auteuil hoping for, what were they doing and what became of them? And what of Chateaubriand and Mme de Staël? What could a handful of men, 'the depositories of human conscience and reason', achieve in this country dazzled by martial glory? What could philosophy and talent accomplish against force? This is the crux of the matter. Before replying, one thing must be made clear. Napoleon's position, at the height of his triumphs, was not dependent on force alone. He was not only irresistible because he was invincible in war and because of the might of his Armies, nor because of the omnipresence of his police and the solid framework of the State, the zeal of his prefects, judges, and clergy, *but by reason of his own genius*. To ignore this would be ridiculous. Genius: not that the heart and mind of Napoleon Bonaparte were governed by the highest motives – far from it. But he was endowed with super-human, phenomenal qualities – an indomitable will, an infallible memory, a stupendous brain capable of swift judgement, a limitless capacity for work. . . . Confronted with such fantastic powers, unknown to ordinary mortals, it seemed useless to combat him; madness to think one could win. But that did not mean to say one had to prostrate oneself before this superman.

Saint-Beuve put together some scattered notes written by Roederer, which gives us a picture of the First Consul presiding over the compilation of the Civil Code and inspiring the Council of State with a respect based on admiration much more than on fear.

'He could work eighteen hours at a stretch, either on one single work or on different projects. I never saw his intellect flag, I never saw him other than mentally alert, even when his body was tired, or when he was engaged in the most violent exercise, or even when he was in a rage. I never saw his concentration distracted from the business in hand. . . .'

Roederer, the author of these lines, was certainly an admirer, but not a worshipper of Napoleon, and much less a grovelling courtier.

In view of the impossibility of any real opposition to Imperial rule (at its apogee), it is not surprising that the *Idélogues* effaced themselves so long from the political arena. Their strongholds had been dismantled: the Tribunate, *Sciences Morales, Conseil d'Instruction publique*, Central Schools had all gone. In the Senate, they were surrounded by an ever growing majority of 'yes-men'. There was nothing for them to do now but retire gracefully and occupy themselves with their own work.

Nothing sheds a clearer light on the more or less resigned, but at the same time dignified, behaviour of these men (*les boudeurs d'Auteuil*, as Napoleon called them) than a letter written to Fauriel by Pariset, a friend of Volney:

'. . . I have chosen the path of silence: not because I have relinquished my principles, but these must be hidden under a bushel. . . . Confine your private beliefs to a small number of tried friends. . . . Work without cease. . . . Work will liberate and console you. . . . It will be a long time before we hear that a good law is worth more than a blow from a sabre. . . . What to do? Range oneself on the side of the leaders, adopt their maxims and their language? Or live without prostituting yourself, without renouncing your opinions? My choice is made, it is irrevocable.'[1]

This is how Volney chose to live under the Empire, disdaining the advances which Napoleon continued to make to him. After his resignation as a Senator had been refused, he came only rarely to the Luxembourg, and then only 'to place in silence his

[1] Quoted by M. Jean Gaulmier in his *Volney.*

opposition vote in the urn', together with other of his friends in the minority. When he married, it was without the authorization of the Monarch – a recently established practice among senators. Questioned by Napoleon on the subject in a friendly way, he cut him short. Although he did not actually refuse the title of Count, this did nothing to alter his attitude. In 1806, Volney retired to Sarcelles, where he had acquired a property, and devoted his time to horticulture and writing his *Recherches nouvelles sur l'Histoire ancienne*, which was a revindication of free thought.

All in all, his conduct was admirable; not heroic perhaps, but neither was he weak. But can we say the same of Daunou, who had given such proof of courage during the Revolution? It is true that at the time of the Directory he had more or less withdrawn into his precious studies, but during the Consulate he had once again, with fresh vigour, upheld the cause of liberty, so much so that he had roused the anger of the dictator.

A victim of the purging of the Tribunate, he was deeply affected by this mortal blow inflicted on the Republic. This fresh grief, in a life which had known so many tribulations, was too much for him. He fell seriously ill; he had no further heart for the struggle. Saint-Beuve, the protégé of the Second Empire, accuses him of capitulation, but would he have done any better in the circumstances?

It is true that, in a moment of great depression and fearful of losing his position as librarian of the Panthéon, Daunou signed a letter drafted by Fouché, which Davout undertook to deliver to Napoleon. The Emperor was evidently satisfied. He not only retained him in his job, but wrote that he 'sincerely hoped to use his talents in a more worthy capacity, and prayed God to have him in His safekeeping' – a formula revived from the *Ancien Régime*. In fact, a year later, after the coronation, Daunou was appointed archivist to the Empire: an inestimable honour for the former organizer of the Institute, since under an absolute monarchy one owes everything to the sovereign's pleasure.

But for this honour thanks had to be given. Daunou paid his tribute. In a long preface to Rulhière's *Histoire de l'Anarchie de Pologne*, he wrote that it was thanks to the *invariably liberal sentiments* of the Head of State that this work could appear in its unadulterated form, and that it was a noble use of sovereign power to demand a faithful rendering of such an important historical work. . . .

The *invariably liberal sentiments* indeed! But, this formality accomplished (essential if the book was to be published at all), Daunou passed from praise to exhortation. This was 1807, the year of Friedland and Tilsit. Daunou appealed for the liberation of Poland, and somewhat in the manner of Bossuet, traced the line which the monarch should follow and reminded him of what constituted 'a worthy use of victory'. We shall see later to what use the Emperor put this advice.

In another work by Daunou (this time a whole book, not merely a preface), published in 1810, he eulogizes the Emperor even more; indeed to such an extent that at first glance we are appalled. But if we examine the very long title of the book: *Essai historique sur la puissance temporelle des papes, sur l'abus qu'ils ont fait de leur ministère spirituel et sur les guerres qu'ils ont declarées aux souverains, spécialement à ceux qui avaient la prépondérance en Italie*, it is clear that Daunou's real purpose was to influence Napoleon towards a rupture with the Concordat.

Apart from its sycophantic conclusion, the work is in the tradition of the *Idéologues*; it is severely anti-clerical and in no way sectarian.

In the years that followed, Daunou may sometimes have been guilty of weakness, but never of baseness. He accepted the Legion of Honour, but refused the appointment of censor (without succeeding in having his refusal inserted in the *Moniteur*). Like Volney, he too remained in the counter-current of the vast clerical wave which was attacking eighteenth-century philosophy. In his *Destin*, he compared, with great independence and broad-mindedness, the classical and Christian concepts of divinity, and continued to demand tolerance in the name of equity and reason. He was to continue to hold these relatively liberal views under the Restoration, which began by depriving him of his posts, but later, when appointed Professor to the Collège de France, he protested against the *Ordonnances* and resigned.

Cabanis, perhaps the most disappointed of all the discontented Brumairians, was also obliged by the Empire to devote his time to his own intellectual work. True, his real vocation was not so much politics as medicine and philosophy. Although still unable to express his thoughts freely, the work he accomplished in this field shows he was a man of much more independent mind than Daunou. In 1802 he had published *Rapports du physique et du moral*, which Benjamin Constant considered one of 'the finest works of the century', and which, moreover, anticipated Darwin. Three years later, he published another edition, but with a preface which, compared with the first, seems as though he was on the defensive. The passages on fanaticism and despotism are played down, and the indirect but violent satirical attacks on Bonaparte's Government are omitted altogether . . . a terrain which had to be relinquished if he was to fight at all.

But, on the other hand, in his last years this disciple of Condorcet conducted a very noble campaign in the cause of freedom. His letter to *Thurot sur les poèmes d'Homère* is written in defence of 'philosophy' as against Chateaubriand's *Génie du Christianisme*, while his *Causes premières*, addressed to Fauriel in 1806, is in praise of stoicism, 'the simple and consoling religion of Franklin and Turgot'.

In consequence of his disappointments, Cabanis suffered in health no less than Daunou. His final days were clouded with melancholy, but the 'angelic Cabanis' had the consolation of being surrounded by friends. . . . In April 1807 he was persuaded to give up his studies and 'even those philosophic conversations so dear to him', and to retire from Auteuil to stay with Madame Condorcet. In the following spring he went to live in solitude in the village of Reuil, but because of his devotion to his calling this was not really a rest. Accompanied by his nephew, he insisted on visiting neighbouring villages on horseback to attend the sick in their humble homes, dispensing medicines, and bringing gifts of bread and meat. On 5 May 1808 he had a [second] stroke and died. Thus, one of the last, and perhaps the most endearing, of the peaceful Auteuil group, flattered and later spurned by Napoleon, died in obscurity.

Did the Emperor remember the warm support which Cabanis had lent to him in Brumaire? Be that as it may, Napoleon considered it expedient that the Empire should mourn the passing of this great Frenchman and ordered that the remains of this celebrated doctor should be conveyed to the Panthéon.[1]

[1] Their relations had in fact never been completely severed and, from time to time, they had met to discuss philosophy and religion.

The gesture was appreciated: at least, the formalities had been observed. On 21 December 1808, Destutt de Tracy, who had been elected to the Académie française to take the place of his friend Cabanis, made a speech in honour of the doctor which concluded with a eulogy of Napoleon: 'May I add to so many wonderful tokens of respect one to which none other is comparable? I have seen the hero, who is the admiration of the whole world, enjoying the conversation of M. Cabanis, I have seen him appreciating his vast knowledge and delighting in his kindly and noble company, ... and I am happy to see the memory of your illustrious colleague and my esteemed friend linked in some way with the immense fame of the Hero, whose exploits will be an everlasting source of conversation for centuries to come.'

Once again, we find ourselves profoundly shocked, completely confounded by this panegyric coming from a man to whom the word flattery was unknown and whose past record was beyond reproach. Let us try to examine the case further.

Picavet, the author of *Idéologues*, stresses the importance of Destutt's *Mémoire sur les moyens de fonder la morale d'un peuple*, published in January 1798. In this work Destutt preconceived an independent magistrature, as well as a reorganization of the law based on humanitarian and rational tenets. Reading this *Mémoire* helps us to understand 'why the Idéologues refrained from attacking mercilessly a Government which was reorganizing the civil, military, and legal services, a Government which was putting down crime and promulgating the Civil and other Codes. ...' When Destutt made his speech praising Cabanis, part of the programme he had been advocating ten years previously had already been realized by Bonaparte, now Emperor. 'Had he not constructed canals, docks, high roads, bridges, and embankments? Had he not promised a million to whosoever invented a spinning machine and a million to whosoever could replace sugar cane by beet; had he not given Jacquard a pension and decorated Lenoir and Oberkampf?'

Only, adds the same author, in many other respects, Napoleon had refused to apply the concepts of the *Idéologues*.

Very true. But what next?

The explanation which we have sketched for the behaviour of Cabanis and Daunou also applies to Destutt. Rather than be

exiled, rather than lose the tools of their trade, their libraries, these
scholars were prepared to burn a pinch of incense at the altar of
the Caesar whom they had called to power. They could not condemn him absolutely, because not everything he did was damn-
able. Once this rite was accomplished, they could continue with
their own work. The years in question were particularly produc-
tive for Destutt. Between 1801 and 1805 he published the *Projets
d'Éléments d'Idéologie* and numerous works on the formation of
languages, the origin of writing, a *Grammaire*, and a *Logique*.
The last two were the second and third instalments of *Les Éléments
d'Idéologie*. The fourth and fifth parts were published in 1815.
Stendhal 'adored' their works – he had met Destutt in 1817 – and
in his own *Souvenirs d'Égotisme* wrote: 'He is the man I have most
admired because of his writings, the only man who has revo-
lutionized me' ['*le seul qui a fait révolution chez moi. . . .*']

But it is in particular Destutt's *Commentaire sur l'Esprit des Lois*,
written between 1806 and 1807, which calls for attention. In this
work we find not only an ideal constitution, but a complete
exposé of the author's political doctrine, a methodical and profound criticism of hereditary monarchy (obviously inspired by
the Napoleonic régime) and his belief that religion must be a
strictly personal affair. But what emerges from this work is a
sense of pessimism: that under the circumstances it was impossible to resist further.

On the other hand, it is stimulating to find Destutt putting
forward ideas well in advance of his time. For example, on population expansion: 'The problem is to make people happy, not to
increase their number'; and again on colonies: 'It may be profit-
able to establish colonies. . . . But they must be emancipated as
soon as they can stand on their own feet.' It is a pity that these
words of wisdom did not inspire France and the West in the nineteenth century. Destutt was obviously thinking of the disaster of
San Domingo and of all 'the absurd and ruinous wars' made to
conserve conquests: 'an orgy of authority run mad'. This pro-
phetic, liberal *Commentaire*, so hostile to the Napoleonic régime,
was published in 1811 in an English translation in Washington,
and not until 1819 in France.

In 1809, Destutt, who, like the other *Idéologues*, corresponded
regularly with Jefferson, sent him his manuscript with a letter

asking him to have it translated, adding: '. . . but it is of the ut-most importance for me that it should never be known – or at least, not until after my death – that this is my work. If the men-tion of Condorcet's name might lead to suspicion that I am the author, perhaps, it would be as well to suppress it.'[1]

How significant are these lines, written a year after his election to the Academy! And the forbidden name of Condorcet, sufficient to arouse the wrath of the Emperor! Are we not right to have placed Condorcet in the van of the fight for freedom against Bonaparte?

And what of the Emperor? Although he seemed satisfied with the academic homage paid to him, and the apparent submission of Destutt and Daunou, he still regarded these 'metaphysicians', whom he so contemptuously termed 'ideological trash' and 'addle-pated Utopians', with insurmountable antipathy, a criticism all the more unjust since Destutt, the leader of the Ideological school, completely rejected speculative metaphysics and based his concepts on positive and concrete ideas. Today, France possesses a national school of administration, a revised version of the *École libre des Sciences politiques* first conceived by Destutt de Tracy. In 1800 he had pleaded for the institution of a school equivalent to the present-day French polytechnic. But to this he received no more than a formal reply. Bonaparte was no longer interested in science of that sort.

It would be superfluous to discuss in detail the conduct of the other members of the ideological school – Garat, Andrieux, and Ginguené. A word, though, about Jean-Baptiste Say, one of the 'purged' members of the Tribunate. He remained uncompro-misingly hostile to the Emperor, and was later to write: 'Bona-parte reversed the march of civilization . . . it was his ignorance of political economy that led him to Saint Helena. He did not see that the inevitable results of his system would be to exhaust the nation's resources, and alienate the affections of the majority of Frenchmen.'[2] Like Cabanis and Garat, he also maintained a corres-pondence with Thomas Jefferson: the *Idéologues* indeed continued to regard the United States as the 'Hope and Example for the

[1] Gilbert Chinard: *Jefferson et les Idéologues.*
[2] Picavet: *op. cit.*

World', but they were careful not to say a single word to Jefferson of the political situation in France.

The other implacable opponent of Napoleon was Grégoire. At the time of the institution of the Empire, he had been one of the most outspoken members of the minority in the Senate. When hereditary rule was instituted on 12 March 1808, he alone voted against sending a congratulatory address to the First Consul. Two years later, he refused to attend the Emperor's marriage to Marie-Louise. To flatter the Emperor, the police denounced him as a conspirator. Napoleon, however, refused to believe this, and even summoned him to discuss ecclesiastical affairs, but nevertheless continued to reproach him bitterly and put him in the same category as his friends, the *Idéologues*.

The last member of this group with whom we are concerned is Chénier. We have seen him protesting energetically, even violently, in the Tribunate against arbitrary rule. No one had exasperated the First Consul as much as he. Mme de Staël, it will be remembered, on one occasion had even thought it expedient to help him flee the country. But he was not arrested, merely excluded from the Palais Royal, and, although given a university post in 1803, this former *conventionnel* was gravely affected by the decree which ended his political career. He was, moreover, seriously ill at the time, and had to contend with family troubles and loss of fortune. If only he could once again write a play for the Théâtre Français! To this end he sought the sympathetic ear of Fouché. Fouché persuaded him to write a play which ended with a coronation scene. Anxious to see how the public would react, the Emperor approved. Chénier weakly agreed and wrote *Cyrus*; a clumsily constructed play, filled with flattering references to the Emperor, for which Chénier tried to compensate by verses extolling Liberty. The Emperor was not satisfied. On his orders the play was hissed off the stage; it did not even satisfy the liberals. *Cyrus* was given only one performance. Chénier was filled with remorse and chagrin, which were to embitter him to the end of his life.

Nevertheless he still tried to fight on and come to terms with himself. With a proud acceptance of his poverty, he steeped himself in the Greek tragedians and in Tacitus (who was one of Napoleon's pet aversions). He tempered his inspiration and talent, and wrote, in rapid succession, *Tibère* and *l'Épître à Voltaire*.

No sooner was *Tibère* finished than Napoleon ordered Talma to read it to him at Saint-Cloud. To begin with he was very impressed; but before long he rose from his chair and began nervously to stride up and down the room. At the conclusion of the reading he seized Talma by the arm and said: 'Chénier is mad. You can assure him that this play will never be performed.'

But Chénier was by no means mad. Did he really believe that the Emperor would allow verses such as the following to be declaimed in Paris:

> *Là, du nouveau tyran j'ai connu l'âme altière.*
> *J'ai vu les chevaliers, le Sénat, Rome entière,*
> *Tout l'Empire à l'envi, se faisant acheter,*
> *Briguer la servitude et s'y précipiter.*[1]

Chénier was naturally banned from the theatre, and after the publication of the *Épître à Voltaire* (a long, vehement, and sarcastic poem which begins by glorifying the ideals of the *philosophes*) he was dismissed from his job as a civil servant. But in literary circles this was considered Chénier's masterpiece. The *Décade* even dared to praise it, although the rest of the Press treated it with contumely. Chénier was destitute and began to sell his library; Daunou, however, came to the rescue and found him a modest situation in the *Archives*. 'Here's a nice trick Daunou has played on me!' was Napoleon's remark on reading of his appointment.

Ill, in debt, obliged to support a mother, Chénier was soon forced to appeal to the Emperor for help in a letter (dated 22 May 1806) in which he retracted nothing, and in which he never demeaned himself.

The tone of his letter could only command respect. The Emperor gave Chénier a pension of 8,000 francs annually and, better still, as the ailing poet neared his end, sent him 6,000 francs from his own purse. Magnanimity? Liberalism? No. In return, Chénier had been obliged to confine himself to 'pure literature

---

[1] which, roughly translated, with no attempt at poetry, might be rendered as:

'I understood the haughty spirit of the new tyrant. I have seen knights, the Senate, the whole of Rome, the entire Empire, bought and cajoled into servitude.'

and erudition'. He buried himself in solitude and study. The man to whom France owed the *Chant du Départ* was condemned to silence. He produced nothing more during his lifetime. One of his last poems, the very last perhaps, is *La Promenade d'Auteuil*, 'an elegy composed under the imperial régime', published in 1817 under the author's name. Looking back nostalgically on that 'hallowed home of poets', Chénier recalls the evening in Brumaire when the *Idéologues* waited anxiously in the garden of Madame Helvétius for news from Saint-Cloud:

> *Le soleil affaibli vient dorer ces vallons.*
> *Je vois Auteuil sourire à ses derniers rayons . . .*
> *Ah! de la liberté tu vis le dernier jour.*
> *Dix ans d'efforts pour elle ont produit l'esclavage:*
> *Un Corse à des Français a dévoré l'héritage.*[1]

The sun sinks. A voice from the lonely valley summons the poet:

> *Viens; tes amis ne sont plus sur la terre:*
> *Viens; tu veux rester libre et le peuple est vaincu.*[2]

Marie-Joseph Chénier died on 10 January 1811, aged forty-six. Now the question arose: who should replace him at the Academy. Napoleon's choice was Chateaubriand, which provoked a fresh incident in the latent struggle between the Emperor and the intellectuals.

Since his resignation in protest against the execution of the Duc d'Enghien, Chateaubriand's conduct had often been inconsistent. On 8 March 1806, just after the triumphal return of the victor of Austerlitz, he had written an article for the *Mercure* (apropos of some historical book) extolling Charlemagne and the conquering genius of the Gauls. This had pleased the Emperor, who, overlooking his former lapse, authorized and even assisted him to undertake a voyage to the East. But, like Volney twenty

---

[1] The sinking sun gilds the valleys.
I see Auteuil smiling beneath its dying rays . . .
Ah! You saw the last days of freedom.
The years of struggle in her name have brought forth slavery:
The heritage of France has been devoured by a Corsican.
[2] Come, your friends are no longer on this earth:
Come, you would remain free and yet the people are in bondage.

years earlier, Chateaubriand returned from his journey (May 1807) profoundly moved by the sufferings of peoples under despotic rule.

This was the time when the usurper suffered his first defeats at Eylau and on the battlefields of Poland. Chateaubriand, always faithful at heart to the Bourbon cause, had learnt on his way home that the royalists were looking to him for a lead. On 7 July, interpolated into an account of a voyage in Spain, published in the *Mercure*, which he had just bought, Chateaubriand defined the role of the historian, probably one of the finest pieces of journalism inspired by Napoleonic tyranny:

> 'When in the silence of abasement no sound is heard but the voice of the informer and dragging of slaves' chains, when all tremble before the tyrant and it is as dangerous to incur his favour as to deserve his disgrace, comes the historian, entrusted with the vengeance of the nations. In vain does Nero flourish, Tacitus is already born; he grows, unknown, beside the ashes of Germanicus; and even now a righteous Providence has delivered up to a humble and lowly child the glory of the master of the world. Soon, the author of the *Annals* will unmask all false values; the deified tyrant will be revealed as nothing but a ham actor, an incendiary, and a parricide. . . .'

The author this time was openly challenging the Emperor – not personally (Napoleon was then at Tilsit), but his Government and his police.

The article caused a sensation. On 27 July came the news of Friedland and Tilsit, and yet another triumphal return of the Emperor. Napoleon, it was hoped, would be too preoccupied to pay attention to newspaper articles published in his absence. Alas for Chateaubriand, Cardinal Fesch [who, it will be remembered, was the Emperor's uncle] brought the *Mercure* of 7 July to the Emperor's notice. Napoleon was furious and told Fontanes that he would have Chateaubriand put to the sword on the steps of the Tuileries. 'Does he think I am such an imbecile that I don't understand what he means?' Although threatened with arrest, Chateaubriand suffered nothing more serious than an order forbidding him to live in Paris. But what little liberty was still left to the Press was further restrained. The censors and editors of the *Débats*, *Publiciste*, and the *Gazette de France* were replaced and the *Mercure* and the *Revue Littéraire* (formerly the *Décade*) were amalgamated, a further turn of the screw first applied two years previously.

Deprived of his paper (though perhaps well indemnified?[1]) Chateaubriand bought a 'cottage' at Vallée aux Loups, where he disconsolately spent his time planting trees and finishing writing his epic novel, *Les Martyrs*. This time he had to be careful. There was no question now of being a second Sartorius [the Roman hero of Corneille's play, the defender of Republican liberties]. Fouché warned him that the work would be confiscated if it gave the slightest offence to the Emperor.

The Emperor, in fact, was in no way insulted: on the contrary. In *Les Martyrs* he was not compared with Tiberius, but with Diocletian, but a better Diocletian, as Chateaubriand insisted, than the one described by contemporary Roman authors. But some of the characters described in *Les Martyrs* are not cast in such a happy role. These are the 'sophists', in other words the *parti philosophique*, the Ginguenés and the Chéniers, who still enjoyed too much prestige in the Academy. Furthermore, in the character of Hierocles, pro-consul of Achaia, everyone recognized a portrait of the 'hideous Minister of police'. 'Something indefinably cynical and shamefaced emanated from every feature of the sophist. *It was obvious that his infamous hands were ill-suited to wield a soldier's sword, but rather the pen of an atheist or the executioner's axe.*'

Having taken the side of Diocletian, the writer believed that he could insult the pro-consul with impunity. This was a tragic mistake which was to cost the life of Chateaubriand's cousin.

At the time of the institution of the Empire, royalist resistance in the west had not been completely suppressed. From time to time a Chouan leader was caught and shot. In September 1808, seven agents of the Princes were condemned to be shot at Rennes, convicted of dealings with *émigrés* in England. Another of these

---

[1] Joubert maintained 'that gold rained on the dispossessed'. In any case, Chateaubriand, who had been penurious until that moment, was now able to buy a country house. (Translator's note. c.f. *Chateaubriand* by Maurois).

agents had disembarked at Saint-Cast, where he had lived clan-
destinely for several months. This was none other than Armand
de Chateaubriand, the cousin of the writer. On 6 January 1809,
he had embarked with a companion in an attempt to recross
the Channel, but was caught in a storm and driven back on to the
French coast. At the beginning of February, Chateaubriand, the
writer, learnt that his cousin had been arrested and taken to
Paris. He immediately wrote to Fouché, who replied that he was
mistaken; no Chateaubriand figured in the list of prisoners.
Reassured, the writer discontinued his enquiries. It was only at
the end of March, when he learnt for certain that his cousin was to
appear before a military tribunal that Chateaubriand wrote to the
Emperor, enclosing a copy of *Les Martyrs*. Napoleon read the
letter and threw it on the fire. 'Chateaubriand asks for justice', he
said, 'he shall get it'. On 29 March he addressed a second letter to
the Emperor: 'Deign, Sire, to let your clemency redound on
behalf of the family which for centuries has shed its blood for its
country. . . . Had I won more repute in the field of letters, I might
perhaps have had some claim to appeal to your renown. But I
bring to the foot of your throne only a nameless grief and tears of a
faithful subject!'

Hoping for an audience, he did not undress all night. At four
o'clock on the morning of Good Friday, 31 March, Armand was
shot by a firing squad on the parade ground of Grenelle, together
with two of his companions, condemned on the previous day.
On learning this verdict later in the morning, Chateaubriand
hurried to the scene, arriving only seconds too late, and prostrated
himself before the corpse of his cousin. Such at least is the version
given in the *Mémoires*, which has towards the end the epic quality
of *Athalie* [Racine's great Biblical tragedy].

Chateaubriand was accused of wearing his weeds with 'insulting ostentation'. It was a courageous and theatrical gesture.

Fouché's rancour was by no means appeased. Having recognized his own portrait in the character of Hierocles in *Les
Martyrs*, he had the book pilloried mercilessly in the newspapers
under his control and did his best to discredit it in Catholic
circles. But in this he failed. Chateaubriand, the darling of
duchesses, the illustrious *gentilhomme*, remained the favourite of the
Faubourg Saint-Germain. He continued to frequent Government

circles and remained the friend of important officials such as Fontanes. Fontanes was no longer as zealously opposed to the Consular apotheosis as formerly; as President of the *Corps législatif*, it was his duty to pay homage to and congratulate the new Caesar, although as the years went by his speeches reflected more and more the growing concern of a country faced by an endemic threat of war. On 27 October 1808, in the presence of leading members of the Government and other notabilities, he had the courage to make a speech to the Emperor, seated on his throne, a speech which, although filled with fulsome praise, was nonetheless a lecture:

'... The greatest of captains knows that there is something more heroic, more noble than victory. Yes, Sire, we have it from your own lips: authority based on wise legislation and national institutions is more lasting than authority based on armed force. ... The *Corps législatif* must, first and foremost, celebrate peaceful triumphs, which can never bring aught but blessings to mankind.'

This was not the language of unconditional praise. Fontanes even went so far as to criticise Napoleon, who had only recently returned from Erfurt, for leaving almost immediately again for Spain. It was as though he already foresaw the outcome of that disastrous venture.

Grand Master of the University since 1808 and President of the *Corps législatif* since 1804, Fontanes was not to retain the latter post after 1809, but adopted 'almost the attitude of an opponent'. His speech was one of the first signs of disaffection among Napoleon's immediate entourage. When the Emperor returned to France in 1809, he knew that there were plans afoot to overthrow him, and was convinced that Talleyrand and Fouché were betraying him.

The victory of Wagram, at least for the time being, cast fresh lustre on the Imperial régime and restored confidence. It confounded the pessimists and disconcerted the conspirators. But the turning point in Napoleon's internal policy, as we have seen, came with the Austrian marriage. The sumptuous ceremonies which made the niece of Marie-Antoinette Empress of the French inspired the people with no enthusiasm: Paris had become bored with pomp and ceremony. But the great aristocratic families of the *Ancien Régime* now rallied in ever greater numbers to the Emperor. The last remnants of the revolutionary era were 'liquidated', or at least all who were suspected of Republican leanings. The regicide Fouché and Dubois were dismissed. True, France lost nothing by this, but what did she gain by the appointment of Savary, the terrifying 'Duc de Rovigo', of whom Napoleon is quoted as saying, 'If I ordered him to kill his own father he would do so'? But Savary was ordered to reassure the people and he obeyed. He was to treat the Faubourg Saint-Germain with the utmost consideration and to ensure the co-operation of writers. The Emperor told him, 'Treat men of letters well, they have been prejudiced against me by the reports that I dislike them. . . . They are useful men and must be singled out for distinction, since they bring honour to France.' Napoleon had Chateaubriand, in particular, in mind.

Savary's first plan was to share 100,000 francs among poets willing to celebrate the Imperial marriage, but the response was negligible. It was, therefore, decided to put into practice a long-standing plan of Napoleon's, first proposed in 1804. The Emperor had founded decennial prizes of 10,000 and 5,000 francs to be awarded to writers, scholars, and artists on the recommendation of the various classes of the Institute. The first distribution was fixed for 10 November, the anniversary of the Coup de Brumaire. Laplace, Lagrange, Cuvier, and Berthollet[1] were all selected for the award. When, however, the choice of the Second Class (Académie Française) for literature was made known, the Emperor was highly indignant. Chateaubriand, who was the *bête noire* of Marie-Joseph Chénier (who still dominated the Academy), had been passed over.

This came as a shock. Napoleon had earnestly desired that Chateaubriand, the most illustrious writer of the age and defender of Catholicism, should be awarded the prize, counting on it to effect a reconciliation between himself and the author. Montalivet,

---

[1] LAPLACE (Pierre-Simon, Marquis de), mathematician, physician, astronomer. LAGRANGE (Comte Louis de), astronomer and mathematician. One of the founders of the metric system. CUVIER (Baron Georges), founder of comparative anatomy and palaeontology. BERTHOLLET (Comte Claude-Louis), chemist. Discoverer of chlorination and bleaching processes for textiles, etc. (Translator's note).

the Minister of the Interior, urged the Academy to reconsider its decision, but to no avail. Savary thought of a way out of the dilemma: to propose Chateaubriand as the Emperor's official candidate for the next Academic vacancy. By an irony of fate, it was then that Chateaubriand's chief enemy at the Academy, Marie-Joseph Chénier, died.

Chateaubriand hesitated to accept the proposal, but grudingly allowed himself to be persuaded by Fontanes. He stood for election and was accepted. Napoleon was pleased and smilingly said to Fontanes, 'So! Gentlemen of the Academy, you have been foxing me. You have taken the man instead of the book [*Le Génie du Christianisme*]'. He hinted, moreover, that there might be some distinguished 'literary post' for the new member, the 'Controllership of the Libraries of the Empire for instance'.

But there still remained a thorny point: the Oration. The author of *Le Génie du Christianisme* would have no difficulty in opposing his religious views to the atheistic views of the deceased Voltairian, but the rest of his task was hedged round with difficulties. Chénier had been a regicide. 'Could a royalist deliver Chénier's encomium? If he did, should he not, in honour bound, proclaim his fealty to his kings and his abhorrence of the crimes of 1793? Did not that constitute another provocation to the Emperor?'[1] Perhaps he could extricate himself in a peroration glorifying Caesar's ascent to the Capitol and extolling his conquests and the marvels of his reign?

He was mistaken. The Commission whose duty it was to listen to the reading of the speech were appalled; far from being an encomium, it was an indictment of Chénier. Napoleon himself, when the text was submitted to him, was furious. He ordered Daru to send for the author. Chateaubriand recounts how he went to Saint-Cloud, where Daru returned the manuscript, slashed by the Imperial pencil. The peroration was left intact (with the exception of a few words), but all the rest was scored out, the word 'liberty' with a double line through it.

'The lion's claw had been dug all over it and I had a kind of pleasurable irritation in thinking that I felt it in my side', wrote Chateaubriand.

[1] cf. Maurois; *Chateaubriand*.

Daru suggested alterations. When Chateaubriand refused to change a single word, he advised him to write another speech. It was a waste of time. 'There is no remedy for this ill', replied the author, 'if I cannot deliver the speech as it was written, honour forbids me to write another.'

This was undeniably an act of defiance, but dictated by very different sentiments from those of Chénier and his friends. If the Left of the Academy rejected the speech, it was because they saw in it a profession of Catholic and Royalist faith, an indictment of the regicide revolution and an attack on the *parti philosophique*. The 'eulogy' had been a condemnation of the principles and conduct of the deceased poet. It was a strange speech, which exalted religion, legitimate monarchy, and liberty. Napoleon told Daru that, had it been delivered, the doors of the Institute would have been closed for ever and Chateaubriand cast into the lowest of dungeons for the rest of his life.

Napoleon made an even more violent scene with Philippe de Ségur, President of the Académie Française. 'Are all men of letters bent on setting France ablaze? I have done all in my power to pacify the parties and bring calm. Now the *Idéologues* must needs wish to set up anarchy once more. How dare the Academy speak of regicides when I, who am crowned and should have more cause to hate them, dine instead in their company and sit beside Cambacérès!' He even threatened to dissolve the Academy and told Ségur that he deserved to be sent to Vincennes. But the next day he admitted that his anger had been feigned. 'I am not angry with you', he said, 'this is only my policy. What I told you yesterday is what I want repeated.'

Did Chateaubriand really run this risk of imprisonment? It is not improbable, but it has been impossible to establish anything very clearly on this point. All we know is that Savary alternately used threats and bribes in an attempt to rally Chateaubriand to the Emperor's cause. It would seem that the author refused the money. Continually harassed by clandestine police intrigues, the impoverished Chateaubriand retired to his 'humble cottage' in the Valley of the Wolves to write his *Mémoires* and his *De Buonaparte et des Bourbons*. It was his hope that this pamphlet might pave the way to the return of the Bourbons, but so quickly did the fall of the Eagle trace its 'lightning furrow' that events outran the prophet. By the end of March 1814, the Cossacks were at the gates of Paris.[1]

*   *   *

Madame de Staël: we have lost sight of her since the summer of 1802, when, as was her wont at that season, she had visited Coppet but had been refused permission to return to Paris, due to the implacable resentment of the First Consul. Bonaparte was unable to forgive her for Camille Jordan's provocative pamphlet which she had inspired, nor for the *Derniers vus* by M. Necker, nor for her own *Delphine*, which seemed to scoff at everything he stood for. Apart from anything else, Napoleon's irritation was further inflamed by other literary blue stockings jealous of her success, particularly the witty Mme de Genlis, who maintained a *salon* and was a gifted teacher (she had been 'governess' to the children of the Duke of Orleans, including Louis-Philippe). She also had opportunities for spying, which made her one of the most valuable of Napoleon's informers.

Madame de Staël, however, did not give in. She protested that she had in no way inspired her father's book and argued that 'it would be impossible to guide the pen of a man with thoughts so high.' The First Consul was not to be mollified. 'Since she is at Coppet, let her stay there! We'll see next year!' From this it is clear that he was scared of her and recognized her influence. Mme de Staël for her part, who was frightened of nothing so much as indifference and neglect, confided to Lacretelle: 'He fears me. I am proud and rejoice in the fact, but it also frightens me.'

Relying on the support of Joseph, she left Coppet on 16 September 1803 with Mathieu de Montmorency. Forbidden to live in Paris, she installed herself in a house lent to her by her notary, at Maffliers, near Beaumont-sur-Oise, and close to *Des Herbages*, the property of Benjamin Constant, some eighteen miles from the capital.

Benjamin Constant, having been 'purged' from the Tribunate, had been obliged to economize and relinquish his estate of Hérivaux and install himself in the more modest residence of Herbages. This is enough to contradict conclusively the theory

[1] A. Maurois; *Chateaubriand*.

that he entered politics only because of a vulgar love of money.

Benjamin was none too pleased with his new surroundings, but did his best to disguise his feelings. Other visitors followed to Maffliers, and Germaine, who had not abandoned all hope of soon re-opening her *salon* in Paris, felt almost happy. Madame Récamier had even left her Château of Clichy to be nearer to her. The two women had become close friends in Paris in the previous year. Juliette, like Germaine, was a friend of Camille Jordan and had even hidden him for some weeks (he had nearly been arrested after the publication of his book). Her father, M. Bernard, had been imprisoned in the Temple in August 1802 for clandestine Royalist activities, but, thanks to the intervention of Bernadotte and Joseph, he had been released. Madame Récamier had nonetheless joined the opposition and was later openly to express her sympathy for Moreau.

But to return to Maffliers. It was not to bury herself in a cold and gloomy country house that Germaine had made the journey; she counted on returning to Paris as soon as possible. Before leaving Coppet, she had written to Bonaparte:

'Citizen First Consul,

Having learnt last winter that my return to Paris would not be agreeable to you, I have condemned myself, without any direct order from you, to eighteen months in exile. Since then, a few kind words that you have said about me convinced me ... that this exile has lasted long enough and that you would be willing to take into consideration my family interests which make my presence in Paris absolutely necessary. ...'

Germaine went on to promise that she would never write a single word relating to public affairs during her stay in France. On 4 October she returned to the attack, but this time addressed herself to Joseph. Joseph hastened to Saint-Cloud, but his reply, though kindly, was unhopeful. Bonaparte's decision was not long in reaching her: he informed her by Regnault de Saint-Jean d'Angély that her residence was too close to Paris and that she must leave it before 7 October on pain of being conducted back to Coppet by four gendarmes. Police reports, emanating in particular from Mme de Genlis, had considerably exaggerated the number of visitors to Maffliers.

A visit from Benjamin Constant to Fouché had no effect. On 7 October Germaine appeared to obey, but instead of removing herself, she found asylum with Mme Récamier at nearby Saint-Brice. From there, still refusing to consider her cause lost, she wrote again to the First Consul. 'I was living peacefully at Maffliers, assured that you would allow me to stay there, when I was informed that gendarmes were coming to escort me and my two children away. Citizen Consul, I cannot believe it. . . . If you wish me to leave France, do me the honour of giving me a passport for Germany and grant me one week in Paris. . . . It is not like you, Citizen Consul, to persecute a woman with two children; it is impossible for a hero not to protect the weak. I beseech you once more to give me the benefit of your leniency; let me live in peace in my father's house at Saint-Ouen.'

Neither of these letters are mentioned in her *Dix années d'exil*. In the eyes of posterity they would hardly seem glorious examples of resistance to the despot. But, although she begged, did she really bend the knee to the tyrant? There is a note of protest in the second request. She was not merely 'soliciting', but demanding her rights. She could not imagine that the despot would dare to banish the daughter of the illustrious Minister of Louis XVI. Believing herself invincible, protected by the image of the former idol of the people (for whom, now, no one cared a jot), she calmly returned to Maffliers. On Saturday, 15 October, as she recounts in her *Dix années d'exil*, she was seated at table with three friends when there was a ring at the gate. But let her speak for herself. What she says is so evocative and simple that one feels oneself to be in this lonely house. She sees a mounted man dressed in grey. 'He asked to see me. I received him in the garden. As I went towards him, I was struck by the perfume of flowers and the beauty of the sun. . . . He told me he was the Commandant of the Gendarmerie at Versailles, but had been ordered not to wear uniform for fear of frightening me. He showed me a letter signed by Bonaparte, ordering me to move myself forty leagues from Paris, and instructing me to leave within twenty-four hours. . . .' She replied very calmly, or so she says, 'It may be all very well for conscripts to leave in twenty-four hours, but not for a woman and children.' She proposed therefore to the gendarme ('the most literary of gendarmes') that he should accompany her to Paris, where she needed to stay at least three days to arrange for her departure. The gendarme agreed and mounted her carriage. Madame de Staël stopped at Saint-Brice just long enough to embrace Juliette de Récamier, who swore eternal hatred of Bonaparte, and long enough to soften the heart of Junot, who was staying there at the time. He too went to Saint-Cloud to plead her cause. But it was a waste of time. The interventions of Regnault, Fontanes, and Lucien only redoubled the Consul's anger, who repeated:

'Yes, yes, I know her, *passato il pericolo, gabbato il santo*.[1] Between us two there will never be either a truce or peace. She has only herself to blame, let her bear the consequences.'

In the apartments, which she had been careful to acquire in the rue de Lille, she imagined she could once again resume her former life with her friends, recalling the beginning of the revolution and the glorious days of M. Necker. But on the following morning the gendarme was back to remind her it was time to leave. She begged for one more day's grace and yet another, and to gain a little respite accepted the hospitality of Joseph (who once again pleaded in vain on her behalf) and his wife at Mortefontaine. Would she return to Coppet? No, she decided definitely to go to Prussia.

The ever-devoted Joseph, whom she awaited at an inn at Bondy (did she still hope that Napoleon would change his mind?) came with news from Saint-Cloud that the French ambassador in Berlin would give her a warm welcome. She finally left, accompanied by Benjamin Constant, who sustained her 'with his astonishing conversation'. On the morning of 26 October 1803 they were at Metz, where the Prefect gave receptions in their honour. She stayed a fortnight in this town, where Charles de Villers, the *émigré* officer who had initiated her in the works of Kant and with whom she had been in correspondence for a year, came to meet her.

Brought up on the *Encyclopédistes*, Germaine had studied seriously the new philosophy and foresaw how much her forced stay in Germany might enrich her. From here she would raise all Europe against the tyrant. If *he* had his armies, *she* had her ideas,

[1] *When the danger's gone, the saint is forgotten.*

her talent, and powerful connections, not forgetting the writers who would be pleased to meet her. But were they all really so pleased?

At Weimar, which captivated her, and where she stayed two months, she met Goethe, Schiller, and Wieland. Her assurance astonished them. Schiller, who spoke French badly, admitted that he found her perpetual questioning 'a torture'. She summoned Goethe, who was convalescing at Jena, to return to Weimar – 'If you don't come back on Monday, I confess I shall be somewhat hurt' – and to whom[1] she said, when he suggested that perhaps she did not understand him perfectly, 'Monsieur, I understand everything that deserves to be understood; whatever I don't understand does not exist.'

It was in Weimar that the idea came to her of writing a book on Germany, on an intellectual and pacific Germany. In Berlin, where she was treated like an Ambassadress and presented to the widowed Queen Mother of Frederick William II and to the beautiful Queen Louise, she missed the *salon* of Weimar. Berlin was full of spies, plots, and intrigues. The English newspapers spread calumnies about France, not only about its leader. The news of the execution of the Duc d'Enghien was spread abroad and 'German national pride was wounded by the manner of his arrest'. Passionate interest was taken in all whom Bonaparte had persecuted or driven out. Germaine was now even more of a celebrity than when she had first arrived; when the death of her father obliged her to return to Coppet (24 April 1804), she had already become the symbol of opposition.

She set out for Switzerland accompanied by Benjamin Constant and Wilhelm Schlegel [brother of Friedrich] whom she appointed tutor to her son. He accompanied her everywhere and ended by 'Germanizing' her, as it were, and helped her to develop the important book which she already had in mind.

Six years, however, were to pass before *De l'Allemagne* was published. In the meanwhile she visited Italy (December 1804–June 1805) which was to result in *Corinne*. After which began 'the great years of Coppet'. Among the succession of celebrated

---

[1] In fact to Henry Crabb Robinson, from whom she was taking lessons in German metaphysics. (Translator's note).

visitors who came to see her here was Chateaubriand, to whom she confided her homesickness for Paris. But Chateaubriand, who was not yet the stubborn enemy of Napoleon, was irritated by her complaints. 'In my eyes, what had she to be unhappy about, living on her estates, surrounded by all the comforts of life? What sort of misfortune was it to possess fame, leisure, and peace in wealthy retirement, in comparison to the thousands of victims without bread, without a name, without help, banished to the four quarters of Europe, while their relatives perished on the scaffold.'

'Exile': a word constantly on the lips of the Châtelaine of Coppet. Misery, solitude, and unhappiness! 'No matter where, the exile is always alone', said Lamennais. But all the greatest intellects of Europe continuously flocked to Madame de Staël's princely home, and every day thirty guests sat down to her table. Despite the debt of two millions, which Napoleon still refused to pay her, she was enormously rich. Chateaubriand, for his part, had nearly died of hunger in a fireless garret in London in 1793.

At last, in April 1806, she packed up her things and left for Auxerre. She did not remain there long, however. It made no difference, wherever she was – at the nearby Château de Vincelles, Blois, Rouen, or the Château d'Acosta, where she finished *Corinne* – the Emperor, though now in East Prussia, never lost sight of her. 'That woman is a real crow . . . pack her off to Lake Leman', he had said.

Fouché, however, who found it very useful to keep himself informed by intercepting the letters she wrote and received, showed himself more indulgent and allowed her to slip into Paris.

What was she doing? Was she plotting? She saw many men of letters and had given a few dinners. . . . She certainly did not discourage the spirit of resistance which was smouldering, nor the hopes of royalists who were speculating on the defeat of the usurper in East Prussia. While busying herself with the production of her forthcoming book, she still obstinately clung to the idea of establishing herself near Paris, where she might receive visitors. On her behalf, Benjamin Constant solicited Fouché's permission to buy a property at Cernay. Fouché made one condition. Madame de Staël must introduce some eulogy of the Emperor into *Corinne* – and even hinted that in that case the two millions would be refunded to her.

She refused. She was prepared to delete passages, but she would
not add a word of flattery. Although in March 1803 she had been
ready to slip in 'a printed eulogy' into the new edition of *Delphine*,
this time it would be difficult to accuse her of playing a double
game. She was now the Emperor's implacable opponent and
realized that she could not remain so with impunity. At the end of
April she left for Switzerland. Her departure corresponded with
the publication of *Corinne*, which caused a sensation.

The Emperor was not indifferent to this literary success. After
his victory at Friedland 'he had planted his eagles on the banks of
the Niemen. He was in camp at Osterode when he received a
copy of *Corinne ou l'Italie*. It was night. He thumbed through the
pages and then sent for Talleyrand. The ex-bishop arrived,
yawning, rubbing his eyes. . . . "Read me that", said Napoleon.
But after listening for a few moments the sovereign grew impatient. "Rubbish", he said, "it's a waste of time!" '[1] In Saint
Helena he took the book up again only to reject it once more.
This new novel, even more so than *Delphine*, contained everything displeasing to him: it was a vindication of the rights of
women, with a theatrical identification of the author with her
heroine; it expressed sympathy for England, represented by the
handsome Oswald, and the superficial side of the French character
in the Comte d'Erfeuil; it extolled the opening up of Italy and
foreign cultures.

At the end of 1807, Germaine de Staël left again for Germany,
still accompanied by Schlegel. She visited Munich and was
presented to the Court of Vienna, and was received everywhere
with the honours due to the 'adversary of the detested enemy'.
Her triumphal progress only resulted in redoubling Napoleon's
hostility towards her. Only six months earlier he had been reassured to see her on the farther banks of the Rhine. In December
1807, at Chambéry, on his way back from Milan, he had granted
an audience to young Auguste de Staël, who had come to ask
him to put an end to his mother's exile (and to reimburse the two
millions). Admitting that she was not a '*méchante femme*', he nevertheless flew into a rage when her son told him that she wanted

[1] Françoise Eubonne, *Une femme témoin de son siècle: Germaine de
Staël* (Flammarion).

to devote herself to literature: 'To talk of literature, morals, the fine arts, and everything under the sun, is to indulge in politics. . . . Women should knit. If I let her come to Paris she would make trouble; she would lose me the men around me; she would lose me Garat. Was it not she who lost me the Tribunate? . . . Let her go anywhere she likes – Rome, Naples, Vienna, Berlin, Milan, Lyons, even London, to make "libels". Only your mother could be miserable when she has the whole of Europe at her disposal!'

He had left her free of all Europe, believing her harmless once away from Paris. Now he saw that she was a ferment of European resistance.

Madame de Staël returned to Coppet in June 1808. A year later she made a brief visit to Lyons, where she met Madame Récamier (whose Parisian *salon* had become the centre of all the opposition and in which Benjamin Constant cut a brilliant figure), but her chief preoccupation, apart from her incredible sentimental involvements, was to finish *De l'Allemagne* and prepare for its publication in France. Authorization to live in France, provided she did not come near Paris, still held good, and in 1810 she again left Switzerland with all her court – Juliette Récamier, Mathieu de Montmorency, Benjamin Constant, Schlegel, etc. At the château of Chaumont and later at the neighbouring château of Fosse, she corrected the proofs of her work and once again almost found happiness in the satisfaction of a work completed.

Alas, she was soon to learn that her book had been condemned to be destroyed. This was in the year 1810, the year of tightening restrictions, of the establishment of literary censorship, of the replacement of Fouché by the unmitigated scoundrel Savary. With regard to the censor, Madame de Staël had believed herself to be in order once having obtained a permit to publish the first two volumes of the work. Juliette Récamier took the proofs of the third volume to Paris on 25 September, with a letter from Germaine to Napoleon, appealing to him to read it and give her an audience. But on the 27th Germaine was asked by the Prefect, on behalf of Savary, to leave France within forty-eight hours and to hand him the manuscript and proofs. Moreover, the copies printed by Mame of Tours were already under seal. Feverishly,

Germaine multiplied her pleas and protests. But there soon arrived a letter, dated 3 October, signed by the Duke of Rovigo. It accorded her no more than a week's delay. He went on to say that it would be an error on her part to think that it was because she had made no mention of the Emperor in her book that he had ordered her exile; the book was not worthy to include his name. 'Your exile is the natural consequence of the conduct you have consistently followed for several years. It seems to me that the air of this country does not suit you at all; we are not yet reduced to seeking as models the peoples whom you so admire. ꞏ 'Your last work is in no way French. It is I who stopped its publication. . . .'

Several days later *De l'Allemagne* was destroyed. Nevertheless, the author had succeeded in saving her original manuscript. As for the copy sent to Napoleon, he had thrown it on the fire.

It is easy to understand his fury. The praise lavished by Madame de Staël on the vitality of the Germans, which she sums up in one word, 'enthusiasm', (that is to say a spiritual, inner *élan*), cruelly brought to light the moral and intellectual poverty of a France perverted by despotism. The last sentence of the book rings out like a reproach, an appeal to the French peoples to reclaim their heritage. 'O France, land of love and glory! If "enthusiasm" is once extinguished on your soil, if all is calculated and reason alone inspires a scorn of dangers, of what use are your beautiful skies, your brilliant intellect, your so fruitful nature? An active intelligence, a well tempered impetuosity would make you masters of the world; but all that you leave behind are torrents of sand, terrible as a flood, arid as a desert.'

This much said, is there any encouragement in this book for German national resistance to Napoleon? Certainly not; Madame de Staël was not writing political propaganda, but painting a vast picture of a great neighbouring people of whom the French knew practically nothing. It is a dazzling grandoise essay on the genius of a nation, which later was to inspire the youthful fervour of Renan and Michelet. Since Voltaire discovered England, had anything more *important* ever been read? And since the post-humous work of Condorcet, what French work had paid greater honour to France's vocation—which is to lead the whole world intellectually.

By destroying *De l'Allemagne*, the *Idéophobe* won his greatest victory over the spirit.

* * *

Madame de Staël's account of her return from Blois to Coppet contains an extremely evocative picture of the Empire under the iron sceptre. 'At fifty leagues from the Swiss frontier [she writes] France bristles with fortresses, prisons, and towns serving as prisons. One saw nothing but captives everywhere. . . . Dijon was filled with Spanish prisoners who had refused to swear allegiance. At Auxonne there were English prisoners, and at Besançon more Spanish and also 'exiled French' held in the citadel. . . . On crossing into Switzerland one caught sight, on a high mountain, of the dread fortress of Joux, where state prisoners are held and where Toussaint-Louverture died of cold. . . . Nothing can convey to the few free nations that remain on this earth the complete absence of security which was the normal condition of all human creatures under Napoleon's Empire.'[1]

Coppet had seen the last of its great days. Barante, the Prefect of Leman, and Corbigny, the Prefect of Loir-et-Cher, were both dismissed for allowing the manuscript and several copies of *De l'Allemagne* to have escaped their vigilance. Barante's successor forbade Germaine to travel more than two leagues from Coppet. In August, Mathieu de Montmorency, who had come to visit her, was punished for his pains by an interdiction forbidding him to come within forty leagues of Paris. Soon Juliette Récamier suffered the same fate. The village of Coppet was crammed with spies. Germaine's servants were bribed to report on all the happenings in the château itself; her correspondence was read by police agents. Life became untenable in Switzerland. But where could she go? She was refused a passport for America and forbidden to live in Italy. In 1812 she decided to tour Europe. One can only be astonished by such stubbornness, by such courage.

On the afternoon of 23 May, Germaine, after ordering the dinner, climbed into her open carriage accompanied by M. de Rocca[2]

---

[1] *Ten Years of Exile.*

[2] Her second husband, a young Genevese officer of Piedmontese origin, wounded in the Spanish war. She had just borne him a child and had married him secretly. The Baron de Staël had died in 1802.

and her daughter Albertine, with no other visible luggage than a fan. 'They did not return for dinner until July 1814. The afternoon drive was an immensely extensive one: it took them to Vienna, Kiev, Moscow, Saint Petersburg, Stockholm, London, and Paris before they saw Coppet again.'[1] It was not until 2 June, ten days after her departure, that the police were aware that Germaine was missing. By that time she had crossed into Austria.

*   *   *

October 1812. It was only a month since Germaine de Staël had stood on the walls of the Kremlin admiring the gilded cupolas of the Muscovite churches and the sinuous course of the river Moskva, 'unstained with blood since the Tartar invasions'. Now Napoleon himself was standing on the self-same spot, watching the capital of all the Russias burning. No historic picture is so indelibly inscribed on the imagination of the French as the slow retreat of the Grande Armée from the burning city, stumbling through the snow, each day bringing fresh disasters. When the army set out it had numbered seven hundred thousand men, only a third of whom were French, the remainder being made up of Germans, Poles, Italians, Illyrians, and Spaniards. Its losses in dead and prisoners finally amounted to five hundred thousand. While Ney, in the rearguard, held off the Cossacks and partisans, the Emperor remained at the head of the long column. From time to time, messengers brought him dispatches from France. On 6 November, between Vyasma and Smolensk, he received an incredible report of an event which had occurred in Paris a fortnight previously.

'An obscure General [Malet], who had been under arrest since 1808, after escaping from the sanatorium to which he had been transferred, presented himself at a barracks, dressed in General's uniform, and furnished with false papers which he had forged in prison. He announced to the Commandant of the barracks that Napoleon had been killed in action at Moscow and that the Senate, secretly convened, had decided to re-establish the Republic. He ordered the Commandant to call up his troops,

[1] J. C. Herold: *Mistress to an Age.*

and putting himself at their head he marched to the prison of La Force to liberate Lahorie and Guidal,[1] two Generals imprisoned there. To them he communicated the news of Napoleon's supposed death and persuaded them to accept the false decrees of the Senate. He then went on to arrest the Minister of Police, the Duc de Rovigo, and the Minister of War, the Duc de Feltre, and brought them to the Conciergerie. He instructed Frochot, the Prefect of the Seine, to prepare a room in the Hotel de Ville for the provisional Government and ordered a Colonel of one of the regiments garrisoning Paris to picket all the entrances to the capital. All these orders were carried out without a hitch. The success of the enterprise was only foiled because he himself lost his head after shooting and wounding Hulin, Commandant of Paris.'[2]

Jules Barni, to whom we are indebted for this summary of events, has also quoted M. Thiers's comments on this extraordinary attempt by Malet.

'So much credulity in believing the strangest orders, so much readiness in obeying them, reflects no discredit on the protagonists, who were so constantly misled and who were accustomed to blind obedience, but rather on the régime which made such things possible. Under a régime . . . in which one man, and one man alone, combined in his person Government, Constitution, and State, a man who every day played with his own fate and that of France . . . it was quite natural to believe in his death, and once his death was accepted, to seek some sort of authority from the Senate and to continue meekly to obey without question. . . . In a despotic State, it is the man

---

[1] It will be remembered that it was Guidal who treacherously arrested Frotté, the Norman Chouan leader. (Translator's note).

[2] This scene took place at night in the Place Vendome, where Hulin had his residence. Half awake and impressed by Malet's aplomb, he was prepared to obey just as Frochot and the others had done. It was his wife who put a spoke in his wheel by shouting from an alcove, 'Ask him if he has a warrant'. Malet's pistol shot fractured Hulin's jaw, hence his nickname *Bouffe-la-balle* ['nosh-the-bullet'] by which he was for ever after known in the army. General Lahorie was former Chief of Staff to Moreau.

brave enough to lay his hand on the rudder of State who is master; this is what gives rise to palace plots. . . . But, and this is something of which no one even thought, Napoleon had an heir. It was this fact that angered and disturbed the Emperor. Caulaincourt,[1] who was one of the very few men whom Napoleon took into his confidence at the time, recounted that "he seemed wounded to the quick". "The French are like women", the Emperor said, "one must not absent oneself from them for too long." '

It was only on 4 December, at Smorgoni, that the Emperor summoned his Marshals to tell them of his intention to return to France with all possible speed. True, his Marshals, Dukes, and Princes, knowing that their own fate depended on his crown, were unanimous in persuading him to leave immediately. Murat and Prince Eugene, indeed, had already urged him to so do earlier. On this occasion he had feigned one of his famous rages, claiming that only a mortal enemy could propose such a thing, and even drew his sword on Murat.

The following day in 30° of frost, Napoleon departed with Caulaincourt by coach, which he quickly exchanged for a sledge. During the journey he confided a thousand and one reflections on the current situation, on his plans and on mankind in general. When talking to this scion of a great feudal family, one of Napoleon's favourite themes was the role of the aristocracy in the State, the umbrageous attitude of the Faubourg Saint-Germain, and the obstinacy of the petty nobility: 'They'll come back because they like power and, above all, the court. . . . But it will be too late if they tarry. Today they are almost on the side of addle-pated fellows like La Fayette and Tracy, who inveigh against despotism, as though there was despotism in a country where they are free to shout, intrigue, and criticize as they please.'

As they approached closer to Paris, fresh dispatches brought the conversation round to the Malet affair. No sooner was Malet arrested than he had been tried and shot with his accomplices. But who was right? Savary, who maintained that Malet had

[1] CAULAINCOURT (Louis, Marquis de), Duc of Vicenza 1772–1827. Master of Horse and Ambassador to Russia. He represented Napoleon at the Treaty of Châtillon.

worked alone, or Clarke, who, on the contrary, believed that the plot had ramifications in the Senate?

On 18 December, at fifteen minutes past midnight, Napoleon arrived in Paris, only thirteen days after leaving Russia – a record for the time. On the following morning, indefatigable as ever, Napoleon received his Ministers one by one, beginning with Cambacérès and ending with Savary, whom he retained for two hours. Savary excused his conduct in the affair – how could he, he protested, clad only in his dressing gown, resist five armed soldiers? He explained that Malet had worked alone and that there was no question of a plot, a statement which prompted Napoleon's remark: 'With us everything is organized in such a way that at a time of crisis a corporal and a few men could seize the rein of Government.'

Who was this Malet? Had he really worked alone? Everyone knows his reply to the President of the Court when asked if he had any accomplices: 'You yourself, Monsieur, and the whole of France had I been successful.'

Claude-François de Malet, a young musketeer of the Maison du Roi before 1789, had embraced the Revolutionary cause with enthusiasm. During the Consulate he had continued brazenly to air his Republican views and at the time of the coronation had refused to illuminate the garrison town of Angoulême of which he was Commandant. He was always in conflict with the Prefects of the various garrison towns to which he was posted. In Rome, in 1807, he was accused by the Ambassador of embezzlement, but how many officers in Italy had clean hands? He was, however, recalled to Paris. Deprived of his command, he frequented secret meetings of Jacobins, who like himself were mostly natives of the Jura. This group was politically unimportant. It was a different matter, however, with the group centred round Servan, the former Minister of War, which comprised such liberal senators as Grégoire, Garat, Destutt de Tracy, Volney, Lanjuinais, and Lambrechts, and important officials such as Jacquemont of the Institute, who, in 1802, had acted as intermediary between Moreau and the Auteuil circle. These men were carefully planning the restoration of a Republic in the event of Napoleon's death in battle. Fouché, aware of what was going on, but no doubt in agreement, turned a blind eye to their activities. One is reminded of his more or less lenient attitude at the time of the *dîners du Tridi*. But, in 1808, Servan died. Malet succeeded in contacting Jacquemont, who disclosed to him the existence of a project to re-establish the Constitution of the Year VIII.

Having learned what he wished to know, Malet, it must be confessed, acted in a thoroughly disloyal fashion. He planned his first *coup* in 1808, unknown to Jacquemont and the others, but in such a way as to turn suspicion on them should things go awry. Having gained the support of a number of embittered officers, he planned to imprison Cambacérès and bring out the Paris garrison. He had printed a fake *Senatus Consultum*, which outlawed Napoleon and instituted a 'Dictature' consisting of ten members, including himself and Moreau. He prepared bills to be posted and an 'order of the day' for the Army. But through an indiscretion, all was revealed to Dubois, the Prefect of Police. Malet was arrested and imprisoned. In his report, Dubois exaggerated the whole business, accusing all the liberal senators and Jacquemont (who was arrested on the false testimony of Malet) of complicity. Fouché, on the other hand, played the matter down. A police committee, convened by order of Napoleon, completely exonerated Garat and Destutt. But, in Napoleon's eyes, the matter was not quite so simple. '. . . unlike you . . . I can see that there is obviously a plot somewhere. What society do these people frequent? Benjamin Constant must be mixed up in this in some way. Is that guttersnipe still at large in Paris? . . . I don't suspect Garat, but he is weak-minded. I would not be surprised if he were to become involved in some ill-considered scheme and end by compromising himself.'

Fouché's point of view, nonetheless, prevailed in Paris. The senators mentioned in Dubois's report were not questioned, and in 1809 a number of arrested suspects were set free, including Jacquemont. Malet remained under lock and key, but was later transferred to a sanatorium, from where, as we have seen, he was able to prepare his second and better plot of 1812.

His apocryphal *Senatus Consultum* named the fifteen following as members of the provisional Government: General Moreau, President; Carnot, ex-Minister, Vice-president; General Augereau; Bigonet, ex-legislator; Destutt-Tracy, senator; Florent-Guyot, ex-legislator; Frochot, Prefect of the Department of the Seine;

Jacquemont, ex-tribune; Lambrechts, senator; Montmorency (Mathieu); Malet (General); Noailles (Alexis); Truguet, vice-admiral; Volney, senator; Garat, senator. Two names on this list, Montmorency, the friend of Mme de Staël, and Noailles, represented the Royalist faction. The National Guard were entrusted to La Fayette, the Army to Masséna. What strikes one most about this list of names is that Malet still placed the little group of *Idéologues*, the nub of liberal senators, at the heart of the Government.

Were they aware of the role destined for them? Apparently no more than in 1808. But was this Napoleon's opinion?

On 20 December 1812, when Lacépède, as spokesman for the Senate, headed a delegation assuring the Emperor of their loyalty, Napoleon had insisted on the hereditary character of his Empire. 'Our forefathers', he declared, 'had as their rallying cry, "*Le roi est mort, vive le roi!*" These few words sum up the principal advantages of monarchy. . . .'

And later, in an address to the Council of State, after expressing his satisfaction with the love of the people for his son, and his belief that the people were convinced of the benefits of monarchy, he once again blamed all the evils that had befallen France on the *Idéologues*. Who, he asked, had proclaimed insurrection as a duty; who had sung the praises of the masses and raised them to a sovereignty which they were incapable of exercising; who had destroyed the sanctity and respect for law; who had formulated laws no longer based on the hallowed principles of justice . . . laws which were determined solely by the whim of a handful of men ignorant of the civil, criminal, administrative, political, and military legal codes?

Thus, just as in the days of the Consulate, it was 'Ideology' and Ideologists, that is to say Republican ideals and free thinkers, which he still bitterly resented. For twelve years he had been obsessed by Ideology and *Idéologues*. When he first heard of the Malet plot, had he not exclaimed 'What, another Ideological *coup*!' Had he not immediately thought of arresting, not only Jacquemont, but Tracy and the other so-called accomplices of 1808?

To rid his régime of democracy once and for all, Napoleon in concluding his address showed himself even more trenchant.

'Behold then the principles from which the Council of State of a great Empire should never depart; it should be courageous in the face of adversity, taking example from Harlay and Molé, and be prepared to die in defence of its sovereign, its throne, and the law.'

The war he was asking Frenchmen to continue had started twenty years previously.

> *The Republic summons us,*
> *For her a Frenchman must be prepared to die.*

But it was no longer a Republic which summoned Frenchmen. Now they were being sent to their death to defend a throne.

8

Treachery and Loyalty

✦✦✦

THE Emperor once again nervously resumed the machinery of State. He tightened up the nuts and bolts, he organized a regency, and reduced the role of the *Corps législatif* to practically nil.

With Malet shot, Chateaubriand in disgrace, Madame de Staël in exile on the shores of the Baltic, with the Press gagged, the intellectual élite more discouraged then ever, could one still speak of internal resistance?

The clergy were disenchanted; officials and men of property alike were worried and, even more serious, a new opposition was making its presence felt – the people themselves, a frightened and sobered people. Nowhere was this more obvious than on the Eastern borders, on the roads leading to a Europe plastered with battlefields, roads which once had carried waves of exultant warriors and repatriated, victorious regiments, but roads which now, after the Battle of Beresina, fought against the Russians, saw nothing but armies of spectres returning.

On 8 January 1813, hundreds of thousands of conscripts were called to the colours. Erckmann-Chatrian in his *Histoire d'un Conscrit de 1813* paints a moving picture of the mood of the people in Lorraine at this time. It was not so much that the people wished to rise in revolt against the Emperor, but that they no longer wanted to fight for *him*.

What was the proportion of malcontents? What is certain is that, from the beginning of the war in Spain, there was widespread dislike of and resistance to conscription – and not only in the West, where a refusal to serve had become the rule. In 1808 it was estimated that more than 300,000 men called up had refused to join the colours, not counting the thousands who deserted. A little known, but very significant, fact was the desertion in 1810 of the future Curé d'Ars, at that time a young recruit in the neighbourhood of Lyons. Taken by a comrade into the Maquis, he first had scruples and went to report to the local mayor. 'This man, like many Frenchmen at that time, was against Napoleon and had hidden a certain number of mutineers. He persuaded the newcomer to do as the others.' The young seminarist, after careful reflection, returned to the Maquis, only escaping the vigilance of patrols with great difficulty. One day, while hiding in a pile of hay, he was wounded by the probing sabre of a gendarme and was only just able to restrain a cry of pain. Later he showed no contrition for his behaviour nor, would it seem, was anyone else in the least bit shocked.[1]

*   *   *

It is not surprising that these wars in Spain, Russia, and Germany seemed unjustifiable to many an honest Frenchman, who in consequence refused to obey the Imperial commands. But even more serious was the feverish activity on the part of Mme de Staël in St Petersburg, Stockholm, and London, where she strove to enlarge and strengthen the coalition against Napoleon and to stir up enemies against him; there was also the tragic return of Moreau to the scene.

Exiled to the United States in 1804, Moreau had lived a tranquil life and seemed no longer interested in French affairs, until one day in 1808, when his old compatriot from Rennes, and former aide-de-camp, Colonel Rapatel (the first recipient of the famous 'libels in the crocks of butter') came to seek him out. Although Moreau had not become a reactionary (we have this on the testimony of President Jefferson himself) he nonetheless advised Rapatel to leave America and take service in the army of the Tsar. On 6 June 1812, Rapatel embarked for Sweden. Thus began for Moreau himself the denouement of what can only be termed the 'tragedy of his dishonour', if one identifies the cause of France with that of Napoleon.

[1] Fr Lorson, S. J.: *Un Chrétien peut-il être objecteur de conscience?*

The hero of Hohenlinden had had no reason to change his opinion of that other General who had taken the destiny of the Republic into his hands only to destroy it. When Bonaparte treasonably seized control of France and hurled his armies and those of his subjugated peoples against Russia, it meant the end of liberty, should he be victorious. More than ever, Moreau felt it his duty to oppose him and that his only course was to join the ranks of the Emperor's enemies. It was a decision worthy of a drama by Corneille, exaggerated perhaps, but nonetheless a morally irreproachable decision. Perhaps Moreau would not have carried his decision to its ultimate conclusion if he had not been urged on by Mme de Staël, who was certainly French at heart, but whose real country was Liberty, a country which knew no frontiers.

Madame de Staël had left Moscow for St Petersburg, where she was given a triumphal reception and hailed as the 'conscience of outraged Europe'. The young Tsar Alexander, her 'dear Alexander', in whom she recognized nothing but 'nobility, goodness, dignity, sagacity, and wisdom', conversed with her 'as though with an English statesman'. He was about to meet Bernadotte, the Swedish Crown Prince, at Åbo in Finland, a meeting on which much depended.[1] Madame de Staël's part in the negotiations was considerable; no person did more than she to push Sweden into the Fourth Coalition. She wrote to Moreau in America and in the name of Bernadotte and Alexander asked the hero of Hohenlinden to take a command against the Emperor. But, in fact, Moreau had not waited for her letters before putting his sword at the service of the coalition; he was already military adviser to Alexander, Commander-in-Chief of the Allies.

On 27 August 1813, the Battle of Dresden was fought. Napoleon had only 70,000 men under his command against an Army of 150,000 Austrians. True, he had two other Armies, one in Silesia, the other in Brandenburg, facing a Russo-Swedish Army corps commanded by Bernadotte. Yes, it had come to that: it was no longer merely a question of a mutinous garrison at

[1] The scheme was no less than the formation of a European coalition under Russian leadership and, from Bernadotte's point of view, the establishment of a liberal monarchy in France with Bernadotte as King.

Rennes or a duel in the Bois de Boulogne. Bernadotte was now ordering foreigners to fire on the French soldiers of Marshal Ney, while Moreau, a few hundred miles away, on horseback at the side of the Tsar, was under fire from French cannon. Moreau observed to the Tsar that he was exposing himself unnecessarily. Alexander rode away. Moreau, who lingered on, was struck by a ball which broke both his legs. He was carried to the rear. 'Cut off both of them!' he ordered. He underwent the operation without flinching, but died a few days later. Before dying, he had the strength to write, in his own hand, a reassuring letter to his wife:

> 'My dear friend, at the battle of Dresden three days ago I had both my legs carried away by a cannon ball. That rascal Bonaparte is always lucky. They operated on me as best they could. Although the army retired, this was not a reverse, but a manoeuvre to join up with General Blücher. Excuse my scribble. I love you and embrace you with all my heart. . . . V.M.'

*   *   *

Naturally, we repeat, it is easy to dismiss Moreau as a traitor, but is it not perhaps Napoleon who was responsible for this 'treason' and that he was the guilty one? Purely from a common-sense point of view, was it not the act of a madman to aspire to crush all resistance on the Continent, from the Tagus to the Urals?

On 29 January 1814, as the Allies prepared to invade France, it was announced that this time they intended to reduce its boundaries to those of 1792.[1]

1 The so-called Frankfurt declaration, which was drawn up on 1 December 1813:
'. . . the allied powers are not at war with France, but with that haughtily announced preponderance, a preponderance which, to the misfortune of Europe and of France, the Emperor Napoleon has for too long a time exercised outside the boundaries of his Empire. Victory has led the allied armies to the Rhine. The first use which their Imperial and Royal Majesties have made of victory has been to offer peace to His Majesty, the Emperor of the French. The allied sovereigns desire that France should be strong, great, and happy. . . . The powers

On 30 January Benjamin Constant completed his book *On the Spirit of Conquest and Usurpation*, which was forthwith printed in Hanover [this book was unique in the history of propaganda inasmuch as it survived the occasion for which it was written and was quite appropriately reprinted several times in World War II]. Benjamin hoped that this work would contribute to the fall of Napoleon.

Twelve years had elapsed since the purging of the Tribunate. After his visit to Germany with Madame de Staël in 1803–1804, Benjamin's relations with her had cooled. Subsequently he had gone to live in Göttingen and had remarried. In November 1813, he visited Hamburg to meet Bernadotte. Bernadotte flattered and

---

confirm to the French Empire an extent of territory which France never knew under its Kings, because a valiant nation should not lose rank for having in its turn experienced reverse in an obstinate and bloody conflict, in which it has fought with its usual courage. But the powers also wish to be free, happy, and tranquil. They desire a state of peace which, by a wise distribution of power and just equilibrium, may preserve henceforth their peoples from the innumerable calamities which for the past twenty years have weighed upon Europe.

Ref: *British and Foreign State Papers*, i, *911, 1813.*

On 28 December the *Corps législatif* sent an address to the Emperor: '. . . Such proposals seem honourable for the nation, since they prove that the foreigner fears and respects us. . . . Let us not dissemble: our ills are at their height; the fatherland is threatened at all points along its frontiers; commerce is annihilated, agriculture languishes, industry is expiring; and there is not a Frenchman who has not in his family or his fortune a cruel wound to heal. . . . Conscription has become for all France an odious scourge . . . a barbarous and aimless war has swallowed up youths torn away from education, agriculture, commerce, and the arts. Are the tears of mothers then the patrimony of Kings? . . . It is true that thrones should be strengthened and that France should cease to be reproached with wishing to carry into all the world revolutionary torches. . . . The genius of a true hero, who spurns glory at the expense of the blood and repose of the people, finds true glory in the public weal which is his work. . . .'

Ref.: Buchez and Roux, *Histoire parlementaire*, XXXIX, 456–458 *et al.*

Napoleon, not unnaturally, dissolved the Chamber and forbade the publication of this address. (Translator's note).

courted him and invited him often to dine; he hoped that Constant would persuade his old friend Germaine to intercede on his behalf with the Tsar, and persuade him that he, Bernadotte, Crown Prince of Sweden, was the right man to rule France in place of Napoleon. Although nothing came of this plan, it brought the authors of *Adolphe* and *Corinne* together again. Germaine fired Benjamin's ambition and enflamed his hatred of the tyrant. Indeed, for some months Benjamin acted as Bernadotte's adviser,[1] and for a while Constant, Bernadotte, and Madame de Staël were actively intriguing between London and Stockholm.

In March 1814, *On the Spirit of Conquest* was published in London, but it appeared on the scene too late to affect the tide of events. After the Prussians had crossed the Rhine, even a Bourbon restoration seemed preferable to the ruin of France. Germaine had hoped for the downfall of Napoleon, not an invasion. The presence of foreign soldiers on French soil was unbearable, particularly those of her 'dear Alexander'.

* * *

Leaving aside Constant and Germaine de Staël, how did the French as a whole react to the invasion? Some reacted as in the old days of 1792. Carnot, for example, who had always refused to serve the Empire, wrote to Napoleon on 24 January: 'Doubtless it is of little use to offer you the arm of a sexagenarian, but I thought, perhaps, that the example of an old soldier, whose patriotism is well known, might rally many a hesitant arm to your eagles.' Carnot was to defend a beleaguered and bombarded Antwerp, resisting valiantly until 18 April, even after the capitulation of Paris and the abdication at Fontainebleau. In Champagne, in the East, there were peasant resistance movements, provoked by the extortionate and brutal behaviour of the Russians and Prussians. But on the whole, the people were tired of fighting.

[1] At Bernadotte's request, he drafted a concise outline of a campaign of psychological warfare to isolate Napoleon from the French and to prepare France for a constitutional monarchy under Bernadotte. While still in Hanover, Bernadotte drafted a proclamation to the French closely following Benjamin's outline and announced his pretensions to the King of Prussia. (Translator's note).

Would it have been possible for the Emperor to appeal to the whole nation to rise, as he had boasted to the deputies? Did he even want to?

At the end of March, he fought his last battle on French soil at Arcis-sur-Aube. All was lost ... unless, unless. ... At his side 'in the midst of battle' the Corsican Marshal Sebastiani suggested to him this ultimate recourse. The Emperor interrupted him: 'Dreams, dreams borrowed from the example of Spain and the French Revolution. What! Call on the people to rise in a country in which a Revolution has destroyed the nobility and clergy, and where I, myself, have destroyed the Revolution?'

On 31 March the allied troops entered Paris. On 1 April, at the invitation of Talleyrand, and in conformity with the wishes of Tsar Alexander, the Senate nominated a provisional Government. On the 2nd the Senate was presented [by Lambrechts] with a motion in favour of the 'fall' of the Emperor, which was proclaimed on the following day, with the concurrence of the *Corps législatif*. The senators then hastily drew up a new constitution, not forgetting their own interests. This Senate, which by its obsequious votes had constantly abetted the despotism, was now stigmatizing the very rule it had encouraged. A heart-breaking prelude to the recantations, treachery, and repudiations which were the distinguishing features of the ruling classes of France in the years 1814–15. 'The difficulty was not to do one's duty, but to know where one's duty lay', as a distinguished soldier was to say later. A noble scruple. But for the most part, for soldiers and civilians alike, the problem was to seize the right moment, and, above all, not too late, to switch their 'inalienable and willing loyalty'.

Once again the part played by the Senate *conservateur* in April 1814 inspires us with the most profound contempt. But it should be emphasized that our contempt should only be reserved for the majority; the minority, whose opinions had been formed at Auteuil, had no need to indulge in spectacular demonstrations of repudiation, for the little flame of opposition had never been entirely extinguished.

'... This small group of honourable and independent-minded men, who by their continued, albeit silent, opposition to the despotism of the Emperor when he was all-powerful, had earned the right to desert him when he succumbed to his errors. More enlightened and more far-seeing than the others, these men from time to time foregathered during the early months of 1814, either at the house of M. Lambrechts or elsewhere, to discuss the wisest course to pursue in the event of the Emperor's defeat. One of them, Grégoire, even went so far as to prepare an Act which would prorogue the Senate and deprive the Emperor of his despotic powers. . . . [This Act] would give a provisional Government the duty of appointing Ministers, preparing a constitution, and negotiating with foreign powers. As the situation grew ever more serious, this little group increased in size and, during the days of 29 and 30 April, semi-official meetings were held, first at M. Lambrechts' and then in the Senate itself, which were attended by some twenty persons.'[1]

What was the best course to pursue in the event of the Emperor's defeat? One recalls that the preoccupation of these same men in 1808 and 1812 was to guarantee by peaceful means the principles of 1789 and to re-establish liberal institutions. Thiers, who can scarcely be said to have liked them, recognized that in their negotiations with Talleyrand they showed much more spirit than the others, and refused to allow themselves to be led captive to the feet of the Bourbons. Assuredly it was not Grégoire who worked for the restoration of the *Ancien Régime*, nor was it the Netherlands-born Lambrechts, who before the Revolution had been rector of the University of Louvain. Although Lambrechts had never belonged to the Auteuil circle and had played no role in France until after Fructidor (when he was appointed Minister of Justice by the Directory), he had never denied his republican principles. Appointed senator in 1804, he had consistently taken his seat beside the *Idéologues* of the Luxembourg.

Having proposed the motion in favour of the 'fall', it was left to Lambrechts to formulate the grounds for his proposal. A commission, over which he presided, was appointed for this purpose, consisting of Garat, Lanjuinais, Barbé-Marbois and, believe it or not, Fontanes.

[1] Prosper Duvergier de Hauranne: *L'Histoire du Gouvernement Parlementaire en France*, Vol. II (1813–15).

Another commission of five senators was charged with preparing a new constitution: Lambrechts, *Destutt de Tracy*, Lebrun, Barbé-Marbois, and Emmery. We have purposely italicized the name of the leader of the Ideological school. Although it could be often wished that the resistance of the members of the Auteuil circle had been more active and vigorous, yet they never betrayed their cause in either the Senate or the Tribunate, and the most eminent of their representatives, in this twilight of the Empire, behaved with honour. While notabilities, dignitaries, and Marshals were falling on their knees to pay homage to the Capet monarchy, the Constitution of the Senate still remained faithful, in these early days of April 1814, to the principles of the sovereignty of the people.

Although it was impossible to prevent the return of Louis XVIII, nonetheless these senators insisted that he should not return as an hereditary King, but should be invested by the choice of the people and that he should swear to observe the Constitution.

This raised violent opposition among the reactionaries, especially the Abbé Montesquiou, the confidential agent of Louis XVIII, who had been placed in the provisional Government by Talleyrand. Louis XVIII, summoned to the throne on 6 April (the same day as Napoleon signed his abdication at Fontainebleau), rejected the constitution and replaced it with his own Charter.

*   *   *

It is true that the Bourbons returned in the 'baggage trains of foreigners', but they were also accompanied by a wave of propaganda, honouring the legitimate dynasty and insulting the vanquished usurper. Dominating this propaganda was Chateaubriand's pamphlet, already mentioned, *De Bonaparte et des Bourbons*. It appeared on 5 April and had an immense influence. According to Chateaubriand, Louis XVIII told the author it was worth more to him than an army of 100,000 men.

The history of the First Restoration is not within the scope of this book. It is enough to recall the excessive pretension of Louis XVIII, King by the Grace of God, and the arrogant and provocative attitude of his brother, d'Artois, and of all the 'noble fools' who had learnt nothing and forgotten nothing. It required prodigies of stupidity and mismanagement to change the attitude of the nation once again. But this miracle was achieved. France, which was to greet the return of Napoleon in March 1815 with transports of enthusiasm, was the same country that had learnt with relief of his departure only a year previously. Some of the most intelligent men in the country had expected much of the constitutional monarchy. Volney, with his friends Tracy and Daunou, hoped that Louis XVIII, intelligent and sceptical as he was, 'would re-establish the throne, but "without altars" '. They were soon disillusioned. On 17 October Volney resigned from the Society of Antiquaries when its President solicited royal patronage. But he did not attempt to reconcile himself with Napoleon, his former friend, when the exile returned from Elba.

Benjamin Constant, on the other hand, made a spectacular volte-face, but it is difficult to elucidate his motives, since his personal interests were so confused with his principles. In his *Journals Intime* we read: 'Liberty is not lost: let us try to find a suitable position (*une place commode*) in a peaceful system; it is worth the trouble.' But, in fact, Constant never solicited any 'position' from the re-established monarchy. His political activities were confined to writings (*Réflexions sur les Constitutions*, etc.), but when, on 6 March, he learnt of Napoleon's landing in the Gulf of Juan, he wrote an article (published in the *Débats*) as vitriolic in tone as Chateaubriand's pamphlet of the previous year, comparing the Emperor with Genghis Khan and Attila [and even to Teutates, the devourer of men, a terrific diatribe in which he extremely rashly vowed that he would immolate himself to the infernal deities rather than bow his head to the tyrant].

On the night following this phillipic, the King quietly slipped out of one door of his palace; twenty-four hours later, the Emperor entered by another. What was Constant to do? Kill Attila, take flight, or immolate himself? Nothing of the sort; he sought out Attila, who made him a Councillor of State. A pretty business, surely one of the most successful recantations in the whole of history.

This episode, which has its comic side, nevertheless requires some serious examination. The extremely serious question with which Napoleon was faced was whether to impose a liberal constitution on the nation or a revolutionary dictatorship. He decided in his own interests to grant a liberal constitution (another recantation?). Apparently the Emperor was converted, or at least resigned to the necessity of such a measure. Under the circumstances, Constant could hardly refuse the Emperor's invitation to draft a new Constitution. Only on one thing was Napoleon intractable – on no account would he disavow his past, and he insisted that the new Constitution be entitled *Acte additionnel aux Constitutions de l'Empire*.

The Act represented a considerable change, inasmuch as it substituted parliamentary rule on the English pattern for Imperial autocracy. In future, legislation would not be wielded by the Emperor alone, but by two Chambers (*Pairs* and *Représentants*) equivalent to the 'Lords' and the 'Commons'. The first were hereditary and elected by the sovereign, the second (690 in number) were to be 'elected' by the department and district electoral colleges. The Chamber of Representatives had the right to initiate and amend laws and make financial decisions. Any Minister [or any Commander of the Army or Navy] could be accused by the Chamber of Representatives and tried by the Chamber of Peers. All Frenchmen were equal before the law, no one was to be prosecuted, arrested, detained, or exiled except in cases provided for by law and according to prescribed forms (Title VI, Article 61). Liberty of worship was guaranteed to all (Title VI, Article 62). Every citizen was to have the right to print and publish his thoughts in signed form without prior censorship, subject to legal responsibility, after publication by jury trial . . . (Title VI, Article 64). Conscription could only be authorized by law; military offences were to be under the jurisdiction of military tribunals (Title V, Article 54).

The *Acte additionnel* was debated and approved by the Council of State (to which Constant had been appointed on 20 April), and was promulgated on 22 April. It was coldly received; its title alone had a bad effect. In Republican circles and among the people, it was felt that it still smacked too much of Imperialism and monarchy. Constant himself was none too happy about it. On leaving the Elysée, he met La Fayette, to whom he made the following strange confession: 'I have entered on a dark and dubious road. . . . I can scarcely answer for myself any longer in his [Napoleon's] presence. Remember what I tell you now; watch him [Napoleon], and if you think he is once more becoming a despot, do not believe a word I tell you later. Confide nothing to me; act without me and against me.'

It is not altogether surprising that Madame de Staël, too, rallied to the side of Napoleon. Although the fall of the Emperor had allowed her to return to France again after ten years of exile, she had been extremely shocked by the invasion. On her arrival in Calais from London, the first sight to greet her eyes 'were men in Prussian uniform; they were masters of the town by right of conquest. . . .' Continuing on her road to Paris, she saw nothing but Germans, Russians, Cossacks, and Bashkirs. She felt she was living in a nightmare, torn between conflicting sentiments. '. . . to see Paris occupied by foreigners and the Tuileries and Louvre guarded by troops from the farthest confines of Asia was insupportable.' She had the same feelings as she mounted the staircase of the Opera, lined with Russian guards – feelings very understandable to any French man or woman who lived through another occupation 130 years later.[1]

A year later, the news of Napoleon's landing afforded her no more pleasure. 'If Napoleon wins,' she said, 'liberty is done for; if he loses, national independence is done for.' Feeling that the earth was about to swallow her up, she fled to Coppet on 10 March. But the turn of events, the guarantees obtained by Constant, and the threat of another invasion, helped to dissipate her fears and doubts. She supported the *Acte additionnel*, wrote to King Joseph, and also to Benjamin Constant. Better still, she sent her son, Adolphe, to see them both. Joseph, who had never disguised his sympathy for Germaine from his brother, presented the young man to the Emperor, who received him most graciously.

Perhaps this reconciliation (or should one say truce?) between Germaine and the usurper was not unconnected with the famous

[1] This however did not prevent Mme de Staël from entertaining the victorious sovereigns and commanders. Tsar Alexander, Wellington, Schwarzenberg, Bernadotte, Canning, Talleyrand, Fouché, and La Fayette all attended her teas, dinners, and assemblies at her home in Clichy. (Translator's note).

debt of two millions,[1] money which Madame de Staël urgently required for her daughter's marriage to the Duc de Broglie. Napoleon, for his part, realizing that he needed the solid support of liberal opinion, particularly that of Madame de Staël, whose prestige in Europe was higher than ever, dangled the promise of restitution before her eyes as a bait. A little later, he asked her and La Fayette to mediate in an affair on which much depended – nothing less than to dissuade the English Government from making war. La Fayette's friend, William Harris Crawford, the American Minister in Paris, was about to return to America by way of London, where his opinion was much respected. La Fayette, on Joseph's suggestion, willingly undertook to persuade his American friend of Napoleon's liberal and pacific intentions and request him to take a package of letters to London in the diplomatic pouch. Crawford agreed. Accompanied by La Fayette, he visited Joseph, who briefed him on what he should say in London, in order to encourage the pro-Bonapartist wing of the Whigs to assure British neutrality. Among the letters he was asked to take was one written by Madame de Staël, which he was to show to the Prime Minister, Lord Castlereagh, and to the Prince Regent. In this letter Mme de Staël forcefully and eloquently argues that France, if left in peace, would develop under a liberal Government, and that if war broke out the whole French nation would rally behind Napoleon. The letter, highly favourable to the Emperor, concludes with a plea for peace.[2]

But only six weeks later (8 June 1815), ten days before Waterloo, she was again turning to the Tsar Alexander, to whom she wrote that France and all Europe placed their hopes in him, and referred to Napoleon as 'the man we all detest'. After the second fall of the Emperor, she again assumed her role of 'Third European power', valiantly protesting against the invasion of France and her threatened liberty. Unwilling to revisit Paris under

[1] On 17 April she wrote to Mme Récamier: 'If Napoleon accepts the liquidation [of the debt], he may be sure that my gratitude will prevent me from writing or doing anything detrimental to him.' (Translator's note).

[2] The authenticity of this letter has hitherto been a source of controversy, but recent authorities tend to accept it as genuine, notably Paul Gautier in his *Madame de Staël et Napoléon* (pp. 386 ff.). It is published in the *Letters and Dispatches* of Lord Castlereagh (Vol. II, p. 336).

Prussian occupation, she set out for Italy late in September, and did not return to the capital until October 1816. Surrounded by liberals, such as Camille Jordan, Barante, and Guizot, all hostile to the Bourbons, she spent her last years in declining health, finishing her ultimate profession of faith, *Considérations de la Révolution française*. On the anniversary of this Revolution, 14 July 1817, Germaine de Staël died.

To return to the Hundred Days and the *Acte additionnel*: the genuine confusion, paradoxes, and subterfuges of the new situation did not make for unanimity among the left wing. The contradictory reactions of Napoleon's former opponents are therefore not surprising.

Ginguené, ex-director of the *Décade*, accepted Napoleon's mission to court La Harpe, former adviser to the Tsar Alexander, in order to detach the Tsar from the new coalition.

Volney, although disappointed in the Bourbons, did not lend his support to the Emperor on his return from Elba. 'What is this wild beast up to now?' he was fond of saying. 'France will pay dearly for the little good he has rendered her.'

Destutt de Tracy, on the other hand, more bitterly opposed than ever to the Bourbons ('by behaving like the Stuarts, they will perish like them') rallied to the side of Napoleon, just as did Ginguené and Constant.

Carnot surrendered Antwerp to Louis XVIII (*not* to the Allies). He subsequently asked the King for an audience. Louis's cold reception, however, infuriated him. He then wrote his extremely violent *Mémoire au Roi*. On Napoleon's return to the Tuileries, he was appointed Minister of the Interior and elevated to the peerage, with the title of Count. Carnot accepted, but soon demanded that the appellations of 'subject' and 'monseigneur' should be deleted from all decrees; he also made modifications to the *Acte additionnel*. Up to the last he opposed Napoleon's abdication. When it was announced he was seen to 'bury his face in his hands to hide his tears'.

Grégoire (of whom Napoleon said 'He is incorrigible') remained 'incorrigible' until the very end. In June 1815, he voted against the *Acte additionnel* in the register of the Institute.

This marked the end of the story of the French opposition to Napoleon Bonaparte.

INDEX